D1498330

THE PSYCHOLOGY
OF RE-EDUCATION

Other books by PAUL DIEL

THE PSYCHOLOGY
OF RE-EDUCATION

Paul Diel

Translated from the French by Raymond Rosenthal

SHAMBHALA
Boston & London
1987

To my wife, my best friend, with profound gratitude

Shambhala Publications, Inc.
314 Dartmouth Street
Boston, Massachusetts 02116

9 8 7 6 5 4 3 2 1

FIRST EDITION

Printed in the United States of America

Distributed in the United States by Random House
and in Canada by Random House of Canada Ltd.

Library of Congress Cataloging-in-Publication Data
Diel, Paul, 1893–1972
   The psychology of re-education.
   Translation of: Les principes de l'éducation
et de la rééducation.
   1. Educational psychology.   2. Remedial
teaching.   3. Child psychotherapy.   4. Self-actualization
(Psychology)   I. Title.
LB1091.D513   1987   370.15   86-29687
ISBN 0-87773-367-8

CONTENTS

CONTENTS

Foreword to the French Paper Edition

After being in print for fifteen years, this book, the fourth published by my husband, has today more than ever a burning actuality. So I hoped that published in paperback it would reach a larger audience. And now it has appeared. I feel sure that it will be able to help the many parents who are grappling with the serious responsibility of the education problem, which they generally face bewildered and unarmed.

One must not expect to find easy recipes in this book. Each individual's psychic system is unique, even though it is subject to the law of psychic functioning. This text, which rests on the scientific foundations presented by the author in *The Psychology of Motivation*, will help those parents who wish to delve deeper into the problem, so as to discover what is actually at stake in education. It is material far removed from hypocritical moralism, that destroyer of youthful impulse and sower of rebellion, and is also far from the other, presently dominant convention, banal amoralism.

These false, ambivalent valuations, whether moralizing or amoralizing, dominate and divide all of society and introduce disorientation into the secret hearts of individuals and the family cell, where the child should be healthily educated. The child whose vital impulse has been deformed by inadequate education too often becomes the nervous adolescent or adult who turns to the re-education therapist. In many cases the psychotherapist will not accomplish his task if the only goal he sets for himself is to adapt his patient to a society that is itself ill-adapted to the evolutionary meaning of life. He will be unable to awaken in the analysand the biologically profound impulse toward harmony, which in the nervous person is deflected into vanity-inspired tasks.

This means that the therapist himself must be capable of dissolving his own resentments and false motivations, with the help of an introspective method. Paul Diel experimented with this method for many years in his position as therapist at the Laboratoire de Psycho-biologie de l'Enfant, which at that time was directed by

Henri Wallon. Paul Diel also trained pupils who continue his work. And so the method has given proof and continues to give proof of its fruitfulness.

Insofar as it presents the principles of re-education, this work of necessity contains theoretical expositions that are addressed more specifically to therapists.

In order to locate succinctly Paul Diel's position in modern psychology, I believe that I can do no better than quote an extensive passage from Henri Wallon's preface to the first edition of this book:

"A rigorous and original thinker, Paul Diel belongs nevertheless, and moreover quite freely, to the lineage of Freud, Adler, and Jung; even as he points to their invaluable contributions to psychology, he also indicates their mistakes. To Freud we owe the discovery of repression and of a zone of the extraconscious; without him depth psychology would not exist. But Diel contests the theory that sexuality remains present throughout the life of individuals as the source of the complexes that dominate their entire existence and are perpetuated into adulthood through uniformly infantile impressions. Adler is given credit for having pointed out the existence since childhood of the competitive spirit, the will to power, and the desire for domination. But Diel reproaches him for having also traced all of psychic behavior to a single original drive, that of nourishment, from which the will to power supposedly originates, and for also having thought that a person's entire mental evolution is subject to a "plan of life" adopted during the first years of life. Finally, Jung quite correctly showed in myth the fabulous expression of truths or prescriptions that were of capital importance for the existence of the group or the individual but that tended to be unintelligible to minds ill-adapted to the processes of conceptual thought and reasoning. However, Jung did not delve into the very root of myth. And the study of myth confined his horizon to a particular historical epoch and in any event to the history of humanity.

"Unlike each of these three authors, Paul Diel furnishes morality with biological foundations that are common to all animals but cannot be traced back to a single, immutable instinct. For Diel morality is an evolutionary process that extends from the basic needs of life all the way to reason, and in the detail of the sentiments that underlie this evolution, their relationships are not to be deduced from each other but are dialectically linked. Unlike animals, which simply disappear if their needs do not correspond with the means at their disposal to satisfy them, man in fact possesses, beyond his sexual and nutritive needs, a need to surpass and to renew himself, which in turn may help him to discover the principles of his own nature.

"Unfortunately, between essential needs and their satisfaction is interposed a fertile imagination that creates false pretenses, chimeras, deceptive desires, degraded or distorted motivations that take hold of activity, break it up, render it incoherent or disharmonious. Then consciousness experiences anxiety but refuses to accept responsibility for it. It reacts, in pride and vanity, to feelings of guilt that haunt it but whose burden it tries to shift onto others.

"And thus is set in motion a whole dialectic of erroneous motivations, of imputations that are not deserved but become so through the use of reciprocal grievances, ambivalent reactions. Paul Diel excels in the analysis of such situations, which are complicated but also cast a clarifying light on much logically inexplicable behavior. A wise and penetrating moralist appears in certain pages of this book. I would point particularly to those in which he reveals how relationships between spouses, between father and mother, can become poisoned to the great detriment of the children. And the vehicles of these mutual attacks can go unperceived by their perpetrators—for example, a grating tone of voice or an irritated pout."

An expression of annoyance, an irritated pout would seem insignificant, and yet, for anyone able to read subconscious intentions, these minuscule aggressive acts of everyday life constitute, by their repetition, the true cause of infantile trauma, the source of psychic deformation. Henri Wallon has grasped the originality of this work, which presents the general psychological law in its full scope just as effectively as it does the details of warped behavior, whose precise description compels one to say: that is exactly the way it happens.

Finally, it would be sad if this book did not provide, besides the analysis of distorting, also the heartening exposition of Diel's therapeutic method.

JANE DIEL

INTRODUCTION

If one were looking for the deepest, most secret cause of youth's present disorientation, one would perhaps find it not so much in social conditions of an economic nature—although it would be unreasonable to deny their codetermining importance—as in the decomposition of values. The very meaning of life is being questioned. Spirituality and materialism—beliefs and sciences—clash and propose contradictory valuations of life and its meaning. Ideological conflicts only result in extremist positions or compromise solutions. Contradictory theories about life and its meaning outbid one another; this activity, a product of the adult world and a sign of its own uncertainty, only deepens the malaise, sowing the seeds of doubt and fanaticism, if not indifference, which threatens to end in inertia.

Youth suffers from the consequences of an existence in a state of larval gestation and incomplete metamorphosis. No matter how much its vital impulse attaches to the idealisms at hand, the reigning ambivalences affect it deeply. Condemned to flounder among the immediate contingencies of a disoriented life, youth tends to accuse the adult generation *en bloc,* whose only legacy has been confusion.

The disdainful opposition to the world made by adults is not without an exuberant pride in the privilege of being young. But if we are confronted by a generation of young people whose impulse to surpass is often flawed, and who in that very way have aged prematurely, become bourgeois or rebels without a cause, it would be short-sighted not to realize that the ultimate reason for their arrogance is, in many cases, the disappointed love of the mind when its valuating function is unable to forge a guiding ideal.

Faced by this derangement of the understanding, the desire for a sensible orientation—insofar as it persists—is often satisfied, in the young as well as adults, with a game of the imagination that issues in a pseudo-elevated and literary verbalism which takes pleasure in turning the derangement itself into an amusement, a juggling with

1

opinions, to which the contradictory valuations lend themselves perfectly. This pseudo-artistic amusement and its alluring images end by offering unrestrained instinct as a gratifying ideal and lure. The valuating mind is devalued, decreed theoretical and sterile, because it is opposed to the anarchic and alluring enjoyments into which some young people fling themselves; disillusioned, they believe in this way to have grasped a new meaning of life. The truth is that the return to the unleashing of instincts has always been a characteristic feature of all decadent periods that are afflicted by a breakdown in the sphere of guiding values. An underlying despair seeks consolation in the overvaluation of materialism and sexuality. Letting go, a lack of self-control, are considered signs of virility. The distinctive feature of the present period is its technical character, which leads to the commercialization of souls who are avid to procure the instruments of comfort, the distractions proposed by the technical application of the exact sciences. What marvels of ingenuity we owe to the inventive mind! But as it concentrates all its creative power on the superabundant production of material goods, it also produces the bitter struggle for their acquisition. This aspect of the problems of the present age is only too well known and discussed. The predominance accorded its material aspect engenders a belief that the solution must be sought exclusively on the social plane, through a more economical distribution of wealth. One tends to forget that the need for justice, and the inventive mind and the avidity of desires, are first of all phenomena of a psychic order: they are inner motives for action. Thus the problem has an additional aspect that could well turn out to be essential. This concerns the inner functioning of the psychic system of those individuals who make up society, and its solution can be found only by an in-depth psychological study. Since the mechanization of the mind no longer gives us the time for true reflection, which alone is capable of resisting contradictory and erroneous valuations, superficial excitements and escapism replace the search for the ultimate reasons for the disarray and confusion.

And yet efforts at revaluation and the renewed search for the meaning of life take place despite the general disorientation. Periods of decadence have always been characterized not only by accumulated suffering and anxiety but also by positive liberating efforts, which try to reconstitute the scale of values by means of new formulations more suited to the needs of the age. The scientific age demands methodical research capable of fathoming the inner functioning of the psychic system. The psychopathic consequences of the general confusion act to remobilize the discredited spirit and compel it to search, by means of deeper analysis, for the secret motives of the malaise in order to discover its cure. The birth of depth psychology is—like the present malaise—a feature character- istic of our time. It is its vindicating sign to the extent that this new form of psychology, shedding the imperfections of its beginnings and delving to the very bottom of its own depths, will endeavor to search for the cause of illness, the causes of the malady of the age, where they reside, not only deep within the psychopath but—at least in germ—in the depths of all human beings, including the educating parents and even the re-educating therapist.

Hence the problem of youth education and of adult educators is not more or less vaguely connected to the ensemble of problems of an age in disorder, but constitutes its crucial focus and central core.

In the process of being formed, depth psychology has elaborated methods of education and re-education. It has proven that a patho- genic disorientation operates from early childhood on paths that are ordinarily hidden from consciousness, and it has made it possible to discern in what way the common malaise is reconstituted, from generation to generation, under the influence of the family milieu. But the most characteristic trait of the age—the contradictions and disorientation that it engenders—manifests itself in the very bosom of this attempt to find a way out by means of psychological orientation. At present too many explanatory doctrines and too many re-educational techniques contend with one another, even though they are all founded on the exploration of the subconsious. This revival of interest in the education problem, which is too recent to have already achieved its definitive form in science, is still in a preliminary stage of groping methods and semi-speculative systems. All these theories and techniques should be subjected to a constant effort at verification; nothing should be excluded *a priori* and on the basis of prejudice, and none should claim exclusivity for itself.

This indispensable exigency comes up against a crucial difficulty. It concerns the method to be employed with a view to the unification of psychological theories. For the task of verification to be accomplished, the psychologist clearly needs to be able to free himself of the affectively blind motives that threaten to lead to an obsessive adherence to this or that doctrine. There is no doubt that each psychologist exercises—even without realizing it—a more or less lucid watchfulness over his own motives, because in this clear introspection resides true psychological talent. However, talent in itself is not enough to establish a science. It must be mobilized and disciplined so as to become a methodical instrument.

The need for clarity regarding intentions concerns not only the choice of the re-educational doctrine but also its use. It presides—or should preside—over the contact between educator and the person being educated, re-educator and the person being re-educated. In short, clarity should preside over all forms of contact between human beings: it determines sanity or insanity, objectivity or lack of objectivity in the relations among people. But it is above all the re-educative contact—meant to combat the unhealthy consequences of the lack of objectivity in the original educational contact—which should be based on the need for objectivity and impartiality. In the therapeutic situation, impartiality is not only to be desired: it is a basic necessity, an indispensable condition for success.

The purpose of the present study is to demonstrate that the elucidation of inner motives for action is possible. This study proposes to present the conditions for its realization and the method for its curative application.

The human being is at one and the same time an object for another and a subject for himself. He should be observed and studied under these two aspects. The objective aspect is manifested through activity, accessible to clinical observation. But actions become comprehensible only if one begins with one's innermost motives, discernible exclusively by way of self-observation.

It is therefore a matter of clearly distinguishing, on the one hand, the motives for action that are stimulated by the milieu and, on the other hand, one's innermost motives, the more or less unconfessable intentions.

If man were only moved by the first type of motive, his response would be no more than an automatic reaction, an act bereft of responsibility. But the response to stimuli is a responsible *act,* because man is affected by deliberate motives that he often bears within himself for a long time before discharging them, and on which he reflects with greater or lesser clarity.

Motive can be defined as action in suspense.

Drives are simply the accidental codeterminants of human activity. *Motives are the essential determinants.* Pathologically deformed actions are symptoms that betray the underlying pathogenic, fundamentally warped motives. Should we not then focus our therapeutic attention on these deforming motives?

Deformed motives, more or less unconfessed but capable of being elucidated, are found in all human beings. What varies from one person to another is the degree of deformity and the capacity for elucidation. In principle every one of us is capable of elucidating the intent behind our motives. The first step to elucidation is the renunciation of a self-deceptive denial that falsifies motives by grafting pseudo-sublime intentions on those motives we judge to be unconfessable.

By combatting this self-deceiving temptation in oneself, one becomes the observer of a deception common to all; by ceasing to deceive, one becomes a self-experimenter. Thus fulfilling the conditions of objectification, indispensable to research in science, man will gradually discover the rules—indeed, the laws—that control the falsification of motives.

The observer-experimenter will be able to understand, beginning with his own progressive objectification, the intentionality—even if pathologically deformed—of the motives of others.

Clinical observation is indispensable for the classification of the myriad symptoms and character traits that have been deformed since childhood; curative self-observation is indispensable for comprehension of the inner motivating cause. This understanding will determine the re-education method and techniques to be used.

Discussions are interminable in psychology—and more generally in the social sciences—because too many theoretical views insufficiently subjected to experiment collide and conflict with each other. Is the absence of introspective experience, which might well be the cause of this discord, inadmissible in science? The discord is simultaneously disguised and betrayed by the fact that all sides are unanimous in denying the necessity for in-depth observation. True enough, the refusal hides behind an apparently valid argument that, however, is based on a misapprehension: *introspection in its affective form is the very cause of the illness.*

The confusion here lies in the fact that the argument against introspection itself rests on an introspective act which remains unconfessed. In fact a secret, introspective experience teaches all human beings—even the person who is knowledgeable on the subject of psychology—how difficult and painful it is to face one's own imperfections and inner motives. But what if these inner motives, inasmuch as they are not elucidated, were precisely the cause for the lack of objectivity? The argument against introspection has the great flaw of explicitly taking note of the existence of an inner functioning of the psychic system and of handing it over exclusively to the realm of blind affectivity. Thus at the very center of social studies a lacuna is introduced, an unexplored domain that is declared taboo. Is it not the very nature of science not to exclude any domain of life from its effort at elucidation? One does not have to be an advanced student of psychology to know that in the interval between an incoming stimulant and its reactive discharge exists the entire inner functioning of the psychic system. The slightest introspective act will teach this to everyone, since during such intervals one reflects on one's future modes of behavior. What should be undertaken during these intervals, although it is often neglected, is an effort at the correct valuation of motives. Reflection upon this undeniable observation might lead us to note that we ought first of all to study this interval instead of constantly turning it into unexplored territory. It could be that in the phenomenon of psychic retention (which creates the interval) are joined, not only the pathological problem but also the moral problem, the problem of guiding values, a problem which—from the psychological perspective—would consist simply in the choice of a propitious moment for the discharge of motives that have been clearly evaluated and sanely chosen in the individual's self-interest. It seems obvious that we are confronting the core of the psychological problem and that the anathema against the only method capable of throwing light upon the interval (instead of turning it into an unexplored blank) is a sin against the spirit of science, a sin that gives rise not only to the clash of theories (the impossibility of binding them together in a coherent synthesis), but also to a relative inadequacy with regard to the problem of education. Are we not all, then, like Oedipus, who, rather than look at his mistake, tore out his eyes?

The introspective gaze is indispensable to psychology. What, if not science, should trust in the mind's elucidating force? When distrust in that force is elevated to the rank of dogma, does it not cut off the possibility of studying the central phenomenon of human life: that is, *to know the conflict between blinding affectivity and the elucidating mind?*

In a letter addressed to the author, Albert Einstein wrote: "The aversion to inner observation is a fashionable disease of our time." In the face of an ineluctable need to attack the essential problem and in view of the refusal of the social sciences to do so, it is not surprising that a voice confirming their failure should come—in a manner that could not be more trenchant—from the exact sciences. Since this failure concerns a general human problem—one that goes beyond any specialized competency—it touches every human being who is searching for the truth. The shortcoming of any science whatever in meeting one of its problems constitutes a breach in the spirit of research that binds all sciences together.

Therefore a question of exceptional gravity presents itself: why is it that modern psychology refuses to understand that *the only weapon against the ravages of morbid introspection is lucid introspection?*

How can we help but take this question to its logical outcome? Man's fate depends on the outcome of the conflict between blinding affectivity and the elucidating mind. It is the question that the individual, and all of humanity, puts to psychology, while anxiously awaiting a valid reply. Is psychology not capable of fulfilling its own destiny? The question goes to the very heart of the educational problem. In every generation many adolescents, in order to prepare for life and find stimulation for their vital impulse, turn to psychology in the hope of finding a teaching that will lead them to an equitable solution of their inner conflicts. Is it conceivable that they learn that the question they pose, the impulse they offer, and the hope that inspires them, are only subjective aberrations, and that scientific objectivity consists in throwing up one's hands in the face of the essential problem? Don't we all, to the extent that we suffer and rejoice, attend the school of life, which subjects us to its exams and presents us with problems that are beyond us, badly prepared as we are? Who is to give us the salutary lesson, if not the science of life that psychology is supposed to be? It can become this only by studying motives, which are the essential cause of our often inadequate activity, and which—precisely for that reason—are material for the educational exigency.

Our innermost motives, it is true, are often vain, illusory, and deceptive. The one constant in the study of motives resides entirely in a clear distinction between vain and authentic motives. The most disastrous error consists in claiming that the existence of vain and illusory motives is proof that the entire functioning of the psychic system is only an illusion. Vain motives, though illusory (that is, not meeting real conditions for being satisfied), are nevertheless a psychic reality with an extremely intense, subconsciously obsessive determining power and are therefore pathogenic. The educational effort consists precisely in understanding the morbid nature of these vain determinations so that they may be controlled consciously by means of the superior force of authentic motives. Not to understand the battle between inner resolutions—does this not reduce the educational task itself to the level of an illusion?

What is education if not self-control necessarily imposed on the child by the family milieu? In order not to see education as mere dressage, let us acknowledge that educational impositions are an appeal addressed to the child in the hope that he will shake off his faults, something that will take place only through an introspective review that will enable him step by step to distinguish between right and wrong. False education is performed when the child is exposed to unjust impositions which he will gradually learn to answer—subconsciously—with imaginary justifications. So in the human psyche are inscribed from childhood on both a tendency to clear introspection and a propensity for affective blindness. If this is so, the whole problem of education can be summed up as the elaboration of a specific technique capable of blocking the determination of vain and blinding motives to the advantage of authentic self-determination.

It is essential to understand that motives are more or less clearly controlled means of self-determination. By having an active effect, they are a psychic reality, despite the fact that their intention can be nothing but an illusion.

The inability to teach control of activity beginning with motives—is this not the secret cause of the unspeakable confusion of our times? The repressive denial of the problem imposed by the existence of motives—imposed by life itself—is not only a theoretical error but also a practical mistake. The consequences of error are only superficially concealed by repression of the essential problem, even if it were doctrinal. The resurgence of error in the form of badly controlled, insatiable desires is all the more destructive when this gap in the social sciences is in such contrast to the constant progress of the exact sciences. Their technical inventions—instead of helping to master environmental conditions—are degraded to the point of merely supplying a lure for unchecked greed.

It is the very nature of the sciences to put themselves at the service of practical life thanks to their technical applications. But in order for a balance to be reestablished, it is necessary for the practical applications of the exact sciences and of the social sciences to complement each other.

What inventive technique is for the exact sciences, the control of motives is for the social sciences.

The present work is the result of a re-educational experiment with maladjusted children, an experiment pursued for a period of about twelve years at the Laboratoire de Psycho-biologie de l'Enfant in Paris. I am happy to be able to express here my deep gratitude to Professor Henri Wallon, who, by opening the door of his laboratory, gave me the opportunity of joyful work that he honored with his constant interest. My gratitude is all the greater since this collaboration was possible despite the divergence of our theoretical positions.

The purpose of this work is to present inner motives as they are born in the child unbeknown to him and under the influence of the family milieu. But since this study ventures into a realm of psychology that is as yet unexplored, it will be indispensable from the very beginning to set forth its theoretical foundations and its relationship with existing doctrines, especially psychoanalysis, which also concerns itself with the inner life but in the belief that it can grasp the causes of psychic deformation not by the study of motivations but by the analysis of infantile sexuality.

This book therefore consists of two parts. The first, theoretical part, necessarily quite long, is devoted to establishing its foundations and guiding principles. Its purpose is to achieve a genetic synthesis of the complex elements involved in the educational problem. The second part deals with the problem of re-education and its technique of application.

No profession can be transmitted exclusively by theoretical instruction. This is all the more true for the profession of re-educator. The plan of this book is to complete the study of inner motives—a subject it has in common with previous publications by the author—with a view to its application to the problem of education. Re-educational assistance is only a special instance of repairing the educational error whose consequences encompass all domains of individual and social life. Thus understood, the expansion of the educational problem, its incorporation into the problem of life and its meaning, are a rigorous necessity. The study of the educational task and of the false motivations that hinder its fulfillment leads not to a collection of empirical prescriptions but rather to the grand directing guidelines of re-education.

Contrary to custom, our text will not be strewn with illustrative examples. Such illustrations certainly make reading easier, and their advantage would be appreciable—if they did not involve a risk. The accounts of actual cases inserted in the text, in a form that is necessarily too condensed, scarcely fulfill their supposed function of providing proof in support of the theoretical argument. Excessive condensation opens the door to arbitrary interpretation. Examples prove nothing, for by eliminating from the account certain details and imparting an exaggerated importance to others, it becomes possible to present any case in such a manner as to prove everything and nothing.

In view of this drawback, it seemed preferable to us to put the case studies in the appendix. There, actual cases will be found, developed sufficiently to serve as explanatory illustrations.

PART ONE

EDUCATION

1

THE INNER FUNCTIONING OF
THE PSYCHIC SYSTEM

MOTIVATION AND EDUCATION

Education is a vast problem that can be viewed from different perspectives. The most widespread point of view insists that only the child need be educated. This way of looking at things is based on the belief that the adult, having become a parent, is necessarily in a position to fulfill the educative function in a satisfactory manner. In this regard, it is appropriate to remember that the renewed interest in the problem under discussion is due to the growing diffusion of the doctrines of Freud and Adler, which, among other things, demonstrate that the causes of adult psychopathology can be traced back to earliest childhood and often can be attributed to the parents' educational mistakes. Thus the need for the re-education of adults as well as children is included in the domain of education.

However, this domain can extend even further. Rejecting the affirmation that a single didactic analysis is sufficient to make one forever able to help others, should one not insist—as is at first sight quite likely—that the very special responsibility assumed by the re-educator and the therapist demands a constant effort at self-analysis? It would in fact not do to replace the influence of badly educated educators with the intervention of badly re-educated re-educators.

Considered in its entire vast scope, the educational task therefore extends from the child's education all the way to the adult's self-education.

It is not a question here of knowing whether self-education is desirable, but whether it is possible. From the point of view of all those—children and adults—who entrust themselves to the hands of a re-educator, it is certainly very desirable not only that the re-educator apply a theoretical view but that he personally attempt the inquiry into the self which he expects from the analysand. However, from the re-educator's point of view such a requirement might seem less desirable. Does it not impose a supplementary effort and a considerable waste of time? And isn't this precisely where the decisive mistake occurs?

Introspective control, when it is methodical, saves energy and time. Time and energy are habitually wasted by *the uncontrolled introspection to which every man gives way throughout the day.*

Turned back upon ourselves during our diurnal reveries, we introspectively ruminate on our bad luck and, starting from these imaginative ruminations, reach decisions which are often full of spite and aggression. Thus from childhood on interactions are often only shocks and traumas. *In general, one can say that the more a subject ruminates on his often purely imaginary troubles, the more morbidly hypersensitized is his introspection.* He elaborates shocking reactions on the part of others and is traumatized by their answers, often when they are not at all aggressive. The intentions of others are wrongly interpreted on the basis of one's own motives of aggressiveness, and this in turn breeds generalized distrust. Of course, within every individual's uncontrolled introspection are intermingled carefully weighed motives along with emotionally hypersensitized motives.

The human being is balanced to the extent that carefully weighed motives prevail. The aim of methodical introspection consists precisely in the control of motives in order to achieve relative mastery over them, so that one is able to maintain a balance that is always in danger of being upset.

It is useless for the re-educator to pretend to be equable in order to appear objective during the treatment. Such deceit would be an abuse unworthy of the situation. The subjects to be re-educated—and children especially—are extremely sensitive to such abuses. They inevitably sense the trickery, become indignant over it, and then take advantage of it.

Etymology teaches us that the term *education* is formed from the Latin verb *ex-ducere*, "lead out of oneself." Out of what and toward what? Out of mental inwardness and its deviating paths and toward sensible exteriorization. If sensible behavior were inborn in the human being, the task of education would involve merely teaching the knowledge necessary to exercise a future trade or profession, that which is indispensable to ensure the material condition of both the individual and society. Character education and re-education would be superfluous.

The essential task of life as a whole—of which education is a function, and undoubtedly the main function—resides in the prevalence of equity.

The human being's character is not always equitable. It needs to be shaped in childhood, led out of the rut of inequitability that is prefigured in everyone, a rut which—without sensible education—runs the risk of orienting all activities throughout life in the direction of the senseless. The task therefore involves one generation after another. The fact is that empirical education often deforms the child's character, leads it toward imbalance, renders it inequitable. If one were to heed the wisdom of language, it would teach us that the *mal*formation of *in*equitable (not balanced) character results in iniquity, injustice in interpersonal relationships.

At the level of society, such injustice becomes overwhelming. But if its essential cause lies in the inequity of characters, should we not recognize that this essential cause is not primarily social but rather individual in nature? It resides in the inner forum of each individual; once this fundamental truth is admitted, it should become clear that the cause of social injustice can only be found in the motives that individually and often secretly determine the behavior of men.

It is obvious that education cannot influence social conditions; at least it can do so only indirectly, through the study of the individual's hidden motivations.

In order to base education on the study of motivations, it is indispensable to distinguish, from the beginning and as clearly as possible, the plane of interhuman reactions from the intramental plane where motives for action are developed in the intimate depths of each of us. Confusion between these two domains is responsible for the fact that the study of motivations has always been neglected.

In order to define the domain of education as clearly as possible, we must stress the fact that education, although it has social import, is in the first place a problem of strictly psychological origin. The essential cause of our reactions, whether correct or vitiated, are the secret intentions, the motives of a just or unjust, sensible or senseless, balanced or unbalanced, healthy or unhealthy character. Science is obliged to trace observable effects back to their causes, no matter how secretly hidden they may be. Hence this methodology will try to uncover the essential cause of character deformation: that is, inner motivations insofar as they are just or unjust.

To pose the problem in this way means taking a position that is radically opposed not only to the generally accepted view of the task of education, but also to the various doctrines and techniques of depth psychology.

What lends itself to confusion is the fact that the relationship between the social and the individual is reversible. The social effect, interaction, in turn becomes a cause that acts upon one's secret motivations. This reversal of effect into cause may have induced depth psychology to study only the interactional effect, in the belief that they had hit upon the sole true cause of character deformation as something that operates—to the exclusion of personal motivation—beginning in one's childhood, in the bosom of the family.

For the child who is to be educated or re-educated, the social milieu and its interactions are reduced to the family milieu. Depth psychology believes it has revealed complexes, residues of traumas, which are supposed to be the cause of character deformation. In these complexes are indistinguishably confused the old traumatizing social interaction and the persistent motivating intentionality on the part of the individual. This confusion incites one to analyze first of all the old injustice, and not pay sufficient attention to the subject's present provocatory injustice. His lack of balance is due not to the old traumas—after all, is there anyone who hasn't suffered them?—but to his subconscious intentions, which continue to exploit the past in order to falsely justify present deficiencies. *It is the hidden tendency to create false justifications that renders the subject unjust and inequitable.* Cure is obtained clearly not by the associative revelation of past traumas, but by the revision of one's still-present, false motivations.

The re-educational technique based on the analysis of motives is not retrospective but introspective. The essential reasons for this radical difference cannot become wholly clear without a preliminary definition of the forming and deforming role that motives are called upon to play in the elaboration of human activities.

Human activity of whatever kind—equitable or inequitable, just or unjust, sensible or not, valid or invalid—is determined by a motivating valuation.

Empirically defined, the goal of education is unquestionably that of making dominant in the child decisions that are equitable, just, sensible, and valid.

But one will not go beyond the conventional level as long as these qualifications are applied exclusively to behavior, as long as one sees justice only as a social phenomenon, life only as a speculative problem, and values only as the imposition of morals.

Conventions are exposed to doubt. And doubt ends by claiming that certain forms of inequitable behavior are in themselves more valid—or at least more immediately satisfying and superficially rewarding—than the equitable act.

How can the educator or re-educator who is assailed by doubt accomplish his task in an equitable manner? Is it not true that education, which transmits value judgments from one generation to the next runs the risk of being falsified in its very essence as long as the question of what is dominant is not put beyond the reach of doubt, as long as values are not based on the very meaning of life, as long as one has not clearly defined on what basis equitable behavior should be considered more sensible, more valid, more satisfying than the inequitable act? As long as the search remains confined to the study of social behavior, so long will justice, the ethical sense, guiding values, all the qualities we regard as positive appear as fragmentary entities, irreducible to one another, incapable of synthesis. How could they ever serve to synthesize and harmonize character? It is this lack of coherence which gives rise to doubt, the false justifier of senseless behavior and thus destroyer of the educational effort.

The first task of a theory of education consists in combatting empiricism and in proving why and how values are based on the very meaning of life. Who, if not the psychologist, can assume the task of plumbing the greatest depths of the psychic system, not only the conscious but also the subconscious. Could psychology thereby discover the profound roots of sane and senseless behavior? Can psychology demonstrate that human orientation both toward the evolutionary meaning of life and toward involuting derangement, are *immanent in human nature and, thereby, subject to laws?*

Only knowledge of the laws inherent in psychic functioning will permit us to combat error and skepticism effectively. It will prove that attributes do not primarily affect behavior. It will prove that reactive behavior is simply the incidental exteriorization of an inner intention made up of the totality of one's determining motives. Lawfully structured by the evolutionary impetus, sensible motives form a coherent whole, a single and unique characteristic within which righteousness, sensibility, and cogency—because vitally satisfying—are only diverse aspects. The healthily motivating force of positive values is a dynamic process toward the satisfying realization of the evolutionary drive, even if this realization is continually blocked by the seductive pseudo-satisfactions of a dissolving and distorting, unjust and fundamentally invalid motivation. The latter also provides a lawful dynamic process, but one with a deforming tendency.

The study of motivation shows that false motivation is bound to the immanent problem of justice: it is false justification. It consists in a subconscious confusion between the sensible and senseless, the valid and invalid, the just and unjust. It tries to present the perverse in the guise of the sublime, error in the guise of truth, injustice in the guise of justice.

The educative and re-educative task consists in combatting false motivation and its falsely justifying tendency.

Having become semiconscious, and by that very fact remaining half unconscious, of this immanent internal conflict, the human being needs to be educated, and this education should be guided by a knowledge of the laws that preside over the functioning of the psyche. If it were possible to discover these laws—immanent because biologically rooted in the unconscious—the theory of education could then be developed in a fashion no longer empirical but scientific. Once the laws were established, all the theoretical details would flow from it in a consequent and economic fashion.

In view of the methodology thus set forth, it is of the highest importance to understand before all else the function of false and just motivations in relation to the overall inner functioning of the psychic system. Knowledge of the psychic laws will permit us to establish an objective value theory.

To the task of self-education with a personal and practical intent is thus added the need for a study having an objective and theoretical bearing with reference to the biopsychic origin of the immanent function of guiding values.

The need for such an investigation might seem surprising, if not superfluous, despite all that has been said. Yet this investigation is indispensable. It alone can open a direct path to the present material, because the study of psychic deformation—one of whose chief characteristics is maladjustment beginning in childhood—will remain forever empirical and speculative so long as the pathological is not understood, starting with psychic health and its biologically natural conditions.

It is therefore important that before going into the details of psychic deformation, which begins in childhood, *we establish the principles that should guide a healthy education and demonstrate that these principles can only be revealed by beginning with the study of inner motivations.*

To begin with, the guiding principles of education—as indeed of all of life—are values. And these values must be shown to be definable in relation to the meaning of life. Even before entering into the study of the biological origin of values, one statement is permissible, because it is indisputable: *guiding values are the motives of action.* The study of the problem of values—and the considerable deep-going research such study requires—is therefore an integral part of the study of inner motivations. Only the study of motives could possibly provide a valid approach to the problem of values. If the only motivating force were that of biologically based and therefore fundamentally sensible values, no derangement, no pathological deformation would be possible. From birth on the child would be guided by such values, the only motives for his activities. But as psychic deformation undoubtedly exists and its danger manifests itself from infancy, it seems clear that there must exist a motivating counterforce, a force capable of falsifying values, a falsely motivating force. It is precisely the existence of false motivation that injects confusion into the problem of guiding values, presenting values as nonvalues and nonvalues as values.

In order to establish the principles that should guide education and re-education, and to base them on the study of inner motives, it is therefore necessary—no matter how difficult the undertaking—to analyze psychic functioning insofar as it is the generator of valid and invalid, sensible or senseless, healthy or unhealthy motives.

EDUCATION AND GUIDING VALUES

The principle of education is the transmission of values. The principle of re-education must be a reorientation toward guiding values.

The science of motives opposes the idea of a social and empirical origin of values. But obviously it will not broach the views of metaphysical speculation, which regard values as an imposition of transcendent and absolute origin.

In order to base the science of motives and its educative application on definable givens, it is important to seek a new line of approach to the problem of values. Psychology must understand that values are a modality of existence. They are a regulating mode that is indispensable to the healthy functioning of the conscious psychic system. Only this understanding, established in advance, can render psychology proof against metaphysical speculation and make the problem of values and the ethical imperative it implies explicable and teachable.

Even if it were true that values have a transcendent origin, it still would be necessary for the human mind to have sufficient reasons to accept them as guiding ideals. These reasons are immanent in the mind. The problem of immanence—knowing how values appear in the course of evolution and why they impose themselves on man—is thus posed.

One thing is certain: values are called upon to fulfill a function.

Values, the motives for sensible action, have a dynamic relationship not only with other motives but with all the intimate functions of the psychic system, from elementary emotivity all the way to the mind's valuing faculty. On the human level the *emotive* is diversified into multiple *motives*, revealed by the immanent need for satisfaction—for valuation by the mind.

The human being's satisfaction becomes semiconscious, and involves the multiplicity of sensible or senseless desires.

All psychic faculties evolve from the world of desires and their need to find fulfillment. Their functions can be defined in relation to this prime exigency of life. *Feelings* serve to stimulate desires and thus intensify their promise of fulfillment: *thought* tries to elucidate affective promises in order to discern their satisfactory or unsatisfactory value; *will* decides upon the discharge of desires and the mobilization of energy for their realization. (See my work *The Psychology of Motivation.*)

The higher functions of the human psychic system are not static entities but diverse dynamic aspects of functioning in search of satisfaction.

As products of the mind's valuing function, values are liable to falsification, because the human mind is not safe from error due to the blinding results of affectivity.

The mind's *value judgments* are exercised within the *representation of goals* proposed by desires. The elucidating mind selects those desires that are judged to be sensible and counterposes them to the desires judged senseless, which, thus condemned by the mind, are struck by an interdiction, and become the cause of a guilt-ridden dissatisfaction. The intentionality of the intrapsychic conflict—its essential and inner goal, often unachieved—is gradually to realize those desires chosen by sensible value judgments, which are thus raised to the rank of guiding values. In this conflict all determinants—conscious as well as unconscious—confront one another and try to impose their motivating forces, albeit to the detriment of values. The study of inner motivations and its introspective method aims to reinforce the mind's elucidating power, in order to render it fit to resist the assault of blind affectivity. This goal—which envisages the realization of values proposed by the mind—sums up the educative and re-educative significance of the science of motives.

Values are our very desires, validated by the mind in a just manner and therefore spiritualized and sublimated.

The terms *spiritualization* and *sublimation,* exactly like the term *value,* are devoid of all meaning—they only indicate a baseless idealism—unless they are defined in relation to desires. It is solely because values are the product of a metamorphosis of desires brought about by intrapsychic travail that their realization is desirable to the extent that it, like desire, is provided with a promise of satisfaction. The mind's valuing function creates values by throwing light on the promises of the satisfaction of desires and by eliminating false promises. The spiritualization process purges desires of their blinding affectivity. It transforms and elevates them by objectifying them to the rank of guiding ideas, which, in turn, become motives for the sublimation of character. Thus the guiding idea is transformed into a guiding ideal, a value endowed with determining power.

The problem of education is bound up with the problem of values, and the latter is tied to the—often blind—dynamic process of desires. Hence the complexity of the educational task.

Usually the sole characteristic of desire is the search for satisfaction. But desires are linked imaginatively, thus permitting a preparatory play with the promises of satisfaction. *Imaginative satisfaction* precedes real satisfaction, which resides in the desires' realization. But the pre-satisfaction procured by imaginative play is detached from the limiting conditions of obstacle-filled reality. The imagination becomes exalted by its own play and loses itself in the mirage of a chimerical, pseudo-autonomous pre-satisfaction, full of unlimited promises and for that very reason unrealizable. *These imaginative reveries, lacking all real satisfying value, constitute nonvalue itself.* Imaginative exaltation is a state of affective obfuscation, evading the control of conscious reflection, the first indication of subconscious activity.

Nevertheless, desires at their origin are solidly attached to reality. Each desire is fixed on its chosen object, which exists in the external world. Desire is an interiorized tension, an energetic intention. But this intention, in order to be healthy, must remain an expectation: a vigilant attention directed toward the object of its choice, stimulated by the object. Such vigilance already bears within itself the need for elucidation. All psychic energy is due to the energetic tension of desires, and this tension, because it is fixed on a real object, is destined to be transformed into a realizing action. But since this tension is a semiaffective, semivigilant intention, the psychic energy, if it does not achieve its active discharge, manifests itself in the form of a prior intrapsychic travail.

Its *raison d'être,* the motive of psychic travail is to prepare the discharge. This innerly motivated and motivating travail results in both increased vigilance and blindness.

Motivating intentions are endowed with determining force only because they share the energetic nature of desire. *Desire itself is the motive, but detached from its particular object. Motive is the pure intentionality of desire,* henceforth generalized and apt to mobilize energy in the direction of any object chosen by the mind or the affect.

The desire for triumph, for example, remains attached to a precise situation and to this or that specific person. On the other hand, the motive of triumph is a habit extended to all situations and liable to manifest itself with regard to any person. The perverse motive of triumph, which seeks superiority in general, is false because its promise of satisfaction is fallacious. The motive is not sufficiently vigilant and lucid to be able to take into account the response of others who, having become the vexed object of triumph, will seek revenge through an aggression that will transform its own vexation into triumph and the hoped-for triumph of the initial aggressor into vexation. *The calculation of satisfaction of the perverse motive is erroneous.*

What is true for perverse motives is also true, but in an inverse sense, for authentic motives. They too are pure intentionality, detached from the specific object envisaged by the desire.

There are only two psychic functions capable of bringing about this detachment that metamorphoses concrete desire into generalized motive: one is the *perversely exalted imagination,* the creator of false motivation. Instead of being directed toward real objects, it detaches itself from them, and its blind exuberance finally becomes determined only by itself, by its vain and unlimited demands for satisfaction. The other force of detachment, which is the creator of sensible motives, is *elevated imagination.* This function detaches desires from their exterior goal, when the latter is considered unable to procure the promised satisfaction, or when the promised satisfaction is considered inferior to that of renunciation. Such detachment is liberating. It frees one from covetousness. It dissolves the desire and regains its energy, which thus becomes available for the elaboration of new plans for the reduction of exaltation and for harmonizing detachment, plans that impart an authentic character to motives.

But imagination, even if elevated, remains intermingled with affective elements. Values, the guides of activity, are sensed rather than clearly understood. Activity can become perfectly authentic only to the extent that the valuing mind, going beyond the partial clairvoyance of imagination, can consciously elucidate the ensemble of determinants and clearly discern all the motivating promises of satisfaction. All motivations would then freely be at the disposal of the subject, capable of deciding their realization or dissolution. *Here is the very definition of freedom; it is freedom of the mind faced by the seductions of perverse imagination. This freedom is an authentically attractive ideal. It is the supreme value.*

Yet the full satisfaction of freedom remains an ideal with a directive but unrealizable significance. Perfection is not within the reach of man, and the perfect ideal can only be approached gradually through the effort at liberation. The supreme value, perfect authenticity, is thus a matter of degree and varies according to a scale of values that permits the gradual approach, the achievement of perfection in proportion to the available forces.

THE LAW OF HARMONY AND ITS BIOLOGICAL AND MYTHICAL BASIS

At the evolutionary level attained by man, value is defined by just and authentic motivation, nonvalue by false and untruthful motivation.

The theory of values proves to be of such importance for the educational problem that it is necessary to delve into it more deeply. Values are the rational products of the deep-seated dynamism of psychic functions; but the functioning of the human psychic system is an evolutionary product. Thus in the last analysis the problem of human values is rooted in phylogeny. The most decisive reproach that can be brought against the educational doctrines elaborated after Freud is that they are too exclusively based on ontogeny.

The sensible direction of life is determined by evolution and its adaptive impulsion, which runs from the most primitive form of life all the way to the most elevated faculty, the valuing function of man, the semiconscious being in evolution toward ever higher consciousness. The sphere of values can find its complete definition only in relation to the directional line that traverses all of evolution.

The directional line tends to ever greater lucidity, the most effective means of adaptation. Lucid orientation in space, which on the animal level is accomplished thanks to the evolution of the sensory organs, is achieved on the human level by lucid orientation in time, ensured by the mind's prescient and valuing functions. What remains to be elucidated on the human level, viewed from this angle, is the persistent affective blindness which is the cause of the dissatisfying inner conflict. The organ necessary for this elucidation is the inward-directed eye.

The progressive adaptation toward lucidity prescribes for life its sensible direction. In other words: *the effort toward elucidation is the point of life.*

Biogenetically defined, *values are a means of adaptation.* They adapt the human species to the purpose of life, and thus guarantee its healthy and satisfactory survival. Adaptation to the evolutionary purpose is more primordial than adaptation to social conditions. The human species, divided into societies, can survive only if the individual members of the community, for lack of an instinct that unconsciously guides them, are subconsciously united by a common ideal which consists in a more or less clearly established scale of values.

On the animal level, fundamental errors, nonvalues, unsatisfactory deformations, condemn a species to its disappearance. Here value is certified by survival and is indistinguishably merged with existence.

Only the human being, incorporated in society and protected by institutions, can survive in a nonvalid, psychically deformed manner that is unsatisfying to himself and others. Thus on the human level the sphere of values becomes separated from the biologically most primitive conditions of existence (materiality and sexuality). Values seems to hover somewhere above life, and as a result they are regarded as an ideal, alien to reality and easily lost sight of because of the difficulty of their individual and social realization. Institutions, meant to protect individuals, become themselves unsatisfactory; societies disintegrate to the extent that individuals are no longer guided by the vision of values.

The individual can survive only in the bosom of society, and the survival of society and its protective institutions depends on the survival of values. The sphere of values, although it soars above life's mutable conditions as an unrealizable but governing ideal, nevertheless remains intimately connected to the fluctuations of multiple desires, precisely because it emerged from these desires and from their elementary need for satisfaction by the path of spirtualizing valuation. Having changed from incidental into essential, the energy stored in values has the directive function as its only goal: the satisfactory harmonization of desires that have remained elementary. Multiple desires are henceforth opposed by *essential desire.* Its elevated satisfaction consists in opposing the excessive multiplication and disharmonious satisfaction of material and sexual desires. This opposition does not create frustration, because it simply envisages the healthy development of sexuality and materiality, which is the precondition for the satisfactory survival of individuals and societies.

The value of life is defined by the need for harmonization.

All values can be grouped in the three categories of harmony: *harmony of thought: truth; harmony of feelings: beauty; harmony of actions: goodness.*

The law of harmony governs life even to its slightest fluctuations, perverse as well as elevated. It determines immanent justice. The law punishes the disharmonious exaltation of desires by psychic disorder and its inhibiting anxiety; and it assigns to the effort of harmonization elevated satisfaction, the joy of life.

The preceding observations permit us to understand the relationship that exists between the dynamic process of immanent values and the ancestral vision that lends them an absolute significance of transcendent origin.

The human species could not have survived unless its half-conscious foresight, too susceptible to subconscious temptations, had not been supplemented since man's emergence from the level of animal instinct by a subconscious prescience, an instinctive certainty regarding fundamentally valid satisfactions. This survival of instinctive certainty is manifested ancestrally as an oneiric vision of guiding values: the mythic dream. It is the intrinsic quality of this collective dream that it transcends values which are in truth immanent. The oneiric aspect of myth concretizes the underlying value judgments through poetic personification. It represents values by means of superhuman figures. (See my book *Symbolism in Greek Mythology.*)

As the immanent consequence of these *symbolically truthful* images, the guide-figures are the transcendent representatives of guiding values. The correct value judgments on which man's fate depends become, in the mythical dream, the judges of human activity. The valuing mind is represented by the supreme divinity. In conformity with the psychological truth that discerns in motives the hidden cause of activities, the divinities—imagined as all-seeing—judge our innermost intentions. Because the mythic dream is rooted in the instinctive certainty of the subconscious, the symbolic images of different peoples, although dissimilar in appearance, all speak about the same vital, most essential problem: the origin of life and the significance of guiding values.

The mythic imagination, capable of formulating immanent values that are truthfully but symbolically disguised by images which lend them a transcendent and absolute aspect, is thus opposed to the untruthful imagination which, with its vain promises of satisfaction, deforms life and its meaning. (In the myth of Genesis, for example, the perversely seductive imagination is represented by the fallen spirit, Satan.)

The imagery of the mythic dream is an ancestral product of the valuing function. Even at the present stage of human evolution, the valuing function still remains half conscious and half imaginative. Thus the conscious is attacked by the two forms of imagination: one truthful, the other untruthful. Progress in the evolutionary direction requires the reinforcement of conscious orientation, so that it can combat the untruthful and deforming imagination, not only with the help of symbolic images (which are too easily mistaken for a real explanation) but more effectively by conceptualized value judgments that conform more closely to the cognition of inner psychic functioning.

Psychologically speaking, value judgments should arbitrate justly the inner conflict between the two forms of the imagination and the valid and nonvalid intentions resulting from it. Myth symbolizes this inner situation by representing nonvalid intentions in the guise of some monster that the human-hero must combat. In reality, understood psychologically, man is assisted in his fight against monstrous dangers—the perverse motives—by his psychic quality, the mind's lucidity; in the mythic image, assistance is given by the divinities, symbol of the lucid mind. The result of the inner conflict is the harmonization of desires or their disharmony, from which come joy or anguish; in the mythic image, the law is represented by the divinity, the dispenser of rewards and punishments.

If it is true that the images of myth know how to express symbolically the inner conflict between the valid and nonvalid, nothing could be less superfluous than to speak, in the introduction to a treatise on education, about the secret meaning of myths.

Visionary imagination has had an educational influence on all of humanity of the greatest scope and significance. The belief in the transcendent image lies at the very foundation of our culture. The most profound cause of cultural decadence resides in the inadequate distinction between mythic image and psychic reality. The confusion that results from it ends by arousing doubt, the destroyer of the sphere of values and therefore, precisely, the destroyer of empirical education based on beliefs.

There is no point in seeking a solution by returning to the ancient beliefs, which, by making dogma of mythical truth, have assumed a mission of compromise, one that was historically inevitable and, from the educational point of view, indispensable. No matter that the compromise remains doubtful and that the doubt, once aroused, will never cease opposing it. This opposition has a double root. On the one hand, doubt is the expression of a banal triumph which, following the collapse of ancient value formulations, believes itself authorized to conclude that all ethical imperatives are meaningless, on the pretext that life's only value consists in giving free rein to instincts and passions. But on the other hand, doubt is the expression of the ineluctable exigencies of elucidating reason, which, in opposing the confusion that has mistaken images for realities, tries to free itself from it by the psychological analysis of the source of beliefs: myth. Reason releases the true immanent significance of values so that their power for cultural education may rise to a new plane.

Psychological foreknowledge of the remote consequences of fundamental satisfaction or dissatisfaction, psychic formation or deformation, is bound to strengthen the attraction of valid behavior and combat the vain promise of unhealthy behavior. An increase in this kind of foreknowledge, brought about by objectively motivated inner observation, creates hitherto unknown intrapsychic determinants, motivating judgments that are bound to direct the individual more effectively toward the satisfying realization of values. Inner observation, insofar as it is objective, is transformed into a formative experience thanks to its prescient power. By thus bringing together the two methodological requirements common to all scientific disciplines—observation and experiment—the psychology of the subconscious becomes the valid scientific instrument of vitally effective education and re-education. As for its theoretic and phylogenetic foundation, the satisfaction principle, would it not be correct to state that this principle alone, because self-evident, can confer upon education an effectiveness capable of placing its ideal goal beyond all discussion: the orientation toward the sphere of values?

THE LAW OF DISHARMONY

As the sphere of values is ruled by a law—the law of harmony—would this not also apply to the sphere of nonvalues? It should therefore be a matter of isolating the law to which nonvalues are subject.

A thought presents itself, however. One would be entitled to say

that the law that governs the totality of values is implicitly understood. No one value can come into conflict with another value:
they must all therefore be harmoniously ordered. Nonvalues are
opposed to values; in truth they are antivalues, and this opposition
is manifested in the very heart of the total body of nonvalues. They
are not harmonious; they are conflictual. They contradict one
another.

But how can this inner contradiction be the result of chance? As
it defines the very nature of antivalues, is it not precisely the law to
which they are subject?

In order to isolate this law—the law of disharmony—it is first of
all important to make a clear distinction between the two forms of
conflict to which motivations are exposed: one normal, the other
pathological.

The norm is the conflictual situation between blinding affectivity
and the elucidating mind. This conflict takes place within every
human being, and introspection easily perceives it because of the
very fact that the mind is involved in it. But it happens that
introspection, out of a need for false self-justification, refuses to see
this conflict and is loath to mobilize the mind and seek an equitable
solution. It is here that the conflict, eluding the mind's control and
misled by affective blindness, sinks into the lower depths and
antivalue manifests itself and prevails. The valuing function is now
exercised only by blind affectivity. Self-evaluation, self-estima-
tion—the esteem which the subject likes to bestow on itself—drives
it to falsify motives. False justification masks inequitable motives
instead of dissolving them and lends them a pseudo-elevated aspect. Iniquity and pseudo-elevation contradict each other at the
very core of each falsified motive, and all the false motives contradict and collide with one another, each imputing to another in turn
the nonvalue that lurks behind a facade of sublimity. False justification has riddled the conflict with guilt, and the guilt is covered up
over and over again by false justification. Antivalues, false motivations, by definition incapable of being harmonized, find themselves
involved in an internal, insoluble contradiction. The conflict, normal at first, has become pathological and pathogenic.

But if it is indispensable to make a clear distinction between
normal conflict and pathological conflict, it is equally appropriate
to observe that in the secret heart of every human being the two
forms of conflict mix and intermingle.

Each of us assumes the role of judge: too indulgent toward our
own false motivations, too harsh toward the false acts of others.
Could it be that because we love justice above all else, because we

recognize it as the supreme value, we demand it from others unremittingly and tend to disguise our own injustices? The confusion between just and unjust exists in the world because motivations are ruled by false justifications.

Here, then, is the principle that presides over false valuation and its pseudo-satisfactions. Its name is vanity. The Latin word *vanitas* contains the root meaning "vain," that is to say: devoid of meaning. Vanity is opposed to the meaning of life and the quest for satisfactions that are harmonious and capable of being harmonized. Vain self-satisfaction is affective blindness *par excellence:* it is an exalted imagining about oneself. Vanity-inspired self-satisfaction is vain and illusory because its promises of satisfaction—by reason of their unreality—are unceasingly transformed into self-deception, into guilty dissatisfaction. Vanity is at the origin of false motivation and its lawful structure, because all false motives are rooted in it and derive from this common source. Vanity has motivating power because it is itself a motive—an intention provided with reactive tension—but by definition it implies an intention too good to be realized. Vanity shuns the recognition of its lying nature and its disastrous consequences, for it relentlessly metamorphoses itself into a multitude of accidental, overly-good intentions and into pseudo-elevated motives with no real value. The ensemble of these untruthful motives—their dynamic process of metamorphosis, which impedes the realization of true values—constitutes the antivalues. Everything depends therefore on understanding introspectively the nature of these metamorphoses.

The law that governs antivalues cannot be grasped so long as we tolerate the dodges of vanity, as long as we persist in remaining our own dupes.

Of necessity the science of motives leads to an educational experience; the problem to be resolved is the painfully felt conflict between values and nonvalues.

The *conflict problem* does not tolerate a purely theoretical solution; it demands a resolution, a decision to be taken. The essentially valid solution would be to stop lying to oneself. It is, however, inscribed deep in human nature that this essential decision is never realized in a perfect manner. Only the effort at progressive improvement is realizable, that is, the effort of self-education. The dissolution of the internal conflict does not depend on a static resolution arrived at once and for all, but on a dynamic impulsion that is able to straighten itself every time it is bent out of shape. Psychic dysfunction is the result if recovery from the distortion is insufficient.

The law of vanity-inspired disharmony and the guilty anxiety engendered by it can only be understood as a form of radical opposition to the law of harmony and its ultimate satisfaction, joy.

The most powerful motive capable of bringing about the essential resolution lies in the promise for satisfaction inherent in the effort at harmonization.

As long as a human being remains alive, he enjoys the possibility of envisaging the gradual realization of this essential decision. The degree of its accomplishment determines value for each person. But the dynamic process of the essential impulsion is continually opposed by the need to elaborate a multitude of incidental decisions, imposed by the fluctuating demands of everyday life and its pressing preoccupations.

Psychic functioning as a whole is determined by this inner conflict, a conflict which is life itself: our very own life with its joys and sorrows immediately felt and reacted to, and therefore transformed into action.

Every day we use the brightest part of our life in search of decisions, and once they are taken we consider these decisions just and valid. These decisions are prepared through a hesitant state of introspection in which the human being, withdrawing into himself, tries to free himself from the conflictual scission in his motives, with a view to arriving at a satisfactory outcome or a preliminary internal reordering, if no immediate outcome is possible.

This introspective debate, or *deliberation,* consists in reflecting on one or another plan as it is prescribed by changes in the environment and in evaluating the possibilities and means for its realization. Deliberation tries to put an end to the conflictual scission, to the indecision, the restless anxiety it engenders. Its goal is descission, voluntary decision.

Healthy deliberation aims at liberation, whose ideal end is freedom.

The liberating decision would take place without any hesitation, without even the need for preliminary deliberation, it would attain its highest degree of certainty and satisfaction in the ideal case that all motives were in reciprocal accord, which is only possible on the condition that they are all valid and sensible. The absence of conflict-related contradiction liberates one from all hesitation. It defines the total decision, the free voluntary act: freedom.

Not only do the so-called higher functions come, as has already been stated, from a single root, the need to master the multitude of desires; what is more, thought, will, and emotions are functionally united in the effort at mastery and in the deliberating dynamism.

They are not faculties that can exist independently of each other. The voluntary act is produced by the forces at play, forces constituted by the disharmony between valuing thought and blindly motivating sentiments.

Promises of satisfaction, elucidated in accordance with their just value, that is, motives, again become imperious desires. Resolution, having become inflexible, concentrates the motives for action on the essential desire. Its objective is not accidental, for it does not dwell in the external world. Freed from environmental conditioning, the essential desire achieves its satisfaction in itself and by itself, because it envisages only its own accomplishment: the harmony of the inner life.

Motives, once harmonized, form a sheaf oriented in the direction of formative evolution. They are magnetized toward the sensible pole of life. (One might liken this perfect liberation to the polarization of molecules that, by magnetizing iron, awaken in it a force of orientation that is customarily alien to it.)

In psychic life, the perfect magnetic attraction to the meaning of life, and the fully satisfying orientation that results from it, remain a never completely realized ideal.

In reality, the voluntary act is always impaired by a certain degree of hesitant disorientation. It is accomplished well or badly without deliberation integrally dissolving or thoroughly sublimating the conflict between motives. Because of this persistent contradiction, the act itself, although it takes place, remains partially blocked, and a feeling of inner dissatisfaction opposes the partly senseless accomplishment, or subsists after the act: it is the feeling of guilt.

Guilt can therefore be defined as a residue of the conflictual scission that persists despite the decision.

Thus the act remains partially unsatisfying. Hence the act—at the utmost—can be entirely blocked, or what amounts to the same thing, the desire for accomplishent is repressed. Guilty dissatisfaction, when its intensity surpasses that of the covetousness of desire, can be changed into an inhibiting anguish that more and more forcefully hinders the decision and ends by preventing its active realization, without the haunting memory of desire having been dissolved by sublimation.

Guilty inhibition thus attains a pathological level. A complete inhibition of activity would clearly be a deadly deformation.

In order to be able to continue to live or—what amounts to the same thing—to react, the stricken subject is compelled to employ a stratagem: he tries to establish the lie of a harmonization of contradictory motives. He can do so only by justifying his nonvalid, guilt-ridden motives.

False justification avoids the inner obstacle by repressing guilt. By imaginatively disguising the guilty motives as noble intentions, it manages to re-establish the path to the ability to react. By thus fallaciously harmonizing his motivation and re-establishing in imagination the condition for ideal accomplishment, the subject— without truly heading in an evolutionary direction—ends by imaginatively and vainly believing himself to have achieved the ideal.

Pathogenic disharmony resides in the ambivalent contradiction between vain and guilty pseudo-satisfactions.

Vanity is nothing but repressed guilt. Not to admit one's faults amounts to being vain. The more deeply guilt is repressed, the greater the vanity.

Thus the law of disharmony becomes definable: it is the law of false, contradictory valuation, *the law of ambivalence.*

The law of ambivalence presides over the deformation of character. Through the repression of guilt, the mark of a nonvalid attitude, that the forceful ascendancy of inhibiting contradiction is vainly camouflaged, instead of being truly dissolved and sublimated. Henceforth shielded from elucidation, guilty contradiction, rendered subconscious, continues to exert its inhibiting power uncontrollably or—and this amounts to the same thing—in an obsessive manner.

This aggravation of the intrapsychic scission—its transformation into subconscious obsession—entails a risk that the path to reaction, instead of being traversed with the help of semiconscious deliberation (semicognitive, semi-imaginative), ends by being negotiated, on the basis of the repressed energy, at a subconscious level where the reactive discharge can only be effected in an oneiric and neurotic form.

Repressed very deeply, imaginative reverie is degraded to pathological daydreaming, which—just like nocturnal dreams—can at this point only express itself in a symbolically disguised manner. The scenes of seduction and anxiety created by daydreaming impose themselves after the repression with the dream's characteristic particular vividness (despite its illogicality). This pseudo-vividness confers on the symbolic illogicality of neurotic symptoms precisely its obsessive and extremely morbid character. The symbolism of these two forms of dreams—the nocturnal and pathological—has as its hidden meaning the continuing conflict between the valid and the nonvalid. Psychopathic symptoms are an explosive discharge of desires and anxiety that have remained jumbled and repressed in the storeroom of the subconscious. Contrary to the nocturnal dream, these psychopathic symptoms preserve the character of activity because motility remains at the subject's disposal.

We can see therefore that there exist functional bonds among the mythic dream, the nocturnal or pathological dream, and day-dreaming. The latter is in turn functionally tied to conscious lucidity (of which it is only a degraded condition, blinded affectively because of the imaginary exaltation). The nocturnal dream is a continuation of deliberation that during its diurnal activity has not found the path toward a liberating decision and its active discharge, or toward the organization, the harmonization of the intrapsychic. The valuing deliberation as regards motives (life's essential effort at obtaining satisfaction, whatever the cost, even by falsification) continues without respite, night and day.

Repression is not always deep enough to produce completely illogical psychopathic symptoms, the symbolically disguised explosion.

At the first stage of psychic deformation, the energetic and active discharge, instead of degrading into a symbolically obsessive dream life, still takes place at the conscious though imaginatively blinded level. The active discharge remains logical in appearance even though an underlying obsessional illogicality betrays itself in the form of idées fixes and stereotyped or unstable attitudes based on whim.

This psychopathic condition, less serious and much more frequent than neurosis, is generally known under the name "nervousness" or "nervous condition."

This condition is typified as much by imaginative exaltation as by a partial active inhibition, and it is due precisely to this—as previously noted—that deliberation is reduced to an incessant effort at a false harmonization of motives, aimed at breaking down the inhibiting barrier. Active discharge made possible by dint of false justification here seems at first sight to be deliberately willed; the voluntary decision appears intact. But the nervous person's activity seems nevertheless marked by an underlying scission of motives whose contradiction is only fallaciously disguised. The illogicality of this false motivation, without being channeled into dreams, confers a senseless lack of adaptation on all activity. Exalted by vanity and inhibited by guilt, each action bears a contradiction within itself. The subject wants and does not want to realize this or that desire; he acts, but in part despite himself. He even comes to hide his unconfessable motives from others, and to save face the nervous person often finds himself obsessively compelled to act in a manner which is utterly opposed to his desire. Anxious inhibition and covetousness frequently manifest themselves simultaneously; they interpenetrate and produce "aborted" acts. Not just this or that action, but the entire behavior, frozen in character traits that have become obsessive, proves to be branded by this underlying false valuation, a *convulsing ambi-valence.*

By dint of false valuation and the vanity-inspired justification of guilty motives, the subject can no longer make a distinction between what is valid and what is nonvalid. What is valid has become nonvalid to the extent that the nonvalid, through pseudo-elevation, is raised to the rank of valid. Finally, the existence of such false elevation renders true elevation itself suspect. This produces complete disorientation regarding values. Deliberation, bereft of all introspective lucidity, turns egocentrically upon itself, is degraded to a sterile vicious circle of morbid rumination, the obsessive preoccupation with insoluble conflicts.

All the faculties of the conscious ego—thoughts, feelings, volitions—are in the end overcome by this initial deformation: disorientation regarding one's valid and nonvalid motives.

As thought gradually loses its healthily deliberative lucidity, one's emotional life disintegrates. By dint of untruthful self-satisfaction and the lack of real satisfaction, feelings lose their integrity. They ambivalently split into sentimentality, on the one hand, contrasted by, on the other hand, insensitivity toward oneself and others. Volitions, insufficiently stimulated by sensible interest, end by disintegrating into indecisive but imaginatively frenzied and capricious impulses. This results in an intermittent explosion of sudden and untimely decisions that only lead to ineffective actions. Social maladjustment results in a chain of constant defeats. Falsely justified by a vanity that represses its own mistakes, one's defeats, instead of serving as experience, simply exacerbate sensitivity and turn it into *plaintive sentimentality.* Through spiteful rumination, self-pity soon produces its ambivalent complement: the complaint against others, who are regarded as the sole guilty parties.

Thus the ambivalent scission of values achieves its disastrous goal. Repressive vanity and repressed guilt become a constant means of self-exculpation; spiteful complaint and plaintive sentimentality serve to project incessantly the repressed fault and cast the blame on others, on the world, or on life.

Vanity-engendered self-exculpation and the *sentimental accusation of others* form two pairs of fundamental ambivalences capable of transforming any and all active deficiency into falsely justifying imaginative satisfaction.

These fundamental ambivalences constitute a pattern of categories of self-idealization that can be used in all of life's circumstances. Thus they become the stereotyped frame for all shades of false motivation and the deformed actions that derive from it.

The categories of false justifying motivation are the result of continuous metamorphoses of vanity, which itself is the self-justifying lie *par excellence,* the overvaluation of the ego, the destroyer of true values and the creator of ambivalent antivalues. Vanity by its metamorphoses creates a dead end, a categorical encirclement: it represses guilt; it seeks triumph in accusing others; it mirrors itself complacently in sentimental complaints.

These metamorphoses of vanity create a dynamic field of perversion whose lines of force are the categories of false motivation. The innumerable shades of false motivation, fixed in character traits, all determining one's activity, are derived from categories which are subject, like the motivations themselves, to the law of ambivalence. Vanity is itself ambivalent; it not only vaunts its triumph, it is also too easily humiliated and vexed. But on the other hand it is capable of an excessive generosity that, too often disappointed, metamorphoses into disdain and distrust. There is no quality on which vanity cannot graft itself, and which it cannot arrange in an exaggerated posture that is diametrically opposed to the original quality. The posture of dignity becomes indignation: the desire for amelioration, inquisition; extreme patience, meticulousness, and so on.

The benefits derived from these vain satisfactions make one blind to the ins and outs of one's situation, one's hidden motives on the one hand and one's maladjusted reactions, which lead to aggressive counterreactions on the other. Hence deliberation, instead of anticipating reality's demands, is continuously intent on a false calculation of benefits and satisfaction. The benefit promised by vanity is itself ambivalent, because vanity is not merely pleasing self-flattery: it is a task too heavy to assume, an exalted task, which compels its victim, seduced and petrified, to prove himself forever worthy of its vain aspirations or collapse in the throes of guilt. The task of vanity—unrealizable because it exceeds the available forces (otherwise it would not be vain excess, but a true impetus to surpass)—is adequate only in imagination, its absurdity continuously put to the test by one's real inadequacies. Vain promises are transformed into disappointments, hope into despair. If at least vanity and its metamorphoses were only an individualized instance, isolated or capable of being isolated. But inner disharmony extends into social discord. One person's vanity provokes the vanity of another, and in both cases arises the need for triumph, rancor, complaint, distrust, contempt, and hatred. Under the domination of vanity, all of life, its essential value lost, is transformed into a nightmare.

Two laws govern life: the *law of harmony,* which presides over the formation of character, and the law of disharmony, the *law of ambivalence,* which determines the decomposition of character. The first is typified by just motivation, the second by false motivation.

Having become conscious, or rather half-conscious, man must assume responsibility for the essential choice and so is exposed to the conflict between the valid and the nonvalid. Man is the only living being exposed to the possibility of error in regard to the elementary need for satisfaction.

The possibility of being falsely motivated is ancestrally rooted and begins to manifest itself—albeit in a still wholly automatic and not imaginatively exalted manner—from earliest childhood. Even a baby is capable of an implicit calculation of motives. As the occasion demands, he increases his crying and outbursts of rage in order, still quite unconsciously, to impose his needs, which are not always exempt from capriciousness.

To educate the child above all means to prevent this germ of false motivation from attaining exalted proportions.

In a great many human beings who have grown to adulthood, nervous exaltation still remains insufficiently dissolved. It continues to exist in a latent manner, concealed by the demands of social adaptation that education emphasizes. The valuing function remains muffled. Deprived of authenticity and vital impetus, it is simply imitative and submissively follows conventions. Social success becomes the single guiding ideal, a fact that cannot fail to have drawbacks. For, removed from higher control, barely contained in the scale of values which are degraded and fixed in institutions, material and sexual appetites are exalted. In the end they demand satisfaction at any cost, even to the detriment of others. Society is divided into oppressors and oppressed. Ambivalences manifest themselves in the form of envy and triumph, solicitude and casualness, poverty and luxury. The elementary foundation of life, material security, is called into question. An unscrupulous struggle for the acquisition of goods absorbs all energies. The pressing need to protect oneself in the end becomes—

in a vicious circle—a false justification for the progressive destruction of impetus.

The usual jeremiads against this state of affairs, and even the best-
intentioned attempts to reestablish justice, run the risk of remaining
exceedingly good intentions, vain intentions, and exalted tasks, so
long as the underlying false motivations persist. And how could
they not persist? Nothing seems more appropriate than seeking an
immediate remedy. The search for it imposes itself as an historical
necessity, compared to which the revision of motives appears
utopian, a much too distant goal.

But is it not in fact utopian to believe that external organization,
necessary though it may be, can eliminate the essential cause of the
disorder that exists in the depths of every human being? Utopia is a
vain hope, leading to the belief that one's goal can be obtained
without the mobilization of means. Vanity consists in believing that
life will yield to human exigencies. The law of harmony stipulates
that the way out lies in the dissolution of inner disorder, and the
law of ambivalence prescribes that individuals and societies decay
when they are stimulated by false motivations. Man may be in a
hurry, but life is patient. It pursues its evolutionary path. Only
knowledge is ameliorating; and still it must not ignore the essential.

The study of false motivation and its consequences, the false
promises that determine false interhuman reactivity, constitutes the
binding link between psychology and sociology. Thus understood,
the need for education does not concern only the individual (child
or adult); it extends to social groups and as a result to all of
mankind. Finally, it merges with the biological needs of the evolution of the species, which, in the face of all its suffering, must
overcome the ancestral scourge of false motivation and its vain
seductions.

The educational evolution of the human species is accomplished
through the revolution of minds. The individual effort at sublimation-spiritualization is accessible only to the person who rebels
against conventions. Only the mind's revolution, lucid and without hatred, can prevent this revolt from being affectively blinded,
from being degraded into banally aggressive plans of expansion, or
from degenerating in a resigned escape into the depths of the
subconscious, an anguished flight from life's problems. Repression
gives rise not only to false actions but also to falsely justifying
ideas, to ideologies of all kinds. When all is said and done, these
two disharmonious solutions—nervousness and banalization—are
both simply forms of submission to convention; since the most

widespread convention is an exalted hope supported by repression and vainly buttressed by justificatory ideology.

THE CURATIVE PRINCIPLE

The educational remedy is the lifting of repression.

Unrepressed objectification leads to the formulation of truth (spiritualization) and the formation of character (sublimation). The formation of character would have a solely individual significance if the experience of self-education did not lead to the spiritual formulation; this latter, because it is objectively valid for everyone, possesses a scientific character and thus becomes the most effective instrument for the education of others.

The effectiveness of this instrument resides in the fact that it is capable of reaching even the deeper layers of the subconscious. Certainly, objectifying introspection must perforce be content with plumbing the superficial layers of the mind's depths, the threshold of the surfacing into consciousness, the level at which lucid thought and blinding imagination intermingle. But the deformed degrees of the imagination are only aggravated states of an imaginative reverie which still possesses the semilucid character of a thought just slightly deformed by affect. To the degree to which one's attention is devoted to observing this first stage of repression, the imagination, instead of becoming exalted, is by this very fact converted into reflection. This decisive reversal is in the long run of double significance. Introspective reflection, thus established, in the first place dissolves the affective thought, the cause of false interpretation of self and the world. But, furthermore, the continued dissolution of burgeoning reveries prevents them from feeding the pathological dream, even when the dream was formed earlier. A circuit of energy is formed in a direction opposite to that of the repressive one. The acts of elucidation, isolated and repeated at the semiconscious level of daily reverie, tend to unite and create a releasing dynamism that in turn reaches successive layers of the mind's depth, where energy removed from conscious control stagnates and by that very fact is ready to express itself in dreams. The subconscious "swamp" gradually dries up. The previously repressed energy is channeled toward the conscious, delivered over to the free use of purified impetus. The psychopathic symptoms, deprived of their energy support, sooner or later disappear.

During the work of objectification, it is important to avoid a trap set by vanity.

Vanity can graft itself even onto the attempt to lift repression.

The repression-lifting process is not indulgence in an incessant pursuit of the self. A relentless attitude toward mistakes would have an obsessive character and simply be the sign of an exalted task aimed at perfection; this would certainly lead to rigid moralism.

Every human being must grant himself and others a margin of tolerance where weakness is concerned.

Obviously, this margin is no less a danger than the exalted task. But it is between these two dangers that man's fate and that of human life is played out.

Too broad a margin is banalization; too narrow a margin is the nervous state. And both lead to ruination.

Too broad a margin results in a tendency to facileness, a slippery terrain that insidiously provokes the fall into mediocrity and platitude, if not depravity. Too narrow a margin forces one to move dizzily on peaks whose height surpasses one's abilities. The nervous person, seized by vertigo, risks letting go at the slightest misstep and falling into the abyss of his vanity-engendered guilt.

To grant oneself a margin, therefore, does not mean to settle into a perverse self-tolerance, the private preserve of depravities. With a view to escaping the two dangers, it is important to understand the necessity for vigilance when making plans and when confronted by mishaps. Such vigilance will permit the meditated dissolution of guilt, in contrast to both nervous tension and banal nonchalance.

Everything rests on the ever-renewed search for the balance between strength and weakness, a balance that can only be obtained by strength watching over weakness, so as to permit dynamism to find its path, starting from a lesser or greater intensity of drive. No one knows his level of equilibrium so long as he has not exerted his strength and given vent to his vital impetus. It is just as vain to set for oneself a specific level of progress as the goal of self-education, as it is to impose on oneself a specific goal in the re-educational treatment. Each person's proper level is different, because it depends on the intensity of one's drive to surpass. The goal of re-education is first of all that of liberating the drive to surpass both from its slackness and from its tension. Very often at the beginning strength seems to fail. It is not always a matter of lack of strength but rather of lethargy due to the loss of confidence in oneself that educational intimidation has caused. The drive to surpass is set free to the degree that new horizons open up as one moves from one stage to the next.

The important thing is to know whether this affirmation is true or false. The problem cannot be solved by discussion. What is the value of any counterstatement that is not founded on an experience of self-objectification? At best it could base itself on the irrefutable fact that since the beginning of human life innumerable experiences at self-education, self-equilibrium, and self-harmonization have been attempted, but instead of reaching a level of harmonious balance, they have almost always strayed down the ambivalent paths of banal laxity or nervous and moralizing tension.

What does this mean? Simply that the experience of self-education was always subjected to the law of harmony, which made it desirable, and the law of ambivalence, which caused its failures.

Only knowledge of the laws of motivation will make it possible to overcome the misdeeds of empiricism.

Knowledge of the law of harmony—the guarantee of real satisfaction—will stimulate the drive for self-objectification or—what amounts to the same thing—the effort to lift repression. The knowledge of the law of ambivalence will permit us to foresee the disastrous consequences of repression and of laxity, and will thus stimulate resistance to the false promises of satisfaction.

But this stimulation due to knowledge of the laws developed up until now is not remotely sufficient. In order to guarantee effectiveness, one would have to reach the point of deriving from it a technique of application.

The entire educational and re-educational self-objectification technique is based on knowledge of the subconscious paths of the ambivalent decomposition of psychic qualities.

It is important therefore to study in the most detailed fashion this destructive aspect of repressive false motivation.

Ambivalence, the effect of a false valuation, is defined by the contradictory scission of a value, that is, of a quality of the psychic system.

Between fault and quality there exists an inverse relationship: a mistake consists in not realizing the quality in a satisfactory manner. This failure is marked by guilty dissatisfaction. As a feeling of dissatisfaction, guiltiness has a rehabilitating dynamic. This dynamic strives to obtain the elimination of the fault by active re-establishment of the quality. It has already been shown that pathogenic ambivalence appears when the fault, instead of being actively eliminated, is imaginatively justified. This pathogenic elimination of the fault—its repression—results in a progressive destruction of the quality. The quality decomposes into two contradictory poles that henceforth mutually exalt and inhibit each other. One of the two poles is constituted by a repressed guilt that has become obsessive, pathologically exalted; the other pole is constituted by the mendacious affirmation of the quality, vainly displayed. The energy that has been invested in the quality cannot be manifested in a sensible fashion: it exhausts itself in pure waste because of its conflictual configuration. The categorized pairs of false motivation (vanity-guilt, accusation-sentimentality) demonstrate in the most instructive manner the contradictory bipolarity of ambivalences.

But starting from these categorized pairs, innumerable gradations of the falsification of motives, their metamorphoses and their combinations, are generated. They all are the result of the progressive and ambivalent decomposition of various qualities. As decomposition progresses, reactivity is no longer assured by psychic qualities but by ambivalent motives. This observation takes in all the reactive effects of false motivation: character deficiencies that have become habitual as well as actions that are either exalted or inhibited. Ambivalence characterizes all of morbid behavior. However, it cannot always be ascertained at first sight. It is the very nature of ambivalence, the product of repression, to elude observation. The knowledge of the law of ambivalence invites us to cast light on the repressive mendacity and to *search each exaltation-producing pole for its hidden counterpole.* The release of morbid motives thus proceeds from one discovery to the next, guided by the recognition of morbid reactions. The morbidity of an action is betrayed by its illogicality, that is, the disproportion between actual excitation and excessive reaction in defense or attack, exacerbated to the point of inhibition (sulkiness, shyness, etc.) or aggression (spite, rage, etc.). This illogical disproportion is proof of the underlying energy factor which, aroused from its repressed somnolence, is added to actual excitation and confers a character of obsessive irritation on it.

The preceding is so evident that in everyday life everybody proves to be enough of a psychologist to intuit from someone else's excessive reaction the existence of certain underlying and unconfessed motives—a fact which, however, does not stop anyone from considering his own exalted reaction to be absolutely normal and justifiable. This rudimentary psychology is often the cause of the poisoning of human relations. In the end, every disagreeable reaction on the part of another, even if it does not display a lack of logic, is suspected of underlying aggressive motives. This produces interminable ruminations which lead to plans of revenge. In cases where such suspicions are verbally formulated, the other person's more or less just aggression arouses no less hazardous countersuspicions, which are often the cause of quarrels and even definite ruptures. These states of unhealthy introspection and pseudopsychological interpretation are the rule of the social game, a rule whose lack of objectivity escapes rectification and even acknowledgement, so that one sees only the reactive effects and neglects their secret motivating causes.

THE TECHNIQUE OF LIFTING REPRESSION

Knowledge of the law of ambivalence permits not only the recognition of a generalized lack of objectivity, but also the analysis of its structure. In this way, it invites re-educative rectification. For the rectification (the releasing elucidation) to be methodical, it must be exercised at the level of imagination where excessive reactions are prepared. It is thus necessarily of an introspective nature. The technique of application must be in keeping with perfectly definable conditions.

1. *Only manifest illogicality* (actions, verbal expressions, voice intonations, mimicry) *justifies the search for false motives.* Without this fundamental rule, the psychology of motives would run the risk of degenerating into vain interpretation and slanderous accusations. Each person carries within himself the tendency to decompose qualities and thereby—under a more or less realized virtual form—the entire gamut of exalting and inhibiting resentments. The more self-analysis strives to uncover and overcome one's own resentments, the better able it makes one to interpret correctly the false reactions of others.

2. *Wherever the illogicality of a reaction is manifest* (whether as an excess of shy submissiveness or as an excess of aggressivity) *the psychological explanation must search for the inner-energy source of the reactive excess.* But again one must not confuse meditative caution with inhibition. To meditate is a balancing quality: equity as opposed to excessive aggressiveness as well as submissiveness. At the present time, when reactive excesses are the rule in behavior, meditative caution runs the risk of appearing to be an excess of submission. This suspicion leads to confusion, and aggressiveness presents itself as an ideal quality. The distinctive difference between quality and its two forms of ambivalent decomposition can only be revealed on the plane of secret motivation, where submissive inhibition is accompanied by spiteful rumination, whereas realized aggression is accompanied by vain triumph. Ponderation, the result of spiritual inhibition (the brake of reason), does not at all exclude firmness. The outcome of a just valuation of the situation, it has no need for triumphant or rancorous false justification. As the consequence of a firm decision, meditative caution does not vacillate

between the ambivalent poles of vain superiority and sentimental or spiteful inferiority. It is sure of itself, and this balanced certainty is manifested on the plane of reactions as well as on the intimate level of motives. *The essential is not what happens to one, but the manner in which one inwardly elaborates the motives for one's actions.* Observed from the outside a just action may appear unjust, and vice versa. The positive or negative quality of an action depends first of all on its underlying motives. The application of the law of ambivalence thus leads to a motivated judgment where one's own actions and those of others are involved. But this judgment based on motives does not yet have the significance of a diagnostic.

3. *The therapeutic value of the knowledge of the law of ambivalence is inseparably bound up with its diagnostic power.* If knowledge of the law of ambivalence permits or even obliges us to deduce the fact that an excessive reaction has false underlying motivations, it is clear that the opposite conclusion is also legitimate. The therapeutic effort does not only trace the excessive reaction back to its motivations; it also inversely establishes the pathogenic motives for future pathological reactions. Introspective observation focussed on motives permits us to foresee their disastrous consequences and thus determines the effort to dissolve the inner energy source (imaginative exaltation) that prepares future excessive reactions. Understanding of the law of ambivalence and its technique of application free one of the *trompe-l'oeil* by which occasionally excessive actions—and even the diverse traits of a deformed character—appear as stabilized and isolated islets. The truth is that these islets emerge from a common ground of falsified motivations. At this depth nothing is stable and nothing is isolated; everything is in a constant state of dynamic fluctuation. But these fluctuations, though illogical and affective, are not without method. They possess a legitimate structure subject to the ambivalent decomposition of qualities. The qualities constantly change into perversions; but it is exactly because of this that inversely the perversions are in their turn susceptible to being retransformed into qualities. The forecast of this forming and deforming dynamic process, once it is methodically guided, acquires therapeutic effectiveness because it creates determinants capable of containing the process of ambivalent decomposition and thus proceeding to the gradual recomposing of qualities.

The *logical* and the *illogical* are two psychological functions, inherent in the psychic system, that interpenetrate each other. Human thought is almost always invaded by affectively formed judgments. The *pathological* is manifested when the valuing function degenerates into ambivalence (for details, see my book *The Psychology of Motivation*).

It is indispensable at this point to exemplify the decomposition process. But such a descriptive analysis encounters a difficulty because of the very nature of ambivalent decomposition, which is an endless process. However far one may push the analysis, it still remains incomplete.

It is true that recognition of the legitimacy of a false psychic calculation raises it to the rank of *psychological calculation* endowed with foresight, as regards the error's inner motives as well as its pathogenic consequences. A means for the release of repression in a treatment situation, psychological calculation is a successive path of approach, which permits one to reveal and make comprehensible the inexhaustible flunctuation of motives. Its verbal use during treatment allows one to take up the theme again and again. The inevitable gaps of an isolated explanation, delivered in the course of one session, can thus be revised during the course of subsequent sessions. Without this possibility for revision, every isolated explanation would necessarily remain incomplete, because obliged to involve itself in this or that direction of the innumerable possible ramifications, the explanation is forced to neglect other paths no less useful for the achievement of the curative lifting of repression. The analyst who can avail himself of psychological calculation has the advantage of being able to take up the explanation again and again, starting with the daily incidents supplied by the analysand and the interpretation of dreams. In a treatment situation, the disadvantage of an isolated explanation is thus transformed into an advantage. The instrument of analysis—psychological calculation—is just as inexhaustible as the analysand's subconscious psychic calculation.

On the other hand, the written explanation lacks this means of pressing closely, by a successive route of approach, on the innumerable facets and shades of false motivation. Thus all written illustrations must necessarily form an incomplete sketch. The process of isolated and isolating exemplification, unable to exhaust the theme, must therefore be regarded rather as a means to highlight, *by its very gaps,* the inexhaustible wealth of the false calculation of satisfaction. So one must see these explanatory passages as an invitation addressed to the reader to detect, thanks to his psychological talent, the inevitable gaps and to complete them by letting himself be guided by the categories of false motivation.

After making this reservation, one may with the help of psychological calculation sketch the analysis of a very complex psychological constellation.

Timidity, for example, is a character syndrome marked by excessive inhibition. The counterpole of reactive inferiority is constituted—as in all nervous states—by the imagination's exalting effervescence in search of a feigned superiority. The illogicality of this pretension is concentrated in an exalted task. The distinctive feature here is that this task, although it almost always has multiple targets (pretensions to an iron will or an exceptional lucidity of the mind, etc.) is in the timid person oriented by preference toward an exalted ideal of goodness. In order to simplify its development, analysis will be content to envisage the morbid consequences of this common form of the exalted task.

Although more or less codetermined by conventional moralism, idealistic goodness is nevertheless proof of a certain drive to surpass. It is a quality that, in the process of decomposition, produces specific ambivalences. Goodness in its natural form is a state of harmony whose superior satisfaction is inclined, by free consent, to renounce conventional satisfactions that are habitually sought for in aggressive plans. (The timid person is frequently someone who was frustrated, even crushed, in childhood. His natural reactions of defense and attack are insufficiently developed. He will, by the path of false sublimation, turn his anguished intimidation into an imagined superiority which is therefore grafted onto the idealist impulse, without which the frustration suffered in early years would unleash excessive aggressiveness.) Unable to realize fully his ideal of goodness—which in an aggressive world would demand an extraordinary strength of character— the timid person vainly sets himself an ideal that has no relation to his available forces. The vain attitude burdens with excessive guilt even the natural defensive reactions, and this turns the timid person ino the dupe in a farce that he plays for himself. The inevitable consequence is the successive aggravation of intimidation. The victim of an aggression provoked by his goodness, the subject becomes filled with impotent rage. Growing anxiety will soon indulge in the imaginative anticipation—often without the slightest reason—of unjust aggression. Unlike natural goodness, the excessive consequences of unbounded renunciation—far from being freely accepted—will awaken, on the secret plane of imagination, hostile accusations and sentimental self-pity.

These fundamental ambivalences, once installed, prepare a cascade of new conflictual scissions. Vanity-engendered superiority will derive its fallacious satisfaction from an incessant adulatory comparison with the condemned environment. But, conversely, at every encounter with others, the timid person is overcome by feelings of inferiority that are exteriorized in attitudes of submission. The more he judges and condemns others, the more he feels judged and condemned by them. Anxiety about the next person's opinion assails him. It is complicated by anxiety in face of the reactions that could result from the contempt he fears he inspires and does inspire. In fact, the timid person offers to others a path of weak resistance, an invitation to abuse.

All these calamities, half real, half the result of imaginary exaltation, or even in part invented, continually stir up ruminations that in the end infiltrate every attempt at confronting the growing difficulties. Plans ripen badly or are nipped in the bud out of fear of having to confront the other, the enemy. Decisions, even if they are sketched out, remain unrealized or are subconsciously sabotaged in the course of their execution, and this furnishes an excuse for the retreat into protective inactivity. In this way the timid person barricades himself in autistic isolation, if not mutism. The social defeat is aggravated, sharpened by anxiety which feeds on the tormenting memories of a multitude of defeats accumulated in the past. But one's shame regarding these social failures is a much less intense torment than the sentimental guiltiness about one's unrealizable goodness. This guiltiness is a suffering in depth, attached to the true core of wasted vital impulse. But, overtaken by ambivalences, even this residual core of the original quality will be dissociated. It splits on the one hand into regret for past good intentions (a regret whose smears of guilt contaminate all of life's situations, all of existence, which is not at all favorable to idealism) and, on the other hand, into persistent vanity about those intentions which, even though unrealized, are still considered a sign of superiority.

Even while he flatters himself for being an innocent victim, the timid person reproaches himself bitterly for his weak attitudes, which no one detests as much as he himself. But he will not pierce through to the motives of his attitudes—his excessive self-inculpation and his mendacious self-justification, his self-exaltation and self-inhibition. He believes he is ready to do anything in order to become free; but in the deepest part of himself he is possessed, and for nothing in the world would he give up the perverse satisfaction derived from the complacent game with his dramatized conflicts, mistaken for exceptional inner wealth and proof of exceptional sensitivity. To free himself of them would signifiy relinquishing his superiorities and the justification for his idleness.

To feel himself drawn out of his autistic shell and see himself exposed to the difficulties of life, regarded as unsurmountable, fills him with anxiety. By means of the refined game of sentimentality, his very anxiety is transformed into satisfaction and morbid delight. How could he renounce the pleasures of his self-pity and the secret triumph of considering himself incomparable and unique? He inflicts on the world his refusal to participate, and his triumphant satisfactions become superlative. He is the proudest, most equitable, most misunderstood person, and how might he not consider himself unique when it comes to justice and goodness? His timidity is equaled only by the most shamefully and secretly hidden arrogance (hidden unless it explodes in aggression against those whom he does not consider dangerous—often those closest to him). But these incessant superlatives are, in sum, only anguished comparisons with others and so carry within themselves a fragility that makes them reversible. If the anxiety is transformed into self-satisfaction, self-satisfaction can be transformed back into anxiety to a superlative degree: he immediately feels he is the most stupid, most absurd, most unworthy, most cowardly, most nonexistent. Even these superlatives of self-accusation bring to a peak the vanity of being unique.

Vain uniqueness cannot fail to aggravate the torments of autistic isolation and thus create a new counterpole of guilt. Excessive accusation of others is transformed into boundless admiration. But from the recesses of his den, the timid person glowers at others, full of the desire to participate in their pleasures from which he feels excluded. His imagination exalts material and sexual pleasures because his appetites are immeasurably famished as a result of the frustrations he has imposed on himself out of exalted idealism as well as social ineptness. People who enjoy the least advantages from nature or social rank, the very pariahs of society, provided they are not inhibited, seem enviable to him because they are endowed with qualities that remain inaccessible to him. They at least know how to let themselves go, let themselves live, approach the next man, speak without fear. Because he has ceaselessly blamed others for their lack of scruples, the timid person in the end believes that only by freeing himself of all scruples would he be able to equal them, be what they are, break through the blockage of his inhibition. The absence of all scruple, the ambivalent attitude of his earlier exalted tasks, becomes his secret imaginative counterideal, which is no less unrealizable.

The timid person, at least if he gets stranded in this path of dead ends, sees himself confronted by a new problem that threatens to obsess him more and more. Do I dare? he says to himself. He makes some attempt to dare, studies audacious and nonchalant poses. He exaggerates them in order to give himself poise. He himself feels ridiculous because of these badly executed poses, and collapses before the ironic and contemptuous responses that he suspects everywhere and that he actually provokes. He feels that he is the world's laughing stock, and he shamefully retreats into the refuge of his autism.

The alternation of these states of hope and despair remains fixed in most cases. In its attenuated forms—a sign that the exalted task is not too obsessive—timidity is one of the most frequent symptoms. Sometimes, in its benign form, timidity disappears during the course of a life when the exalted task is abandoned, either due to the sublimation of the imaginative exaltation that permits a satisfactory realization of the idealist task, or—and this more frequently—by way of banalization. But, conversely, timidity can be intensified to the point of assuming the aspect of a true neurosis.

Under the influence of repeated shocks or a constantly humiliating situation, intimidation threatens to end in an excess of morbid interpretation that verges on the oneiric. The ambivalences become frozen in fixed ideas of megalomaniac vanity (or the vanity of smallness: feelings of complete nullity); ideas of persecution (guiltiness); ideas of vindication (accusation); or ideas of sentimental amelioration of the world (because the neurotically timid person, unable to improve himself, imagines that only the improvement of the world, which he holds responsible, can deliver him from his nightmare). The idealistic exaltation that lies at the origin of his morbid condition—the exalted quality that in imagination lies underneath and therefore is fated to become ambivalently decomposed—thus threatens to sweep him away in the wreckage of lucid reasoning.

It is then that the last stage of ambivalent decomposition can occur. The exalted imagination, becoming oneirically interpretative, borders on the loss of reason. Timidity turns into psychosis. Delirium floods the mind. For example, the *idée fixe* of amelioration will be ambivalently opposed to the desire for revenge. Delirious aggressiveness will tend to concentrate on this or that person, held responsible for all humiliations suffered. In the case of all timid persons, similar ideas can emerge temporarily; they are dissolved by a residue of lucidity. In rare cases the need for revenge abolishes it. The timid person becomes the reckless lunatic. The plan is born in him to reestablish derided justice and put an end to the iniquities committed by the one person responsible for his delirium. In order to prove to himself that he is audacious, the timid person no longer shrinks from an aggressive resolution, even murder.

But in the mind of the timid person who has become excessively reckless, murder is committed solely out of goodness. It is an ideal task to be accomplished, an act of justice, inexorably necessary to wipe out the surrounding ignominy and to give the insensitive world a salutary warning, a striking example of combative courage, unique and rare probity. The timid person, by dint of his goodness, sets himself up as the dispenser of justice.

The exalted task, definitely decomposed into hatred, still remains in the background of a plan of justificatory revenge.

This too-succinct summary aims at emphasizing, first of all, the progressive stages of ambivalent decomposition. Undoubtedly it does not sufficiently take into account the resurgence of qualities which can still persist for a long time despite overwhelming confusion. These qualities manifest themselves in activities that are marked by a tone of exacerbation, due to the fundamental ambivalence between exalted idealism and autistic egocentricity. The timid person is capable of devotion, generosity, and openness. To a friendly and understanding approach he will respond with a gratitude whose overflow is restrained only by his autistic reserve and the distrustful irony of his wounded soul, whose insatiable need for triumph inclines him to perfidy. Very often behind the apparent autistic laziness hides an unsuspected energy, an extraordinary capacity for work, which, however, will only express itself on the condition that it finds a terrain that makes it possible to satisfy idealism. It is true that idealism habitually exhausts itself in efforts at self-justification and self-idealization, and that thus the energy is most often wastefully employed. What ferocious energy it must take to defend ceaselessly the isolated position of one's purportedly unique value against the entire world and its contemptuous assault! But it often happens that the timid person, instead of furnishing his autistic retreat with ruminative ghosts, manages partly to sublimate his sentimental idealism and partly to spiritualize his falsely justifying blindness. Energy, inasmuch as it is liberated, will then be able to concentrate on a valid accomplishment and will often produce a work of art, since exalted idealism, accompanied by hypersensitivity, can go hand in hand with the talents of the aesthete. In this way the timid neurotic will be able to break through his isolation. His message addressed to the world will contain his life's experience. The work will be humanly valid, provided it is not merely the product of a facile talent but a cry of true suffering. Nevertheless, even in the best circumstances, it will lack the fullness of artistic expression found solely in the contrast between the suffering of perversity and the joys inherent in harmony.

A final observation on this attempt to exemplify the ambivalent decomposition of character through a single example: timidity is but one morbid syndrome among many others. None of these syndromes exist in isolation. The transforming dynamic process of life forms a legitimately structured whole. Harmonies decompose into ambivalences, and ambivalences can recompose themselves in harmony. Just as harmonies are linked to each other, ambivalences are also linked despite their conflictual scissions. When all is said and done, there exists only a single unique malady of the valuing mind: *imaginative exaltation*. This, the fundamental cause of all ambivalences, is itself split into two counterpoles: in its actively exalted form, the malady of the mind is manifested by progressive banalization; in its inhibitive form, it leads to nervousness with its states of aggravation, neurosis, and psychosis.

Banalization is not diagnosed by psychiatry as a pathological condition. It is, because of its frequency, generally confused with the norm. But the norm is *banality,* the state of balance and common sense which, however, lacking the drive to surpass, is content to adapt to the reigning conventions. Banalization, on the contrary, is not a stationary psychic condition but a deforming process that tends to the unscrupulous satisfaction of sexual and material desires. It is an imbalance of valuation, a disease of the biologically elementary function of the mind whose goal consists in healthily deploying desires over the entire expanse of valid satisfactions. Unlike nervousness, which by overvaluation of the mind creates the exalted task, thus crushing sexual and material desires, banalization undervalues the harmonizing function of the mind in order to free itself from the brake of reason. But this amputation only succeeds in reducing the range of satisfactions to the sphere of vulgar and mediocre pleasures. Despite this restriction, and because of its invitation to the unleashing of desires, banalization is often mistaken for the ultimate meaning of life and set up as a counter-ideal of unscrupulous ambition and lack of inhibition. The bana-lized person overflows with contempt for the nervous person and his inhibitions; the nervous person detests the banalized because of his vulgarity. Both of them obtain from this continual comparison the sure reward of vanity-engendered triumph. But unlike the banalized person (at least in his most obvious form, that is, the prototype of the banalized-banal whose euphoric triumph is not contradicted by any drive to surpass), the nervous person suffers instead from the backlash of his triumphant disdain: the promises of banal and facile satisfactions attract him. In his shamefully hidden imagination he sees himself unleashed without shame. Inhibited, he sees in banalization the ideal of release from inhibition. And hence he tries at times to play the part of the banalized man. But he will only be a banalized nervous person, or, if he persists beyond measure, a nervous banalized person. His triumph will be manifested in the ambivalent form of cynicism. The hatred of the mind, outrageously displayed, betrays a disappointed love of the mind. The betrayal of his idealism only results in guilty self-deception. This banalized counterideal is perhaps the deepest cause of the disorientation of the nervous person who, in order not to go too far astray, needs a solidly established superstructure of values.

Falsely idealized banalization is included in the calculation of satisfactions; it is one of the most frequent paths. No understanding of psychic functioning as a whole is possible so long as this path of unhealthy deviation is not clearly diagnosed.

ANALYSIS OF THE IMPONDERABLES

Comprehension of the ambivalent lawfulness of false subconscious calculation permits one to uncover not only the secret motivations of character-related syndromes but also the innumerable "tricks" to which vanity resorts, whether constantly or occasionally, in order to assure itself of its feeling of superiority: a myriad of tiny reactions, trifles, but whose irritating power is extremely intense as long as they remain imponderable. It is precisely the perfidy of their imponderability which, leaving the indignant victim without defense, becomes a cause of mutual irritation that in the end extends to all interpersonal relations.

The result is a kind of impotent rage that stagnates at the most profound depth of the spirit. Contained and intensified again and again by further troubles, rage, often accumulated since childhood, becomes transformed in adults into generalized suspicion, surliness, crabbiness, and nastiness, and finally becomes the most unsuspected cause of character deformation.

The constant and insidious pressure of this secret impotent rage is far more traumatizing than any accidental shocks and catastrophes. One could also say that from childhood on the family milieu is the truly traumatizing situation, when contact between the two parents is infested by these imponderables of false motivation. They manifest themselves in gestures, intonations of the voice, verbal insinuations. They are at times accusatory allusions

camouflaged by a mellifluous voice, at times reproaches accompanied by assurances that one does not hold a grudge against the
person, a sign of one's magnanimity. Silences that clamp down
with a sulkiness that gesture and expression strive to convey, the
construing of the other's fault with the help of accusations drawn
from a past that eludes control, ironies disguised as gentle teasing,
petty humiliating acts, impertinences aimed at cutting short an
argument, attacks of willful and exaggerated cruelty, expressions of
impatience over some trifle, endless quibbling for the sake of being
right at all costs—a swarm of small, aggressively hypocritical
attitudes. They "mean nothing," and yet they mean everything.
Because these so-called "nothings" pierce the victim of the perfidious aggression like an arrow and in the long run inflict on the soul
wounds that are all the more poisonous since every attempt at
defense runs up against expressions of boundless amazement,
shrugs of the shoulders, indignant denials, that brand the unhealthy
hypersensitivity of the victim, who finally explodes in rage or who,
in order to avoid ridicule, is obliged to swallow his resentment, and
this leads him in turn to utilize the perfidious weapon of small
imponderable acts of revenge. Out of this war of nerves, conducted
subconsciously with the aid of innuendoes, hatred accumulates and
explodes in quarrels that each partner uses to cast blame on the
other.

It is true that the nervous person, hypersensitized from childhood on, can end by seeing insidious attacks everywhere even if
they do not exist, so that finally the interpretative form of nervousness makes all contact difficult. Morbid interpretation based on
these imponderables can even become delirious. No logical argument succeeds in convincing the interpreter of the morbidity of his
behavior. The logic that tries to make him understand reason—by
proving to him the nonexistence of illogical and imponderable
aggressions—does not reach him, because the patient has very
personal reasons for an excessive belief in their importance. To a
greater extent than others, he has been their target since childhood.
His enraged impotence in the face of their enormous accumulation
makes him lose the brake of reason. They have so often put him
beside himself that he is crazed. Can these imponderables be
insignificant if they can, even if only in infrequent cases, cause the
loss of reason? In view of this possibility, any argument denying
the importance of the phenomenon must be suspected as illogical, a
false intepretation of reality, the repression of truth.

The truth is that these "imponderable" motivations do exist and
are of immense and unsuspected importance in life, even in their

most customary and everyday forms. Not only do they produce interpretative psychosis in marginal cases, they invade all of life with their destructive power. From childhood on they act in all of us to destroy, in varying degrees of intensity, positive character qualities and prevent all of humanity from realizing values. Each person's character is disintegrated unbeknown to him, because he sees himself driven to utilize insidious and falsely justificatory motivations in order to actively defend himself as best he can against mysterious, elusive aggressions.

There is no point in claiming—as the rule of the social game requires—that one mustn't pay attention to such trifles. Of course, good manners are right to teach that one mustn't be affected by them or respond emotionally. But to claim that one is at ease when one is in fact not beyond their reach amounts to pure affectation, a vain pose, a disdainful attitude of superiority, a calculated revenge that is part of the game and countergame of imponderables. Refusing to lend conscious and objective attention to them is but a repressive attitude, with all its terrible consequences. Precisely in claiming to pay no attention to insidious attacks, one becomes used to paying no attention to one's own revengeful counterattacks. The precept of "not taking it lying down" becomes a conventional requirement in defense of one's honor; but the attacks and defenses often continue with the greatest politeness. Under the mantle of exquisite courtesy, spite is discharged, whether by pinpricks that send the other person into a rage or by calumnies against which he is impotent because they occur without his knowledge but have consequences which are certain to be very bad for him. Mutual distrust degrades character, ruins cordiality, breaks up friendships, poisons homes, destroys the life of societies whose members, generation after generation, have been brought up in unhealthy homes.

Even the relations between nations are involved in this. Here, as everywhere else, the illogicality of false motives is puerile and imponderable. But more than elsewhere, the destructive consequences on an international level manifest themselves in all the vastness of their senseless enormity. Technical progress supplies the discharge of aggression with means that transform apparently insignificant motives into a threat that hangs over the life of entire peoples. Imponderable motives end by revealing their vital importance, because they codetermine the decisions of those who are responsible. The false calculation of satisfaction has as its interpretative justification the uncontrolled avidity of economic and material interests elevated to the rank of supreme ideals. The reasonable conciliations desired by the entire world are sabotaged over and over, because they would deprive the game's leaders of the opportunity to exhibit their skill at provocation and force them to renounce the spectacular staging of their protective missions. The need for vanity-inspired triumph over the adversary drives both sides to hurl threats of intimidation, cheered on by their partisans; the fear of losing face makes retreat difficult, if not impossible. Intrigue and the threat of violence becomes the rule. Imponderable subconscious motivations produce a reciprocal lack of meditative caution, which is generally considered to be the only attitude that jibes with the environing reality. But the hidden psychic reality, the more it is neglected and repressed, imposes its law that governs pathology. Interpretative madness is no longer an isolated phenomenon. Affectively blind reasoning produces, to the extent to which the true psychic causes, the false motives, remain subconsciously denied, a generalized anxiety psychosis.

The fault is not that of society's leaders, nor of the crowd that gives them the right to decide its fate; it is the fault of human nature in general. Since this failing involves the entire world, it does not seem imputable to anyone, hence it leads to indignant interprojection, the cause in turn of belligerent conflicts. Indignation cannot change this state of affairs. Indignation and self-justification complement each other because they are the ambivalent result of the decay of authentic dignity, which is to be found only in an objective attitude. Indignation decomposes qualities and leads back to puerilism. Whether it is a quarrel between children, with its stereotypical "Say that again, if you dare," followed by a scuffle, or a family quarrel, or a quarrel between nations, the false motives remain the same. What changes is only what is at stake. We must begin to combat the imponderables of false motivation in the child so that the adult will not become, unbeknown to himself, the victim of puerilism, of indignation and relentless false justifications. The problem is not beyond the reach of education. As long as imponderables are not clearly objectified and actively eliminated, false reactions will continue to plunge individuals and collectivities into a state of anxiety whose effects are indescribable because its secret causes elude description.

The pathological puerilism that stagnates in the depths of the human soul is nowhere revealed as clearly as in the course of the reeducation of maladjusted children. When one speaks to the child—in terms that he can understand—about the imponderables of false motivation, when for instance one shows the child that his disobedience is a form of indignation and provocative revenge, one often elicits a convulsive laugh of admission, even before linking it up with proof of the advantage he derives from this false calculation. This uncontrolled convulsive laugh is a perfect demonstration that the child is able to recognize his false motivation. Sometimes instead of the avowing laughter there is repeated yawning. The child tries to withdraw into repression, pretending that nothing could be more boring to him than this kind of revelation. It is then enough to explain the meaning of this defense for it to radically disappear. The two ambivalent attitudes show that the child has been touched in the depths of his spirit.

In the adult, more able than the child to exert a certain self-control over appearances, yawning is not used to express resistance and the avowing laughter is rare. But the treatment of adults, above all at its beginning, is also marked by exaggerated attitudes of repression and avowal that betray the fact that the revelation of imponderables strikes the subject at the core of his existence. Yawning is often replaced by an exaggerated facial expression of hostile distrust that strains to express how irritating (boring, insufferable) it is to see oneself understood and exposed. As for the attitude of avowal, in the place of convulsive laughter the analyst may see equally spasmodic weeping that suddenly breaks through the barrier of self-control. This happens if, when talking about the patient's childhood, one touches a vulnerable area of secret self-reproach. In the face of the evident contrast between the hopes once nourished about oneself and the present guilty disappointment that has been camouflaged out of vanity, the tears gush forth. This same contrast produces an excess of aggressive hostility rather than sentimental tears, if the subject does not understand that the imponderables of his motivation, repressed up until now, are at the bottom of all his disorientation and despair. Despite its nuance of sentimentality, the spasmodic explosion of tears, like the child's convulsive laughter, is an authentic expression of avowal. We see, too, that in the adult's case the most frequent response to the revelation of imponderables is hope for turning over a new leaf, often expressed with enthusiasm. But this reaction, still a form of exaltation subject to ambivalence, will give way sooner or later to conventional anxiety in the face of the painful revelations and the solitary effort that is required in order to obtain a veritable renewal. This more or less lengthy treatment then consists in reinforcing, with the help of psychological calculation, the first intimations of the existence of imponderables and knowledge of their disastrous consequences. As the patient's initial, vanity-induced enthusiasm subsides, his authentic hope for renewal is strengthened. Little by little, the subject becomes able not only to admit the existence of secret false motivations but also to dissolve within himself all the vanities, sentimentalities, accusations, and exalted feelings of guilt. He ceases to utilize them on the plane of imaginative ruminations as a way of falsely interpreting himself and his environment, or in order to discharge them in the form of more or less insidious and treacherous vengeful reactions. The good he procures for himself in this way finally helps to convince him and causes the selfish motive of false satisfaction to be replaced by a biologically elementary accounting, whose search for just satisfaction was pathologically disturbed. Only inner experience can overcome the cavils of opposition and resistance that are inspired by false motivation and attain to spiritualizing conviction and sublimating renewal.

The laughter of children, just like the tears of adults who are confronted by the revelation of imponderables, highlights feelings of ridicule and pain that have accumulated in the depths of the human soul because of the false ancestral calculation of satisfaction and its perfidious means of attack and defense. Under this unceasing assault, the nobility of the soul crumbles, and its opposite, ignominy, invades all human interactions. Conventional education consists in introducing the child to the conventions of polite society, which in themselves are indispensable but often are no more than hypocrisy. Nobody feels as deeply as the child the absence of generosity, tolerance, authenticity, and righteousness in all vital relations. The child's response to this kind of education is the spasm of laughter and tears that remains shamefully locked in his depths. Laughter is the equivalent of tears. The child's spasmodic laughter, when it explodes in a therapeutic situation, is the expression of his unmasked vanity but also, and above all, the expression of his precocious despair about the life that awaits him and that adults prepare for him.

All of humanity protects itself against the revelation with ironic laughter or by complaining about how inopportune and indiscreet it is. A tacit pact of repression unites all humans in reprobation of any attempt at elucidation. "Don't talk to me about my false motives, and I'll make sure not to talk about yours! Let us bear the consequences of our common repression—the false interactions— instead of exposing the secret causes of our miseries, because those causes are too ridiculous and too lamentable." Would that the consequences were borne! But each man's impotent rage is manifested by his indignation toward others. Each man considers himself the innocent victim and sentimentally blames the other. The ridiculous part of this picture is that, if one were to believe each person's self-justifications, there would not be any innocent victims; the deplorable part is that all the supposedly innocent are victims of their own repressing lie. The life of which they complain is nothing but their common way of living.

The laughter of despair, open to the convulsive tears that each person bears within him since childhood, will cease to exert its convulsive constraint to the extent that each person, having stopped blaming others, will begin to direct judgment at himself. What is comic about the situation will give way to humor and its liberating laughter. Humor liberates us from what is comical and deplorable because it is connected with the tragic aspect of life: it invites us not to exclude ourselves from the ancestral fault inscribed in human nature. Humor is an introspective attitude: it tries to overcome the tragic aspect of motivations that are susceptible to falsification. This liberating humor has existed since the beginning of time. Without it, life would only be a degradation of lofty possibilities. Introspection, when it achieves the intensity of humor, allows us to understand that at the essential level—the plane of just motivation—no innocent victim exists, and the incriminating proceedings brought against others are simply self-deception. This trial against others leads to a verdict and a sanction that turns against the plaintiff. The unjustly initiated trial unleashes, through subconsciously legitimate paths, pathogenic processes: vanity-inspired self-justification is reversed and becomes self-condemnation. The repression of this verdict does not suspend the execution of the sentence, which is unfailingly realized because of the justice inherent in life. Self-condemnation takes place through the ambivalent decomposition of qualities.

Introspective humor is the mainstay of all qualities. It endeavors to harmonize even decomposed qualities. Its educational and re-educational power resides in the fact that it liberates moral courage, which alone dares to confront motivations judged to be imponderable.

INTROSPECTIVE METHOD AND RETROSPECTIVE METHOD

The use of the introspective method has as its consequence a complete reversal of therapeutic and re-educational techniques.

It is hardly superfluous to recall at this point that the works of Freud, Adler, and Jung contain passages, too numerous to be quoted, that sing the praises of introspection. Indeed, introspection is, time and time again, put forward as the indispensable condition for all knowledge of psychic functioning. This fact leads us to believe that inner observation, even though employed by these authors in a nonmethodical manner, lies at the basis of their revolutionary discoveries.

Among the authors who have tried to elevate introspection to the rank of a method, it will suffice in the interest of brevity to cite the attempt by far the most methodical, made by Karen Horney *(Self-Analysis)*. However, this attempt, despite its lucidity, gives rise to an objection that is of capital importance and highly instructive.

Originally a member of the Freudian school, Karen Horney worked with the help of so-called free association, whose interpretation, inaugurated by Freud and developed by Jung, is very difficult even for the expert analyst to manage and leaves, because of this, too much room for the danger of random speculation.

No analytical procedure can completely renounce associations. They are used above all in the interpretation of dreams, and this is often extremely fertile. Nevertheless, one must emphasize that the so-called freedom of associations is often only an illusion. Associations are determined not only by affective memory of the extraconscious (which ensures their revelatory importance) but also by the ideological predominance that various doctrines accord different vital phenomena. One can also observe that in Freudian analysis associations obsessively revolve around sexual complexes, which Freudian doctrine regards as vitally predominant, whereas in Karen Horney's analytical procedure, which is liberated from the theory of sexualization, associations reveal subconscious intentions and obsessive plans that extend over the entire range of inner feelings and interpersonal relations and situations.

Since associations are codetermined by the value judgments set forth by analytical doctrine, their use is advantageous only to the extent that the valuation proposed by the doctrine refers to authentic values and thus to the meaning of life.

Only the preestablished knowledge of the law of harmony (which determines motivations and therefore sensible actions) and of the law of ambivalent disharmony (which determines senseless reaction-motivations) can prevent the analysand from producing obliging associations codetermined by doctrinal suggestion and prevent the analyst from interpreting them in a more or less speculative manner. Moreover, knowledge of the laws governing hidden motivations renders the use of associations in greater part superfluous. The introspective method is not based on the search for associatively revealed *past traumas,* but on the study of *motivations presently active* and determining, revealed by knowledge of their inner calculation of satisfaction.

Since psychic deformation and its various syndromes are the result of an inner deliberation subject to the false calculation of satisfaction, it is important to reveal to the patient the nature of his false subconscious calculation and to awaken him fully to the disastrous consequences that flow from it. The re-educational goal is mobilization of the need for satisfaction in its authentic form. Only the awakening of this need, the most elementary vital need, has the strength to overcome the vain promises of exalted imagination. The means to realize this re-educational goal consist in concentrating attention on the categorized pattern of this repressive false justification.

What is important is not what happens to a person, but the characteristic manner in which he actively responds to it. As the reactive response has been elaborated in a morbid form since childhood through repressive false justification, the re-educational effort must first of all address this essential cause of morbidity, so as to obtain the curative effect, that is, the progressive abreaction of subconsciously accumulated anxiety.

For both Adler and Freud, the pathogenic principle resides in the regressive fixation on infantile trauma. According to Freud, this fixation is determined by insufficiently overcome Oedipal stages; according to Adler, affective retardation fixes the child in a plan of life made up of defense and attack attitudes that render him forever incapable of adjusting to the demands of reality. Jung makes a point of distinguishing between two types of human beings, intravert and extravert, the first to be treated by Freud's method and the second by Adler's.

For both Freud and Adler the curative principle consists in tracking down the traumatizing incidents. The recognition of past incidents allegedly makes it possible to achieve dissolution of the fixation and discharge of pathogenic affectivity. Thus the curative method has itself a regressive nature. It must unfold the history of the past in order to uncover the traumatizing incidents one by one.

Because of the fact that not only the adult but even the child has forgotten the link existing between past shocks and the present unhealthy psychic condition, the only way to reveal this link lies in mobilizing traumatic memories with the help of associations.

Whatever modifications successors may have made in this curative technique, its fundamental principle—associative exploration in order to obtain the *abreaction of affect*—remains unchanged.

It is, however, important to take note of an important modification, feasible only in the treatment of children, that consists in utilizing play as a re-educational tool. The child expresses himself freely only in play. For example, almost all children like to draw, and this sort of play—provided that the proposed subject matter permits it—can incite affectively troubled children to express resentments they have acquired in the family milieu. The re-educator interprets the drawing along the lines of the doctrine he has adopted and thus can avoid the complications of associative exploration. On the other hand, active play is often utilized to achieve the abreaction of repressed aggressiveness. It is always a good idea to let the child play, and the freedom accorded him can thus become the cause of a liberation whose benefits have an influence on family relations. The child affectively linked to the re-educator will, for example, agree to do his homework and in this way avoid being scolded, something that will introduce a new motive for tranquillity in his troubled life and often the start of other efforts as well. So the problem consists in knowing whether the results obtained, attributed to the alleged "abreaction," are not in reality the consequence of an underlying repercussion on the constellation of motives. It will be necessary to return later to the problem posed here.

In the light of the preceding study of motivations, serious objections of a general order militate against the associative technique as well as the doctrine of abreaction.

The discharge of subconsciously accumulated affect does not take place only in a therapeutic situation. The abreaction, whether in the form of a choleric explosion or in that of a tearful crisis, is a frequent phenomenon of everyday life. Such discharges possess no curative value. This is because their underlying motivation remains intact; they form the crystallizing point around which morbid affectivity regroups again and again. In a treatment situation, whether of children or adults, it is therefore important to dissolve this crystallizing point, the knot of resentments. The entire problem of the curative technique is thus concentrated on knowing how this nub of resentment is formed and by what means its dissolution can be obtained most economically.

One thing is beyond doubt: the knot of resentments is formed in childhood. All unhealthy states of the psychic system—whether they are characterized by resigned submission or open revolt—can be imputed to an *impotent rage* faced by the exigencies of reality, which produces an incessant morbid abreaction of a choleric or plaintive nature. This impotent rage has accumulated since childhood as a result of traumatizing frustrations. (In the spoiled child, impotent rage results in excessive capriciousness, which ends by provoking indispensable prohibitions that are judged unjust.) In one case or the other, repressed rage is manifested by hypersensitivity that continually effervesces both on the imaginative plane, in rancorous accusations and sentimental sulkiness, and on the active plane in aggressive explosions or morbidly inhibiting reactions. Affective abreaction, far from being a means of cure, is therefore proof of the persistence of an unhealthy condition; it reveals an underlying erroneous motivation and this motivating error forms the core around which the resentments are always reconstituted anew. It is this morbid error that must be dissolved, something that can only be done by way of just revaluation. *The curative principle resides in cognitive abreaction (sublimation-spiritualization) and not in affective abreaction.* Lucid valuation must be opposed to affective explosions, which only continue to reinforce the rage of impotence again and again. Affective explosions, far from being liberating, are followed by imaginative ruminations that reinforce obscuration and thus are opposed to the curative effort of just revaluation.

In the treatment situation, affective explosions (accusatory or sentimental, choleric or plaintive, submissive or rebellious) focus on the analyst and produce the alternation between resistance and transference. These ambivalent explosions of impotent rage are simply false attempts at abreaction. They are inevitable, because the analyst must attack the cause of enraged impotence, the intrinsic error: guilty vanity, the disavowal of one's mistakes. But an excess of this false valuation of the curative situation, the excess of morbid ambivalence (resistance-transference) manifested by the production of a transference neurosis—which is judged indispensable in psychoanalysis—is precisely the sign that the analysis is badly conducted and that valuation, instead of being objectified, continues to overflow due to blinding affect.

An even greater reason for this drawback lies in the associative method. Associations continually reveal the parents' educational faults (even in orthodox psychoanalysis, where the parents become castrators). They threaten to feed retrospective imagination and imbue it with an accusation so intense that the revealed causes—which belong irremediably to the past—frequently end by being used as a definitive self-justification and thereby render the present unhealthy condition beyond remedy. As long as the core of resentment (false motivation) persists, the associations, supposedly free, are codetermined by it, and memories thus produced are often nothing but false interpretations of the past, screens of false justification charged with renewed traumatizing power. It is true that the analyst—unless, on the pretext of scientific objectivity, he becomes fixed in complete passivity—tries to contain the danger, an irremediable part of the associative method, by trying to reconcile the

62	EDUCATION

patient with the past. But this attempt to change the valuing perspective and to get the patient to assume responsibility for his past and present mistakes is nothing less than an insufficiently methodical incursion into the domain of motives and their false calculation of satisfaction. The educator gifted with true psychological talent will thus obtain results in spite of his method. He will be led to believe that the remedy resides in the associatively obtained revelations and in the illusion of abreaction, instead of understanding that his results, to the extent that they are positive, are due to the underlying revision of motivation, and that amelioration would be attained much more economically by a methodical study of motivations and their falsifying tendency.

The true curative principle does not reside in the abreaction of this or that affect linked to this or that past trauma, as revealed by the path of association.

The child will resist all accidental traumas—or, at least, have a greater chance to resist them—if he feels assured of his parents' affection and of the esteem he deserves.

After the last world war, all children seen in consultation had been traumatized by the air raids and often by racial persecutions. Detailed review of these past traumas was not only superfluous but harmful. In order to achieve readjustment, it was necessary to combat residual false valuations that subconsciously acted as much on the parents as on the children and that brought about—even if in part and accidentally—excessive irritability, the source of continuous family quarrels. In general, it is advisable to realize that traumatization is not a phenomenon of paramount importance. Trauma produces anxiety; but all real anxiety is surmountable and thus becomes a positive element in character formation. *Anxiety becomes pathogenic when the trauma, instead of being surmounted, is utilized as a pretext for self-justification.* This utilization can be subconscious, and the trauma, itself repressed, becomes the center from which the obsessive anxiety emanates. *Yet, the cause of the unhealthy condition is not the trauma but its morbid utilization.* In the past life of every human being there are events that might have been traumatizing. The normal man differs from the psychopath in that he has surmounted them instead of utilizing them morbidly. The child, even more than the adult, is liable to traumatization because of his more active sensitivity and his weak capacity for valuation, which means that he can neither avoid nor resist its harmful influence. But the child living in an affectively united family has the greatest chance of not succumbing to traumatization.

If he is not unjustly scolded and accused or spoiled and pampered, he will surmount his affective troubles instead of utilizing them as a pretext for self-justification. One can nevertheless admit that there are traumatizing instances that are normally insurmountable, even though the psychic terrain is not morbid. They can be of a sexual nature. But they are too rare to justify a generalized doctrine and a curative technique based exclusively on their investigation.

The curative principle does not reside in the abreaction of some affect linked to some past trauma that has been revealed through association. The real trauma resides in the *family atmosphere* created by the parents' false motivations and the false educational activities resulting from them.

The family atmosphere, when false motivations underlie it, creates a permanent traumatization that prepares in the child a morbid terrain in which submissive or rebellious maladjustments can germinate. Any fortuitous event, often the slightest (for instance, a punishment resented as being excessively unjust or a ruse that has permitted the child to escape punishment), can become the occasion for an erroneous valuation capable of generalizing the significance of the event and deducing from it, *once and for all*, a guiding principle for future activity. In this regard, it is imperative to remember that the categories of false motivation are ancestrally prepared in every child. It is only right to observe that the essential fault should not be exclusively imputed to the parents. *It is inscribed in human nature.* It was transmitted to the parents by their own parents inasmuch as they were excessively irritable, and it will be retransmitted to his own children by the child when he becomes an adult. The essential fault—false motivation—is formed in childhood to the degree in which the ancestral predisposition encounters a constantly irritating family climate. Its revivification is actuated in the child beginning with a constant irritation out of which sooner or later springs a still completely emotional and prelogical valuation, all the more incorrigible and principled when it is sustained by indefinable resentments. The child's affective logic does not yet know the modalities "possible, likely, certain" or the gradations "sometimes, often, always." Affect imposes itself on the child as an incorrigible certainty and in the reticent child disoriented affect will impose itself with the force of obsessive certitude. His budding judgment, still lacking all nuance, will in his secret imagination be affectively based on accusatory complaints. *"I* am *always* scolded." The fact of being scolded, perhaps "sometimes" or "often," is deformed, generalized into "always," while the child's offense, which is also a more or less frequent fact according to the degree of disobedience, is repressed (affectively transformed into "never"). The child has a hypersensitive reaction to the scolding and is no longer conscious of the continued repetition of his own provocative misbehavior. This repression incites the child to believe that his misdeeds are matters of no importance that do not deserve the scolding, and at a more intense degree of repression he will be persuaded that he never does anything wrong and that he is nevertheless always scolded. Resentment, when it is accompanied by the generalization of "always" and "never," contains the germ of a judgment. This plaintive and accusatory resentment produces the vanity-induced conclusion "I am always innocent." Thus, starting with its initial affectively false judgment, a tendency is formed that persists in the adult, always to repress his own faults and never to admit them to himself. Having becoming subconsciously obsessive due to the original repression in the child, his fault will produce character traits beginning in childhood that have as underpinnings incorrigible judgments, as for instance "One must never take it lying down"—hence giving rise to a rebellious character able to resist and impervious to all sanctions. But these deformed judgments can take an inverse turn and will then determine apparently exemplary behavior owing to an exaggerated attachment to the parents' good opinion. This form of derangement can go so far as hypocritical submission based on a global judgment of this sort: "One must always seek the protection of one's mother (or father)." In families with several children, these principled judgments will be influenced by the attitudes of brothers and sisters: "One must never take it lying down as my sister does out of cowardice" or "One must never rebel openly as my brother is foolish enough to do," and so on.

Such exalted valuations, the products of subconsciously excessive resentments, are, due to their erroneous excessiveness, accompanied by their own ambivalent corrective. Thus in the rebellious person there will be aroused the anxiety of provoked sanctions, an anxiety hidden by vanity that refuses to yield, just as in the case of the submissive person there will be regret for the amusements and games that they have had to give up in order to obtain, by exaggerated obedience, the other's protection and esteem.

Morbidly ambivalent judgments can produce extremely variable character traits. Underlying all these traits will be the basic resentful emotion: love-hate. The subject may become fixed in a pose that betrays only one of two exalting poles of ambivalence; but often in the same subject character traits will oscillate between one excess and another. Then spite alternates with sulkiness, impertinence alternates with entreaties for forgiveness. On the scholastic plane frantic efforts at work are followed by fatigue and the collapse into idleness, and so on.

All deformed character traits are underlaid by fallacious promises of vanity-inspired, accusatory, and sentimental self-satisfaction; this makes them categoric and difficult to correct. Overwhelmed at their origin by vague, completely subconscious feelings of resentment, affective judgments gradually become conceptualized as the intellect awakens. In the end, they fully acquire their character of false rationalization. They become more or less consciously formulated value judgments, constant motives which, though remaining puerile, in the end determine the adult's behavior. The adult's maladjustment is also underlaid by affective traumas which began in early childhood.

In the exaggerated valuations of the maladjusted and affectively retarded adult one finds the ensemble of past traumatizing events quintessentially condensed.

The process of condensation of all past traumas into a present false valuation is intensified by the fact that every subject, starting with the subconscious choice of his stereotyped attack and defense attitudes, will end by constantly provoking in the people around him counterattacks that are in turn stereotyped (for the child, scoldings and sanctions). The defense system having gradually adjusted in an unhealthy fashion to these provoked counterattacks, the subject will become filled by the falsely justified feeling that his way of acting is perfectly adapted to the exigencies of reality, and that this is the only means of protection against the surrounding hostility. *Fixation and regression are therefore not static but dynamic phenomena.*

The subject, and indeed the child, is not once and for all fixed in past traumas and their residual affect; he remains fixed in his present false valuation which has become justificatory habit, that is, falsely categorized motivation.

False subconscious motivation is the essential cause, and character deformation—senseless activity—is its accidental effect. So long as the cause is not eliminated, the effect will be reproduced obsessively. No abreaction of residual affect can prevent the reproduction of falsely motivated activity. The residual affect will accumulate again and again as the result of false, vanity-inspired, accusatory and sentimental valuations of each current situation. The present false valuation, in which all past traumas are condensed, transforms all present excitations into feelings of irritation and indignation, unendurable traumas. This pathogenic transformation takes place because of imaginative ruminations, which end by obfuscating more and more the valuing mind's lucidity and by creating a more or less constant condition of absence of intellect, which is the real ongoing cause of all character deficiencies. Imaginative rumination, constantly released by a vexed vanity which is searching for triumphant accusations and sentimental consolation, serves to repress the subject's own actual provocative fault. But the fault, precisely because it is repressed instead of being resolved, repeats itself obsessively and thus demands incessant repetition of the falsely justificatory repression.

Repression is also not a static phenomenon, an act accomplished once and for all in the past. It is an endlessly renewed dynamic phenomenon.

The subject finds that he must devote all his energy to the incessant attempt at imaginatively justificatory repression. The repetition of false repressive self-valuations buries the fault, and the guilt linked to it, in ever deeper layers of the subconscious, where the fault repressed in this way is transformed finally into a psychopathic symptom. The fault, or the desire to free oneself from it, is in the end expressed actively but in an oneirically disguised form (for example, obsessively washing oneself and not touching anything for fear of becoming dirty or infected express repressed guilt, the cause of psychic impurity, and an impotent desire for purification).

The oneiric reappearance of the fault: the explosion of the psychopathic symptom, is not the consequence of a static fixation on the affect repressed in the past.

The symptomatic explosion of the repressed fault—which can already be observed in children exposed to excessive accusations—is due to the incessant intrapsychic activity that produces false valuations because it is imaginatively troubled and affectively blinded. False valuation become obsessive habit can no longer elaborate a voluntary decision in a satisfactory manner, and instead of a sensible discharge, logically adjusted to the exigencies of reality, the symptomatic discharge takes place, illogical and senseless, adjusted solely to the exigencies of the pathologically deformed psychic system.

Since neither the fixation in childhood traumas nor affective regression (the cause of the repression) nor pathologial abreaction (which produces character deformations and symptoms) are statically determined by the past, it follows that the curative principle should be founded not on the associative investigation of past history but on the *elucidation of the motivating dynamic process that is acting at present unbeknown to the subject, a process in which the entire past is condensed.*

As long as one is not aware of this true cause of the active deficiency and anguished disorientation, it is obviously preferable not to intervene actively and not to proffer advice that threatens to be conventional and ineffective, if not harmful. Passivity then becomes a therapeutic virtue.

It is above all in the field of the re-education of children that this supposed virtue of passivity has led to a technique that is equivalent to the therapist's abdication. It is customary to claim that the child will become healthy to the extent that his rebellious resentments, focussed on the therapist, are allowed to manifest themselves freely through verbal and even active aggression.

This therapeutic procedure based on the abreaction principle runs the risk of being extremely harmful to the child under treatment.

Because of the ambivalence that underlies the ensemble of false motivations, the child's aggressive impertinence is periodically transformed into submissive guiltiness, which is mistaken for a sign of amelioration. But this temporary docility is itself but a manifestation of a persisting unhealthy hypersensitivity that at the slightest sign of impatience on the part of the re-educator will change into vexation in the child, who tries to obtain his triumphant revenge by increased impertinence. As long as motivations are unchanged, the child will tend to take advantage of the situation. Only the re-educator's sustained patience will have a sufficiently exemplary and pacifying value finally to have an effect upon the child's motivation.

Has it not been observed that patience and the restitution of material love can cure even schizophrenia? (See Sechshaye, *Journal d'une schizophrène.*)

The re-educator who proposes to subject himself to the child's aggressiveness must examine his secret reactions of impatience again and again. For him to repress them would be useless because they would manifest themselves surreptitiously through gestures or the voice's affective intonations and from that moment would result in the child's aggressive triumph. By relying on self-discipline, won't the re-educator be obliged to have recourse to inner observation, even if unbeknown to himself? To guard against one's own resentments and dissolve them before they become active, means simply to *bring to consciousness the flaw common to human nature* and to prevent, by this acknowledgment, the harmful abreaction that destroys contact.

The re-educator who with the help of the so-called abreaction method obtains valid results—in reality because of scrutiny of his own motives and the genuine strength of his patience—nevertheless remains, on the theoretical plane, a very poor psychologist if he does not become aware of the self-observation method that unbeknown to him has operated in a conclusive manner. The sublimating *formation* of character that creates the ability to resist lucidly the subconscious resistance of the child (or any other analysand) must be completed by a spiritualizing *formulation* in order to insure the method's full effectiveness.

The cumbersomeness of Freudian technique, in great part preserved by the schools of Adler and Jung, is due to the insufficiently lawful interpretation of an insufficiently free association. The method of association, when it remains the sole means of investigation, offers no way to concentrate attention on the legitimate residue of old traumas: that is, false motivation. This morbid condition, thus insufficiently examined, cannot help but risk spoiling the therapeutic contact between analyst and analysand.

In every analysis, one must take resistance and transference into account. These two attitudes constantly alternate. Resistance, due to guilty vanity, manifests itself by an accusing projection which, in accordance with the law of ambivalence, alternates with sentimental transference. Sentimental transference is simply a form of resistance. Although the transference may take on sexual tones, its true motive is the attempt to paralyze the analytic attack. All of false motivation is in a state of exacerbation because of the shock caused by the therapeutic intervention.

Such falsified sentiments run the risk of overflowing the analysis and exacerbating the analyst's false motivation (countertransference), if he does not know how to attack false motivation resolutely both in the patient and in himself. Common resistance to the release of deep truth is the cause, on the one hand, for the analysand's transference continuing to be neurotic (the "transference neurosis" being incorrectly considered favorable to the analytical process) and, on the other hand, for the analyst's being driven to respond to it by the countertransference of his vexed vanity, a sign that his own sentimentality and his tendency to accuse others are not sufficiently dissolved and that his guilt in regard to the too-reluctant progress remains repressed.

It is clear that the analyst will be able to handle the countertransference well or badly only to the degree that he is endowed with introspective talent. Between analysand and analyst, insofar as they remain victims of morbid entanglement, a struggle for supremacy takes place. The transference neurosis (the love-hate focused on the therapist) incites the patient either to accept, by sentimental submission, the therapist's interpretation (transference) or to reject it, just as affectively, by hostile accusations (resistance). This latter attitude will be more frequent because it permits the patient to repress his guilt and to transform his humiliated vanity into triumphant vanity and thus create an escape route for himself.

The analytic intervention, if it does not know how to attack false motivation directly, has no other means of defense against the patient's need to transform his guilty feelings of inferiority into vanity-inspired superiority but the transposition of the struggle from the plane of present and legitimate false motivation to the plane of so-called free associations that in truth are codetermined by the therapist's ideology. Thus the therapist is able to triumph over the analysand and his resistance, gradually drawing from the associatively supplied material elements ideologically suggested beforehand. The method demands a whole technique of slow suggestion (transmitted by didactic analysis) whose supposed objective passivity is in reality only prudent preparatory activity.

The countertransference cannot be ascribed to the Oedipus complex (which Freudian doctrine regards as the cause of the transference), since didactic analysis should have freed the therapist from this complex. Surely one must admit therefore that the explanation of the patient's "transference neurosis" with the help of the Oedipus complex is also inadequate. Shouldn't both forms of transference—the patient's and the therapist's—be suspected of being motivated in the same way? Why should the analyst's countertransference, at least in principle, be any less neurotic than the patient's transference?

The fact that analysts who use the Freudian method see themselves increasingly forced to fix their attention upon their own transference to the patient is surely striking proof of the persistence (despite didactic analysis) of too large a dose of affective subjectivity, or—and this amounts to the same thing—false motivation.

The analyst will be able to be objective only to the extent that the countertransference is arrested. And this can only take place through the analyst's constant work on himself, work that will necessarily be of an introspective and self-educational nature.

2

THE TASK OF EDUCATION

ONTOGENY AND PHYLOGENY

If man's psychic life is subject to laws, must we not ask where these laws come from? Perhaps it does not suffice to say that they are immanent in human nature. Psychic functioning cannot be understood as long as one fails to take the results of evolution into consideration. Could the laws of harmony and ambivalence have an evolutionary history? Could they be the end result of more elementary laws that govern life in its preconscious forms?

The educational task can be understood in all its vastness only if one understands its biogenetic underpinnings.

Before reaching maturity, the child traverses a long period of ontogenetic development that lasts not less than twenty years. Throughout the period from birth until adolescence, the child is exposed to educational interventions. This situation requires a great deal of patience and sacrifice on the part of both children and parents. The child remains subject to impositions that often are contrary to his will and even to his true needs for expansion, and the parents collide with the children's disobedient opposition.

Is it excessive to point out that the gravity of the collisions diminishes to the extent that the parents' educational impositions are in keeping with the children's essential needs? But how is it possible to know the essential need so long as one does not take into account the biogenetic root of the laws that govern psychic health and illness?

In the absence of knowledge of psychic laws and their biological foundation, an effort has always been made to define the educational task on the basis of a somewhat moralizing demand for love. Love of one's parents, love of one's neighbor, love of God, the supreme legislator of moral exigency: undeniably an ideal full of beauty. But perhaps we should try to define clearly what characterizes the quality of love; and how can we define it if we ignore its biogenetic foundation? There is a great danger that the educational task based on imprecisely defined love will degenerate into an exalted task and that it will suffer the ambivalent scission into sentimentally exalted, falsely idealized love whose underlying counterpole could only be secret, hate-filled exaltation. It can hardly be denied that educational reality often confirms the existence of this legitimately foreseeable danger.

Moreover, it is this pathogenic decomposition of the child-parent relationship—the consequence of a poorly performed educational task—that brought about the advent of depth psychology. This in-depth exploration consists precisely in the attempt to provide psychology—that is to say, the study of feelings, their sublimation and their perversion—with a genetic foundation.

But instead of first seeking the remedy in a better definition of the educational task in its healthy form (in order to establish on that basis an understanding of what is pathological and a re-educational technique), psychological renewal is content to study only patho-genesis and to follow its deforming power through the stages of ontogenetic maturation (Freud's Oedipus complex, Adler's instinct of domination).

Thus the study of *the phylogeny of the human psychic system* was neglected to the advantage of the study of pathogenesis and ontogeny.

And are not the stages of the child's ontogenetic maturation, although they may be pathologically deformed by the parents' intervention, originally prepared in a healthy manner by the phylogeny of the human species?

The genetic phenomenon at the human level is composed of phylogeny of the species, ontogeny of the individual, and patho-genesis (character deformation essentially due to false motivation).

The newborn child carries within him the germ of the phyloge-netic heritage of the human species. This heritage, insofar as it interests psychology, consists in the capacity for conscious and foresightful choice, a superior means of adjustment in relation to the blind, instinctive foresight that characterizes animal life. On-togeny, through the stages of a child's maturation, should develop the germ of these superior qualities (clarity of mind, voluntary decision, intensity of shades of feeling). But ontogenetic matura-tion cannot take place healthily without educational help, and the educational mistakes (falsely motivated parental interventions) de-termine the child's character deformation, that is to say, the inade-quate development of innate qualities. It is nevertheless important to emphasize here that it would be unjust to incriminate the parents exclusively. The pathogenetic principle, false motivation (the consequence of the fragility of conscious choice), is also to be found in germ in the newborn child along with superior qualities. But whereas the qualities in germ are one's phylogenetic heritage due to the evolutionary drive that traverses all of life, the vital error (the falsely motivated choice, psychopathy) appears genetically only at the human level. The innate rut of false motivation is the heritage of a long line of ancestors and their failure to make reasonable adjustments.

The conflict between qualities and nonqualities is from birth the destiny of all human beings. This biogenetically prepared destiny, immanent in the human species, determines the child's educability and the possibility of educational error on the part of the parents; it defines the educational task. In view of the overriding practical significance of this problem, the search for its biogenetic foundation is not a detour but an indispensable precaution. The empirical fragmentation of the problem, and the temptation to search for a solution by way of moralizing speculation, are dangers too certain not to justify the preoccupation with delving more deeply, which imposes the disengagement of the evolutionary line, starting from the animal's preconscious life and its unconscious instinct. But this sort of delving demands that analysis be pushed ever further with a view to understanding the very genesis of conscious life, which is endlessly threatened by regression toward the pathological unconscious, the subconscious.

The newborn child, a preconscious being, is destined to evolve toward the conscious.

Each new stage of maturation, phylogenetically prepared and healthily overcome, will have as its essential characteristic the acquisition of a higher degree of conscious control. The adult's psychic system will form a structured whole in which are preserved the ontogenetic stages that are phylogenetically prepared, but in part pathologically deformed. These stages, which begin successively, then later become simultaneous and finally form the more or less conscious "layers" of the functional constitution of the adult's psychic system: *instances of the conscious and extraconscious* (superconscious and subconscious).

The essential task of education, understood in all its vastness, consists in watching over and guiding the healthy development of the ontogeny of these instances. Since ontogeny is the prolongation of phylogeny, education itself acquires an evolutionary significance.

If the ontogenetic maturation of the child is the prolongation of the phylogeny of the species, how can we discern the goal of education without knowing in advance the biological adaptative significance of the functions that are to be educated?

The guiding principles of education cannot be established without a prior study of the phylogeny of the higher functions of the human psychic system.

Psychology cannot avoid speaking of the biologically elementary functions (drives, instincts, nutrition, sexuality, etc.). How can it avoid the risk of remaining empirical or speculative so long as it neglects defining these fundamental terms? What would be the point of speaking about higher functions—clarity of mind, voluntary decision-making, the feeling of love—unless we were in a position to demonstrate the genetic link between elementary functions and the evolved functioning of the human psychic system?

It is true, however, that such a broadened picture, developed to the full, would by far surpass the necessarily limited scope of the present study. However, such preliminary studies can be found in an earlier book of mine *(Fear and Anguish)* that deals specifically with the phylogeny of psychic functioning.

In the absence of a detailed study here, it will nevertheless be necessary to isolate the biogenetic elements insofar as they directly concern the educational problem.

In order to find the immanent link between phylogeny and ontogeny, it is certainly not speculative to postulate that the link consists in the need for security (satisfactory survival). Instinctive security is lost with the evolutionary appearance of conscious choice and its possibility of error. On the human level, choice is exercised in regard to desires and the means for their satisfaction. *It is the capacity for choice that needs to be educated.* From the biogenetic perspective, the entire problem of education would therefore consist in knowing how the insecurity inherent in choice can from childhood on be led toward a superior form of security.

These observations will determine the development of the present chapter.

The child needs to be succored. His security depends on his healthy incorporation into the family milieu, and the means of this incorporation is love.

Hence the biologically elementary problem of security becomes considerably broader. It no longer concerns only the material basis of the home (choice of profession), but also the definitive and exclusive choice by which the parents ought to be linked to each other, an indispensable condition for the child's security. But to these two conditions of the home's security is added spiritual security: certainty about the value judgment as regards the couple's life. This condition no longer exclusively depends on the parents. It depends on mores, customs, and above all on the moral ideologies that reign in societies.

The analysis of the educational task must take these various factors successively into account.

Beginning with the analysis of the psychic instances that determine choice and its affective uncertainties, it must extend to the fluctuation of motives which, often extraconscious, influence the social life but above all the private life of the parent-educators and thereby even the stages of the child's maturation.

PSYCHIC INSTANCES

Before broaching the subject of the analysis of instances, a warning should be given. It certainly is not superfluous to remember that we cannot speak of the psychic system and its functioning without resorting to the use of a spatial image. This is all the more true for those instances that linguistic imagery is accustomed to represent as superimposed *"layers."* One must therefore not forget that the term *instances* serves merely to designate the different functional modalities—prelogical, logical, illogical—of the human psychic system.

The *conscious instance* and its logical functioning is subtended by the *unconscious instance,* which man has in common with animals, an instance whose prelogical function is emotive and instinctive. Hence the result is that preconscious emotivity is able to submerge the conscious. These two instances can interpenetrate and deform each other. Thus the conscious loses its lucidity and the unconscious its instinctive assurance. This results in an unhealthy instance: the *subconscious.* However, against the danger of involutionary regression below the conscious level there acts as a corresponding corrective an instance that tends to go beyond the present conscious level. Certainly nothing could be more senseless than to believe that evolution has reached its apogee and end with the appearance of the intellectually foresighted being. The human species, on the basis of intellectualization, could even in certain of its aspects seem very poorly adapted to life, at least in its instinctive form, because the function of the conscious—the intellect and its capacity for choice—disperses the primitive vital need in multiple, often contradictory and conflicting desires. The surpassing instance aspires to a more clairvoyant spirituality than that of the intellect; it no longer envisages simply utilitarian adaptation to environmental exigencies, but the adaptation of desires to the evolutionary sense of life, their harmonizing reunification, the source of ultimate satisfaction and the condition of joy. This instance, which is still in the process of being formed, can be called the *superconscious*.

Thus the functioning of the human psychic system depends on four instances: the *unconscious*, which is instinctive; the *conscious*, which is regulatory; the *subsconscious*, which is involutionary; and the *superconscious*, which is evolutionary.

Thus defined, the superconscious is something entirely different from the Freudian *superego*, which, far from being of biogenetic origin, is only the residue of prohibitions conventionally imposed by one's parents, prohibitions that supposedly above all concern sexual desires of an Oedipal nature. The superconscious is closer to the Jungian "Self." However, one must stress that in Jung the "Self" is simply the residue of the human species' ancestral experiences. Genetically understood, the superconscious is the deployment of the evolutionary thrust. It thus preserves—on a higher plane—the same instinctive assurance that precedes all experience and that, for instance, impels the spider to spin its web with an eye to future satisfactions. The superconscious instinct is no longer expressed organically but spiritually, intuitively. Its most ancestral product is oneiric intuition, condensed in the guiding images of the mythic dreams of all peoples. The instinctive assurance of superconscious vision is disturbed by the hesitant choice of the conscious, from which it follows that the difficult realization of this superior adaptation to the evolutionary sense of life remains an ideal of ethical significance. (Once the problem of education is understood as a prolongation of the adaptative thrust, this raises the boldest questions, which are put to man by his own evolutionary life. Psychology, far from having cut through them speculatively, cannot and must not recoil from the necessity of facing them.)

The task of education, in keeping with its deepest meaning, is to support the evolutionary impulse in such a way that in avoiding the danger of involutionary and subconscious deformation, the vital impulsion succeeds not only in the healthy formation of the conscious self but, depending on its amplitude, in the formation of the harmonizing instance of the superconscious, an instance that alone is able to bring the individual to full psychic maturity, making him into a personality that no longer needs to be guided by education. Adolescence, the stage that precedes maturity, is characterized by an often despairing effervescence of the drive to surpass, by the individually graduated and almost always fleeting effort to go beyond immediate utility and seek an orientation in respect to the meaning of life.

From the biogenetic perspective, we can say that each individual is an attempt on nature's part to realize through ontogeny the forever unfinished pattern of the species' phylogenetic evolution. Linked to genetic psychology and finding in it its biopsychic foundation, education is by this very fact connected with the evolutionary thrust, transformed on the human plane into an ideal requirement: deployment of the harmonizing instance and its vision of guiding values.

The educational ideal is confused with the ethical exigency, because both envisage the most evolved form of biogenetic adaptation. What other goal could education have but that of making the child into a moral being, a being incorporated not only in social convention but also able to fulfill the evolutionary meaning of life? As long as education is considered an empirical process, morality will be mere speculative theory or utilitarian convention. The two domains—education and morality—come together again if one disengages the adaptative substructure that they have in common, and this can only be done thanks to the analysis of instances which are the residual layers of phylogenesis.

Instances constitute the ensemble of conscious and extraconscious psychic functioning. If it is true that psychic life (that is to say, the dynamic process of motivations that often escapes conscious control) is governed by laws, it should be possible to formulate the ensemble of psychic laws, starting with the definition of instances, and thus complete the laws of harmony and disharmony, which were previously isolated. Instances (evolutionary and involutionary), far from being static entities, are sheaves of motives. As such, instances are dynamic, and their dynamism constitutes the intrapsychic work destined to elaborate activity. The motivating dynamic process of extraconscious instances codetermines the elaboration of the conscious voluntary decision.

But the dynamic process of instances, by unifying the psychic system in a functional "whole," no longer resides only in their participation in the intrapsychic work, characteristic of the presently attained evolutionary level. Instances being the product of phylogeny, each instance preserves the memory of the evolutionary dynamism in the form of a law that is specific to it.

If one wishes to define the educational task, its phylogenetic foundation and its evolutionary significance, it is necessary to establish—even at the price of some repetition—the genetic link that joins together the ensemble of laws governing the healthy and unhealthy functioning of the psychic system. Thanks to their common biogenetic root, these laws can be uncovered.

All laws derive from the unconscious, the instance common to animal and human life.

The *law of the unconscious* is a quest for satisfaction. At the animal level this search is instinctive. No deviation from the law is possible. The animal rests in the preconscious mind without the possibility of guilty transgression. No education is required here, save, in the case of higher animals, an apprenticeship in the instincts of attack and defense.

Owing to the absence of all possibility for transgression, the law of the unconscious is constitutive at the animal level. At the human level, where the conflict between evolutionary and involutionary instances appears, the laws that govern the instances are no more than directives: deviation becomes possible; but it is sanctioned by guilty dissatisfaction.

Life, the evolutionary dynamic process, in search of satisfactions, tries to go beyond instinctive blind security in order to attain the higher level of a certitude that is unrealizable without the healthy development of the valuing mind. The search for rest in the mind's assurance is subject to a law that derives from the law of the unconscious and its search for satisfaction, limited and harmonized by instinct.

The *law of evolution* stipulates that despite the differentiation of vital need into multiple desires—life's intensification, thanks to the nuanced diversification of possible satisfactions—one must not lose sight of the unity and simplicity of its origins, where the most elementary satisfaction is ensured by reflex reaction. Evolutionary differentiation progresses toward reflection, toward the mind, because the mind is the means of supremely satisfying reunification.

Life tends toward the authentic unity of the valuing being. Now, unity in differentiation is harmony (both of thought and action), the supreme condition of satisfaction. Thus, from the unconscious, ruled by the search for satisfaction, comes the superconscious vision of values. The elementary need for satisfaction—even though egoistic—is thus sublimated by way of evolution.

The *law of the superconscious* is the ethical imperative, which imposes—with an eye to sublimated satisfaction—reunifying harmonization.

Thus understood, the superconscious is a form of instinctivity, which, however, since it is penetrated by the valuing mind and its possibility for going astray, is inseparably tied to the subconscious, characterized by promises of falsely valued, imaginatively exalted, and therefore fallacious satisfaction.

The *law of the subconscious* is unhealthy temptation, the false valuation that ends in ambivalent disharmony. Each exaltation of desire is matched by guilty dissatisfaction and its consequence, which is anxiety-ridden inhibition.

The two extraconscious instances (superconscious and subconscious) are the necessary complements of the conscious instance, which forms the distinctive trait that separates animals and human life. Having broken away from the animal's instinctive assurance, human consciousness has in it the possibility of choice as regards the promises of satisfaction.

The law of the conscious is the hesitation between motivating promises of superconscious and subconscious origin. *The hesitation is prolonged into deliberation,* which is meant to elaborate the voluntary decision. The deliberation is a calculation of satisfaction which, because it is codetermined by superconscious and subconscious promises, can lead to decisions, either authentic or fallacious.

If the conscious were perfectly lucid, its preferential choice would lead it without prior deliberating hesitation to decide in favor of the authentic promises of the superconscious. The conscious and superconscious would form a single instance, evolutively superior to the animal's instinctive unconscious. Yet man is but a semi-conscious being. His deliberative choice is affected by imaginative distress, the first indication of subconscious deviation. The conscious degrades into the subconscious to the extent that the imaginative distress is exalted and exasperated. The subconscious is the conscious itself insofar as it is imaginatively blinded.

Among the instances—unconscious, conscious, superconscious, and subconscious—no precise delimitations exist. Their radical separation is but an illusion that springs from the inevitable spatial image. This image also invites the division of the superconscious as well as the subconscious into an "imaginative layer" that surfaces in the conscious and an oneiric layer that seems radically separated from the conscious. The latter manifests itself in both superconscious and subconscious through symbolically disguised products. (The superconscious myth truthfully symbolizes the psychic conflicts between values and nonvalues. Due to the fact that they encourage the victorious realization of values, the mythic images of all peoples have cultural and collective significance. Conversely, the symbolic product of the subconscious—the psychopathic symptom—could be called "subconscious myth." At this point the symptom has only an individual significance. It truthfully symbolizes the defeat of this or that individual.)

Just as the pre-oneiric and purely imaginative "layer" of the subconscious is an integral part of the semilucid conscious, the superconscious also breaks into the conscious through a premythic layer and blends into it. This imaginative layer of the superconscious is subliminally creative. Its products are the intuitive visions of harmonies (intuitive vision of truth; philosophical systems and fertile hypotheses in science; vision of beauty, the creative principle of the arts; intuitive visions of goodness, the principle of religiosity). All these visions often prove to be tainted by dogmatizing error, codetermined as they are by the utilitarian satisfactions proposed by the conscious and the vanity-inspired satisfactions of the subconscious.

Beyond the spatial images of instances, nothing exists but the functional fluctuation of the calculation of satisfaction in its various degrees of lucidity and blindness.

From this dynamic fluctuation, which makes psychic functioning into an indissoluble "whole," comes the hope of continuous evolution, whose goal it is to transform blindness into lucidity. The condition of realization consists in broadening the conscious in the direction of the subconscious but also that of the superconscious. In penetrating the imaginative and oneiric "layers" of the extraconscious with its elucidating and conceptualizing force, the conscious will be able to diminish the suggestive power of the fallacious promises of the subconscious and to transform the directive suggestions of the superconscious into wisely based knowledge. At the limit, the functional subconscious disappears—its determining force dissolves—to the extent to which the instinctive superconscious becomes lucid consciousness. The evolutionary expansion of the conscious creates new determinants with comprehensive force, capable of freeing deliberate choice from its hesitation. In expanding, the conscious dissolves the subconscious determinants, which are the perverse motives of false obsessive choice, and it helps the superconscious to fulfill its guiding function no longer by mere instinct but consciously and knowingly.

The evolutionary goal can be realized only thanks to the elucidation of determining motivations, which—insofar as they are subconscious—are nothing but promises of satisfaction in their inauthentic and fallacious forms.

The study of extraconscious motivations is possible because extraconscious instances are not radically separated from the conscious instance.

The evolutionary path on the human level can be opened only by the study of extraconscious motivations, that is, the elucidating penetration of the extraconscious by the conscious. Only this comprehending penetration renders motives and their value of satisfaction capable of being formulated and taught, of being transmissible by education.

It is not possible to understand the fundamental importance of the play and counterplay of instances so long as we do not face the relation between the inner life of instances and the exigencies of active and practical life.

Instances perform the intrapsychic work of evaluative selection in regard to the multitude of desires. They prepare their sensible or senseless discharge. Desires constitute the link between inner life and the excitations coming from the environment. To each instance corresponds a specific function destined to elaborate—at the level of inner deliberation—the reactive response to solicitations from the environment. The individual and the social together form an inseparable whole.

At birth the child is still entirely and egocentrically turned in upon himself. His desires have not as yet multiplied, his reactivity is still completely passive. Instances have not as yet developed.

A still completely preconscious being, the newborn infant evolves toward conscious choice, by which means it attempts to adapt to the environment's variable conditions. The specific function of the conscious instance is the intellect. In its practical form, it attempts to go beyond the infantile phase of passive adaptation to the environment. By gradually disengaging itself from purely emotive preconsciousness, the blossoming of the intellect traverses the preliminary stages in which judgments regarding the environment still are affectively and imaginatively blinded. In the majority of cases, the individual never completely transcends these stages of affective thought. It is, however, of the greatest importance to understand that, starting with the conscious instance and its intellectual function, a complete reversal of the function of adaptation takes place. Man does not passively adapt to an environment; he tries to adapt the environment to his needs and multiple desires.

The entire situation of the conscious being is determined by this ability to change environmental conditions so as to make them conform to his desires. Hence, from that point on, the problem consists in knowing whether the motives that incite the change are fundamentally sensible or senseless.

Due to the necessity for sensible adaptation, there will be created an instance superior to the intellect that is capable of sorting out and comparing the many desires according to their real satisfaction value. This instance, more than conscious or superconscious, is the conscience. Its adaptive function is to serve as a *brake on reason.*

While the utilitarian intellect is characterized by the force of realization (the favorable transformation of environmental conditions), reason—still a very precarious function in the human species—turns toward a higher level of satisfaction. Its adaptive value consists in the dissolution of senseless desires (incapable of harmonization) and in the acceptance of the unsatisfactory situation that is temporarily or definitively unalterable. Acceptance (which must be distinguished from repressive and spiteful resignation) is a liberating force; it works to sublimate desires (which is just another way of saying that they are being brought into harmonious order).

The meaning of education consists in its bringing about in the child the blossoming of two fundamentally satisfying reactions: *to change* or *to accept,* the sole conditions that give one mastery over desires. Not knowing how to change or to accept is the essential cause of vital dissatisfaction, which leads to two senseless reactions: perverse acceptance (resignation) or perverse change (rebellion). Education is senseless and unsatisfactory, it destroys the child's personality, when it does not know how to lead him toward mastery of his desires. Forced to endure his parents, unacceptable as they are, the child cannot change them. His maturation is blocked. His vital dissatisfaction is exacerbated into impotent rage, which he can only succeed in exteriorizing by rebellious disobedience (or by submissiveness, which just as fully destroys his personality).

Outside the two sensible reactions (conscious change and superconscious acceptance) only one path—a senseless and perverse path—exists in the search for the satisfaction of desires, and it leads to no reactive discharge of any liberating significance: I refer to imaginative exaltation. This is the fundamental error *par excellence,* because exalted desires cut off from sensible discharge (realization or harmonization) remain repressed deep within and, becoming more and more charged with guilty anxiety, in the end open the path to subconscious deformation.

Just as the intrapsychic work of instances concerns the fate of desires—their activation, their sublimation, or their repression—just or false value judgments have an eminently practical bearing: *the false becomes the bad, and the just becomes the good* that man prepares for himself and brings about, starting with the intimate deliberation of his behavior, his way of being. Thus good and evil are given their biopsychic foundation, and this divests morality of its speculative character and insures a theoretic basis for education.

Good is the harmony of desires; evil their disharmony. Or, formulated another way: good is vital satisfaction tied to progress in an evolutionary direction, the deployment of conscious control toward the superconscious instance; evil is the anguished dissatisfaction of involution, the pathogenetic transgressing of the conscious by imaginatively falsified and affectively blinded valuation on the part of the subconscious.

Thus the inner functioning of the psychic system as a whole is defined by the instances and their different ways of evaluating desires and their promises of satisfaction: that is, motives.

Desire, so long as it is not satisfied, is a source of suffering. The calculation of satisfaction, the function exercised by the instances, tries to overcome this suffering.

As long as the conscious surmounts suffering by favorably modifying the surrounding conditions, the superconscious and the subconscious intervene only when satisfactory change proves impossible. These two extraconscious instances cause, instead of a change in the environment, the modification (healthy or unhealthy) of the psychic system.

The superconscious appeases one's obsession with unrealizable desire. It surmounts dissatisfaction—whether the desire is temporarily or definitively unrealizable—by the force of acceptance (patience). It thus reestablishes internal peace (the terms *patience* and *peace* [pax], have the same linguistic root). The superconscious liberates the energy collected by the desire, which is recognized as unrealizable, and puts it at the disposal of realizable desires (sensible and not exalted). The conscious and the superconscious join in their liberating effort, since a favorable change in the environment brought about by the conscious is often possible only thanks to an effort of long duration, and this requires—even for intellectual and utilitarian work—the collaboration of superconscious patience. The collaboration of the conscious and the superconscious produces farsighted plans and a mobilization of effort with a view to their lucidly organized realization: *work* (the effort at long-term realization).

As for the subconscious, it tries to overcome the dissatisfaction of unrealizable desires by means of an exaltation of imaginary presatisfaction, the first stage of repression. Dissatisfaction and its suffering are thus temporarily eliminated. But the relief is deceptive. If the energy remains a captive of the repressed desire, the obsession continues to manifest itself, but in an uncontrollable and urgent manner. The persistent obsession creates pathological suffering.

Diametrically opposed to repressive resignation, to the reaction of weakness which leads to impotent rage and indignant rebellion (which renders one unworthy), superconscious acceptance is a psychic force indispensable to the just calculation of satisfaction. Thanks to the force of acceptance with its pacifying and sublimating power, calculation can attain a positive result, whatever might be the givens of the fundamental problem to be solved. Despite the often insurmountable hostility of the surrounding world, the possibility of a pacifying solution always exists in principle, even though human weakness often does not succeed in realizing it. Desires, once they are freed of exalting impatience, harmonize by themselves. Acceptance is a harmonizing force. In the end, the degree of mobilization of the force of acceptance determines fundamental satisfaction or dissatisfaction. Life's immanent justice rests in the possibility of opposing imperturbable psychic forces to the ineluctable postulates found in the hostile surroundings (the natural source of suffering).

Through the instances a constant choice—sensible or senseless—is elaborated in regard to desires. This permanent choice is inner deliberation.

CHOICE AND DELIBERATION

The functional opposition between superconscious and subconscious, an opposition subject to the possible error of more or less conscious judgments, constitutes the capacity of choice.

The entire task of education is concentrated in the influence that parents exercise over the child with a view of guiding his choice and finally making him able to choose without being guided.

As long as instances are not deployed, the child is incapable of conscious choice. Nevertheless, the infant possesses from birth the characteristic of the human species, a faculty—still very elementary and almost organic—of choosing his reactions in relation to the parents' intervention. It would obviously be erroneous to consider the newborn child an automaton; it is animated by needs which, though instinctive at the start, soon become volitional.

The infant's elementary faculty of choosing between sensible and senseless (moderate and exaggerated) actions is, like all instances, a hereditary legacy. Instances form the phylogenetic heritage, as has been pointed out previously, while the prefiguration of choice is the heritage of the evolutionary effort or the involutionary failure of the entire chain of human ancestors. It is characteristic of the newborn's individuality that his choice—elementary because not as yet supported by motivating judgments—is still blind and emotional.

It is therefore important to distinguish as clearly as possible between these two factors that determine reaction to educational excitations: the instances phylogenetically prepared and common to all human beings, and the individual characterological predisposition, the inner choice of the educated being.

From this distinction flows a consequence of exceptional importance to the golden rule of education. This rule is based on relationship: healthy educational excitation—healthy reaction by the child; unhealthy excitation—unhealthy reaction. By virtue of the characterological predisposition, it nevertheless remains possible at least in principle for the infant to respond to educational stimuli of a perverse and involutionary order with reactions that possess an evolutionary value (deployment of the force of acceptance); or that he will respond to stimuli of a formative value with deformed reactions (the latter case presents itself above all with physiologically handicapped children).

The golden rule therefore is not without exceptions. The possibility of exception is itself a necessity of evolutionary adaptation. It is only due to the fact that the rule is not the law that the human being from the moment of birth lives in accordance with the ethical law, the law of responsibility, which in the course of maturation demands that better and better use be made of this exceptional capacity of choice and that one respond to a perverse stimulus with a noble reaction, in order to constitute and reconstitute—for the individual's own good—the unity of the ego, the harmony of emotions.

However, this possibility of exception does not at all diminish the value of the educational rule: the force of noble resistance, rare enough in the adult, is therefore all the more weak in the child (a receptive and passively reactive being). Also—according to the rule—when the child is exposed to an unhealthy and irritating education, his choice will not be one between perverse and noble, but rather between different possibilities for perverse reaction (tearful whining or aggressive rage).

The capacity for choice includes responsibility. It is composed of the child's and the educator's responsibility. The responsibility affects psychic formation or deformation; it encompasses all of life and cannot be divided or partitioned. Both child and adult are completely responsible.

The child and the adult are not two fundamentally opposed beings. The adult was a child and the child will become an adult. The adult's choice was at the outset emotional, and the child's choice will become conscious. Included in the adult's responsibility are the healthy and unhealthy forms of his educational intervention, the consequences of his own formation or deformation, which began with the emotional choices of the child he was; included in the child's responsibility is his future formation or deformation, the consequence of the exaltation or moderation of his emotional response to the educator's intervention.

On the one hand, the child's emotional choice is not unilaterally determined by educational intervention, and, on the other hand, even an adult's more or less conscious choice is not undetermined. It remains determined through his entire past beginning with early childhood, and even by heredity through the life of his ancestors. But as long as life continues the decision is never completed. At every instant of his life, man is not only what he was and what he presently is, but also what he will be. Only at the end of his life will what he was in relation to the evolutionary direction of all of life become manifest. Every moment of life brings new stimulants that are bound to change the choices that determine behavior and to produce evolutionary or involutionary mutations in the psychic constellation.

The entire sense of life consists in this possibility of mutation, the vehicle of evolutionary adaptation that, at the human level, becomes choice and responsibility. At no moment in his life can the individual find himself outside this vital responsibility; in other words, even the newborn is vitally responsible for his emotional choice or—what amounts to the same thing—for the ancestral determination that makes him this unique being, this being capable of choice, characterologically distinct. Emotional and even conscious choice is not free; it remains codetermined by excitations including those undergone by ancestors, to which they have responded with their own reactive choice. Thus the element of freedom that choice contains is inseparable from the element of determination entailed by the excitation, so that in the end it comes to the same thing whether we say that the individual is free or say that he is determined. His free determination, his determined freedom, makes him one with all past and future life, all of life in evolution. The ancestors are responsible for the descendants, and a newborn child is responsible for his ancestors. Life itself renders him responsible by making his choice the determinant of his future life. But precisely because it is a matter of choice, his determination is never decisive and irremediable; it remains susceptible to being revised by increasingly conscious choice. The newborn child has all of his life before him to change in a sensible or senseless manner in accordance with his legacy. Despite the ancestral heritage, his evolutionary capacity, still fresh and intact, offers maximum impressionability. Hence the great importance of the educational intervention, that is, the responsibility of adults as educators.

Education can form or deform the psychic system; but it does so only because the child's emotional choice responds to the educational intervention.

The newborn child is not moved only by his immediate needs. The profoundest motivation of his entire preconscious being strives toward the distant goal of organic growth and psychic evolution. His life is nothing but evolution, and his immediate needs are but a means to sustain the evolutionary thrust. Moreover, the physical aspect of this thrust, the growth of the body, prepares nothing else than the substratum of psychic evolution, the true meaning of his life.

The entire problem of education is posited by this clearcut distinction between the family environment and the child's selective response.

The educational problem would be incorrectly enunciated if one were to attach an exclusive importance to either the child's emotive choice or to familial stimulation.

To neglect the influence of the environment would be tantamount to denying the possibility of education; to ignore the fact of emotional choice between responses—and, consequently the germ of ancestrally preestablished motivation—would be tantamount to considering the child an automaton, or, at most, a purely instinctive being (which, when all is said and done, would equally eliminate the possibility of education).

Excitations are the subject matter on which choice is exercised. But in order to become the subject matter of choice, the exciting stimuli must be impregnated with the inner depth of the psychic system and shape the intentions of future activity, that is, motives.

Only the distinction between emotional choice and codetermination by external stimulants permits us to understand the child's evolution toward the adult's complicated psychic system.

Primitive choice, since it is erroneous, tends to its revision to the extent that the choice which begins as an emotional one, becomes valuing deliberation. Errors committed in the past, the source of deformed reaction, begin to be infused with responsibility; the error is subjected to self-condemnation, a more or less conscious judgment regarding oneself, whence flows *the emotion of guilt, the turntable for the blossoming of instances.*

Provided that the responsibility is really taken seriously, that suffering from guilt succeeds in preventing deficient reactions, the past choice, even when erroneous, can become beneficent by stimulating the desire for revision, by sharpening the distinction between the false and just, between bad and good, and thus accelerating the healthy blossoming of conscience. Guilt is sublimated, dissolved, thanks to true, active justification. But the danger is great (above all to the extent that educational stimulants remain unhealthy irritants) that the conscience and its capacity for judgment, while in the process of being awakened, will be diverted from their evolutionary significance and used to repress the vital emotion of guilt, to repeat—on a level that has become conflictual—the old error of emotional choice and replace self-accusation only by imaginative and vanity-engendered justification. Emotivity wins out over lucidity: thought remains childish, at least where its vitally practical significance is concerned. Surcharged with vexed emotivity, judgment is employed solely to condemn others and make them exclusively responsible. However, this malignant condemnation—because of its emotional blinding of judgment—does not attain the conscious level and remains hidden in the child for a long time by his thirst for love, which is all the more exalted as it remains unquenched. In place of consciousness of his own responsibility, the essential falsehood is installed, *false motivation,* the secret cause of all defective activities.

Efficient education has as its goal the protection of the nascent psychic system from this inner deformation, the essential obstacle to healthy maturation.

Thanks to the analysis of instances, which highlights the problem of emotional choice, it becomes possible in the end to bring together all the formulations outlined above in a final definition of the educational task, which is bound to reveal its ethical meaning even more clearly. This definition rests on the fact that emotional choice is the germ of the adult's liberation (permanent choice) with regard to the motives of action. Evaluative self-determination, that is, deliberation, is an attempt to free the personality. *Therefore the opposite of freedom is not determination but subconscious obsession,* the result of the falsely justifying motivation of imaginatively exalted and vitally senseless desires. The essential problem of education is the freeing of the personality; this effort at liberation therefore concerns the inner life of motives.

The life of motives begins with the child's emotional choice, and in the course of maturation it develops into more or less conscious deliberation.

The task of education is to direct in a healthy fashion the development of emotional choice toward evaluative deliberation, in order thus to prevent the installation of false motivation, the essential danger ancestrally prepared by the constellation of instances.

All instances are involved in the inner work of choice that has become deliberation. Semiconscious motives—the elements of deliberation—are influenced both by the ethical imperative of the superconscious and the blinding obsession of the subconscious. The superconscious imperative is the driving wish to surpass, and what this wish tries to surpass is the subconscious obsession and its false promises of satisfaction. Deliberation is evaluative choice exercised by the conscious mind in regard to superconscious and subconscious determinants. In elevating inner determination to the rank of justly or falsely valued motives, inner deliberation elaborates, through its unceasing work, the reactive response to inflowing excitations. *The entire functioning of the psychic system is summed up in the effort at deliberation.*

Education's error consists in addressing itself exclusively to actions and neglecting the essential fact of their previous elaboration by deliberative choice.

The analysis of this fundamental ability of the human being, that is, choice on its way to becoming permanent deliberation, leads to the ultimate definition of the educational task: the task must be realized through *the education of deliberation,* and this cannot be realized without the elucidation of inner motives.

Founded in this way on the psychological analysis of instances, education acquires all of its profound meaning. It is the most important event in everyone's life. On it depends every individual's way of confronting life. Responsibility, included in emotional choice destined to become deliberation, determines not only what the child will become but what the man will be.

The capacity for choice determines the human being's inner conflictual situation, and it does so from the day of his birth. However, it would be wrong to neglect the importance of social interaction. Life in society determines reality, which is necessarily inferior to the ideal value.

The evolutionary event of semiconscious choice results in a decisive scission between the need common to the species and individualized desires, the material upon which choice acts. The satisfaction of desires that are too individualized ends by opposing the satisfaction of the need of the species and those of social groups. Biologically based, the ethical ideal strives for sociability, the species' harmonious unification. This aim goes beyond the platitudes of utilitarian pragmatism and the too restricted framework of present societies, which are themselves in evolutionary gestation.

Education must incorporate the child in society with its presently inadequate form, trying meanwhile to safeguard the drive to surpass. The essential aim is not to obtain the child's obedience so that he or she will cause the least possible nuisance to the parents (incorporation into the family), and neither is it some distant utilitarian goal to which all the child's present needs should be sacrificed: specialization of skills and attitudes with a view to the future practice of a trade or profession (incorporation into society). Yet these goals do exist, and it would be a mistake to base oneself too exclusively on the biological ideal of evolution.

This requires a sharp distinction between *the ideal task of education* (developed up to this point) and *the real task* imposed by each person's limited impulse and by the current conditions of social life. However, this distinction should not lose sight of the common roots connecting the impulse to surpass with elementary instinctual energy (nutrition and propagation), a root from which branch out the multiple forms of human desire and the diverse directions in the search for satisfaction.

INSTINCTUAL DRIVES (FRAMEWORK OF DESIRES)

While instances determine the nature of choice (vitally just or false), instinctual drives determine the material over which choice is exercised.

From its origins, life is characterized by two instinctual drives of a conserving nature: nourishment and propagation, to which the evolutionary drive is added. Surpassing the conserving need, the evolutionary impulsion successively displays the diversity of the species.

Nothing is more misleading than basing the study of fundamental problems too exclusively on a single drive: on sexuality (Freud) or on socialized nourishment (Adler). Only from the study of the biogenetic relations between the evolutionary impulsion and the two conserving drives can come understanding of the human drives, which, enlarged by *semiconscious foresight,* become the throng of desires whose multiplication renders choice necessary. The relation of drives and the ensuing necessity for sensible choice cannot fail to be of the greatest importance for the problem at stake: the human progeny's educational upbringing.

In the newborn child, the nutritive drive is manifested in the most spectacular fashion, whereas the evolutionary impulsion determines the future, and precisely because of this, escapes direct observation. As for the sexual drive, even at an early age it can be translated into precocious activity. Behaviorists have shown that precocious sexuality is frequently observed in young animals deprived of their freedom. Education by neurotic parents produces a similar situation of deprivation. Far from being a natural phenomenon, infantile sexuality is pathological in nature. It itself needs to be explained and so cannot serve as the basis for a theory about the ontogenetic maturation of the human psychic system. The sexual interpretation of all functions of the digestive apparatus (from mouth to anus) would only be justifiable if it were possible to demonstrate that the sexual nuance already adheres to the animal's digestive functions. For lack of a sufficient phylogenetic basis, the Freudian theory of the stages of ontogenetic maturation is still suspect of being merely an arbitrary construction. The great merit of Freudian psychoanalysis is the discovery of the symbolizing function of the subconscious. On the other hand, pan-sexuality is the error that has made Freudian theory inapplicable to education and above all to the re-education of the child.

The three elementary drives—nourishment, propagation, and evolutionary adaptation—are common to all forms of life. But the means of their satisfaction varies from species to species. In man, the means for satisfaction have become partly conscious, that is, reflective, variable according to circumstances, and in keeping with the individuals' attitudes.

This enrichment of the means for satisfaction cannot fail to have an effect on drives, which are the forms of desire. Human desires, multiple and conscious of their goals, often have a distant aim. Conscious foresight projects past experience into the future. The driven tension, blind in the animal that lives only in the present, acquires, thanks to man's conscious choice, the dimensions of time. The drives expand.

It is impossible to understand the functioning of the human psychic system so long as one bases it on unexpanded animal drives. Only the story of the *expanding* drives can teach us how human psychology is founded on animal biology. The expanding of drives forms the bridge between the unconscious and the conscious, and because of this expansion extraconscious instances are constituted: the evolutionary superconscious and the involuntary subconscious.

On the human level, nourishment expands into a *social drive* that looks to the procurement of satisfaction (social position and property: money). Propagation expands into a *sexuality* that is no longer satisfied with a temporary union through the corporeal act. Human sexuality, when it is in possession of all of its power, seeks satisfaction with a more distant aim. It finds it thanks to a lasting bond with the chosen partner. This soul bond makes the family the framework suitable for the raising of children. As for the evolutionary impulsion, it is the vehicle of the expansion of nutritive and sexual drives. By changing itself into clairvoyant *spirituality,* it becomes the creator of superior forms of life and of its cultural context.

The expansion of drives is of the highest importance to the educational problem. The child is born as a preconscious being, and its drives are not yet differentiated or broadened. (Instances have not as yet been formed.) The child's entire maturation, his ontogeny, is summed up in the expanded deployment of drives (the formation of instances).

Even at the animal level, unexpanded drives are, with a view to their satisfaction, provided with two forms of behavior common to all of life: *attack and flight.*

On the conscious level these forms of behavior remain means of ensuring satisfaction: but where they start as instinctive, they then become semiconscious. The semiconscious tendencies of attack and flight mark the boundaries of man's motivated choice, which, broadened into evaluative deliberation, results in a veritable calcu lation of satisfactions. In the newborn, the attitudes of attack and flight, which are acquired ancestrally, are still only in the stage of rudimentary prefiguration, and their healthy or unhealthy deployment will depend on the regularity of care. The feeling of security, which alone is capable of preventing the unhealthy exaltation of attack and flight attitudes, can only develop to the extent in which the newborn finds tranquility in the parents' affection.

Because of the immediacy of needs and the utter dependency of the nursing infant, his impulses for attack and flight, wholly lacking in effective exteriorization, still only possess the character of impatient emotivity. The absence of any possibility of liberation through coordinated action carries with it the risk of an increase in emotive impatience, which is discharged in screams and tears when the infant's instinctual and imperious needs do not obtain immediate satisfaction. Even these appeals for help, screams and tears, contain a nuance of attack and flight. The only sensible chance for tranquility resides in transforming the emotivity of impatience into loving emotion, a kind of primitive and still completely passive sublimation, which can take place only under the influence of parental tenderness, buttressed by the regularity of care. The newborn child's impatience is intensified due to the deprivation of affection and regular care, or under the influence of an affection devoid of calm (too submissive or too exalted). This perversion of the parents' emotivity calls forth in the infant the underlying bipolar attitudes of attack and flight. It intensifies the infant's natural impatience and transforms it into impotent rage, which is characterized by a convulsive mixup of attack and flight impulses. The emotive convulsion confers on the child's screams and tears—a primitively simple appeal for help—the significance of choleric attack or aggrieved flight. Having become unhealthy, emotivity thus begins to ravish the psyche at a very early age. In the end it deploys the ancestral germ of false motivation: it is easy to observe that even in infancy the child uses the debacle of his emotions for his own profit. This calculation of false motivation adds a nuance of capriciousness to the need for succor: as if the abandoned infant meant to avenge himself for his frustration by forcing the parents to busy themselves with him incessantly. The existence of underlying calculation is observed even more obviously in the case of the spoiled infant who, in order to attract loving attention, cries even when his needs are satisfied; if he had the underhanded intention of further overwhelming his already overwhelmed parents, he could not have hit upon a more effective strategem. It is clear, however, that the process is not as yet charged with subconscious intentionality: it is still completely preconscious, instinctive, and organic.

Beginning in early childhood, the emotive convulsion is accompanied by an organic convulsion of the sympathetic endocrine system, which produces tonic and vascular spasms. Due to the reciprocal interaction of the psychic and organic systems, it follows that when they are repeated and exacerbated, these crises of psychic origin will pave the way for motor discharge, so that the spasms will reach the torso and limbs.

It is interesting to observe that psychic convulsion has the character of regression to the most primitive biological functions. In its biologically elementary form, the convulsive reaction is incorporated for adaptive purposes. Indeed, in the most primitive beings (amoebas), convulsion exists as a means of locomotion, permitting both approach to the excitant (attack) and distancing from it (flight). Convulsion in a form that has become rhythmic is preserved in the economy of the most evolved organisms, where it only presides over visceral movement. But since life's origins, convulsive reaction is also expressed in a disorderly form. This is unleashed when the means of reaction prove to be unsuited to the excitant, so that the primitive being will not be able to respond by attack or flight. The primitive reflex reaction is perturbed but nevertheless preserves an adaptive significance. The convulsion is manifested in the form of contortions which, though at the start only an attempt to get rid of the harmful excitant, are employed in the end as a groping means of orientation. Convulsive groping proves to be the most primitive attempt to explore the environment: the method of trial and error. The infant's emotive convulsion is an erroneous attempt to feel out the resistance of the parental environment when it is experienced, in the absence of regular and affectionate care, as a threatening obstacle.

The first manifestation of exalted desire and its transformation into anxious convulsion, the nursing infant's angry tears, prepare the way to pathological irritability. The attitudes of attack and flight, prematurely awakened and convulsed, can no longer be deployed in a sensible manner: they remain throughout life exalted on one hand and inhibited on the other.

When the child is subjected to verbal prohibitions (education in cleanliness, the anal phase in psychoanalysis), there is a great danger that his emotivity, which until this point has been only sporadically anxious, will become surcharged with a new form of anxiety liable to condense and perpetuate itself. This is due to the awakening of the imagination.

IMAGINATIVE PLAY

Precisely like the play of animals, imaginative play—predominant in childhood—has as its natural and adaptive function the training in sensible attack and flight attitudes.

To the degree that the child's desires, hampered by excessive prohibitions, are not allowed discharge and are tinged with anxiety, imagination runs the risk of being deflected from its natural function and becoming a means of vain consolation (flight) and of rancorous blame (attack). Attack and flight already begin to be perverted in childhood; thus is created—by way of imaginative exaltation—a constant source of endogenous self-exaltation, more or less independent of any present and external excitation. Instead of performing its natural function—the regrouping of desires in keeping with real possibilities—imagination threatens to escape into the unreal and the impossible. From the time of their first premature appearance, the rancorous and sulky ruminations of the infant, who lacks all real defense, prepare the ground for future escapist reveries. These imaginative flights and attacks will sooner or later lead to a perverse discharge: disobedience that is no longer simply sporadic but constant and obsessive.

The only way to avoid this perverse outcome lies in not restricting the infant's budding imagination, so that it can find its natural outlets for discharge: affection and active play. The child's imaginative play finds its natural discharge through active play, which trains him in the exercise of motor and intellectual skills. It is of capital importance that active play not be inhibited by too frequent and untimely prohibitions. For the child, who is still enclosed in an unreal and imaginary world, active play possesses the charm of a magical power. It absorbs his entire being. Calls to order tear him away from its fascination and cast him forthwith into a utilitarian world that in the first moments of his sudden awakening is resented as refractory and hostile. Prohibitions that are repeated too often solidify these emotions of hostility and end by provoking the refusal to adapt.

Cut off from active discharge by the prohibition of real play, the child sinks into a magical and imaginary world. He escapes into the consoling satisfaction of imaginary games that become more and more frenetic.

The opposition between imagination and reality—the cause of future insoluble conflicts—becomes established in the child's psychic system.

The healthy maturation of the nascent psyche cannot be accomplished unless imaginative training is transformed into more conscious foresight, ensured by the reflective preparation of future action. Having become a daydreamer instead of learning little by little to apprehend clearly the surrounding reality, the child tends to withdraw egocentrically into himself. The egocentric imagination finds satisfaction only in what is prohibited by the environment. Egocentricity is a flight into the center of the ego with a view to escaping the exigencies of the environment, exigencies that for the child are educational impositions. Disoriented, the child cannot distinguish between what is permitted and what is not. His entire nascent psychic system is suffused with the anxiety of hearing the voice that calls him to order explode in his ear. Crushed by reproaches and punishments, he flounders in inhibiting anxiety. He cannot explain to himself what is happening to him and cannot explain to others what he feels. Injustice—even though partly provoked by the child himself—overwhelms him to the point that soon he feels nothing but his desolation. Lurking behind a hypersensitized sentimentality, even at this early age, is attack, accusing indignation, which will be all the more distressing for being as yet unconscious and incapable of formulation.

Self-justification and the incrimination of one's mother (or parents), remain for a long time below the level of evaluative reflection that—by way of conceptualization—transforms indignant resentment into the intentionality of aggression, into more or less consciously motivated disobedience. Long covered entirely by affection, the aggressive goad of indignation is turned by the child against himself; it becomes self-aggression, self-incrimination. The prohibition against playing, anxiously feared, thus is finally interiorized. In the child's secret heart, anguished disorientation acquires a new, very decisive character, one of the most decisive where present and future deformation are concerned: it becomes the *emotion of pathologically exalted guilt.*

As behaviorist observations and experiments have demonstrated, animals prevented from exercising attack and flight instincts through play perish prematurely. In the human being, insufficient employment of intellectual attack and defense attitudes is no longer a mortal danger: its outcome is persistent infantilism. The inhibition of maturation—externally observable due to the absence of adaptation to life's exigencies—has as its inner, shamefully hidden cause the emotion of vital deficiency: guilty anguish.

The guilt-ridden conflict, once introduced in the child's psyche, becomes more and more serious.

The guilty scruples are matched, in accordance with the law of ambivalence, by the excessive insouciance of the dreaming child. Sooner or later it will collide with the parents' exalted preoccupations. Since they are conventional, the parents can see nothing but the child's distant future, his social position in days to come. They become more and more insensitive to his present suffering, and this incites the child to exaggerate more and more his indifference about the future. He lives from day to day the hours of restless pleasure that he reserves for himself in the midst of his despondency. The child's tendency to live in the present degenerates into a laziness with which he counters the refrain, "What will become of you?" The parents' preoccupations are of a social order (expanded material drive); they concern the indispensable basis of material security and as such are justified. But their exaltation is proof of an unhealthy derangement of the educational intent due to excessive attachment to material necessity and thus is proof of the stagnation of the evolutionary drive. In the background of the child's rebellion often exists a savage courage that—despite all sanctions—defends his evolutionary need against the parents' utilitarianism. In the end,

all restraints cluster around this initial opposition between the
carefree quality of the child's play and the parents' social ambitions.
The parents' love is expressed now only by their preoccupied
badgering, and the opposition between them, from early childhood
on, is worsened as conflict follows upon conflict.

But the pathological consequences of the initial opposition are
not only manifested on the plane of the external success demanded
by the parents; they strike the child in the profound depths of his
inner life. The guilty conflict, once introduced into the child's
psyche, results in the progressive decomposition of his emotional
life and the disintegration of his character. The outstanding trait of
a child lost in the guilty frenzy of active or imaginative play is
affective imbalance, nervous irritability which finally causes the
lack of affect from which he suffers.

The deprivation of play—at first a solitary, later a collective
exercise—a deprivation originally due to the absence of sensible and
understanding love on the part of the parents, will end by becoming a necessity, because of the frenzy with which the frustrated
child infuses his play. (The spoiled child, from an early age, is just
as disturbed by his need for play as the frustrated child. The
parents, in order to enjoy as long as possible their child's exclusive
attachment, often shower it with toys that end by boring him and
keeping him away from collective play. They are inordinately
afraid that he might hurt himself, that he might get dirty, that he
might catch a cold, that he might get bad habits, etc.) The
deprivation of collective play prevents the development of qualities
of character (courage, perserverance, initiative, cheerfulness, sincerity, etc.). The child's nascent ego cannot succeed in being
integrally formed.

Having become capricious due to the exalted or inhibited love his
parents show him, the child does not succeed in crossing the
threshold that leads from the love freely granted during early
childhood toward the love-esteem that he must make an effort to
deserve. Thus from an early age the conflict between self-love and
the need for esteem is awakened. This conflict will find its just
solution—love-esteem—only to the extent that the parents are able
to respect the child's nascent will so that he learns in turn to respect
the parents' educational will.

The child filled with guilt is unable to obtain esteem or to esteem
himself. Guiltiness, which in the beginning is a vague and diffused
feeling of disorientation, is exasperated and becomes a lack of self-
esteem. Appearing whenever previously conceived good intentions
are defeated, the lack of self-esteem consolidates for that very

reason into a motivated resentment that wants to define and formulate itself. But this attempt at definition and formulation will only make it more unbearable, and the excessive sense of guilt, the negation of his own value, will evoke—by the path of ambivalence—an attempt at excessive self-justification. Thus already at this stage one will see arise the first signs of the tendency to free oneself through repression, the ascendancy of guilty self-negation. Inner deliberation, instead of becoming objectified, threatens to remain the imaginative play of false exculpation, an obsessive inducement to negate all faults. (Sooner or later one sees the surfacing of verbal expressions of this inner process of false justification: "What did I do now?," "I didn't do anything!," "It wasn't me," etc.)

The child's self-love, not having found the natural path to satisfaction that is opened by the search for merited esteem, remains all the more vulnerable as it is endlessly wounded by excessive reproaches from the family circle, which is often too impatient. Swollen with vanity because of the accumulation of vexations, self-love explodes, and from its explosion spring the original false attitudes of attack and flight, the forms of false motivation.

From the ambivalent decomposition of the child's need for love arises his false estimation of himself and of his parents. The false attitudes of attack and flight due to the decomposition of the bond of affection into love-hatred can be more clearly defined starting from this falsified estimation: repressed guilt appears as underesteem, repressive vanity as overesteem of the ego; accusation appears as underesteem of others, sentimentality as overesteem of others.

Nothing is more important than protecting the human being in childhood from psychic crippling, the wounding of soul: from the ambivalence of excessive attack and desperate flight which, seeking refuge in imaginative play, ends by losing itself in the labyrinth of the subconscious. Instead of being aggressive toward the child in the hope of obtaining his abdication, which can only lead to introjection of the guilty conflict, nervous irritability, or banalized discharge, it is important to love the child's nascent personality and assist in its blossoming. Only love—the nourishment of the soul— can impart vigor to the child's psyche and render it fit to discipline desires. The pleasure found in love is for the child the compensation that he needs to discipline the pleasure of play. To love the child is to respect his natural need for pleasure and at the same time to teach him to economize it, that is, to socialize and subsequently to sublimate it.

Love—in its double aspect: received and given—is the most sublime form of pleasure. Not to find pleasure in loving, what is it if not to sink into egocentrism? Healthy love is perfectly reconcilable with sensible egoism and its search for healthy pleasures; but it is opposed to the egocentrism of unhealthy pleasure.

In childhood, love is the condition of psychic health; but to condition the child's psyche healthily, the love binding parents and children must have free play; it must be enjoyable play. To radically separate love and pleasure is to render love unenjoyable and falsely moralizing.

Pleasure and Love

Prejudices regarding love are extremely harmful in the educational situation because they deform the relationship between parents as well as that between parent and child.

The entire educational problem is falsified—falsely motivated— by a sentimental lie regarding love.

The rooting of love in pleasure—which is the same as saying in the calculation of satisfaction—is a biologically profound phenomenon.

The human psychic system, through the blossoming of instances, is differentiated into the lower "I" (material and sexual drives) and a higher "I" (the evolutionary drive that has become a sublimating and spiritualizing instance). The consequent egoism finds its satisfaction in surpassing the lower "I" and in the blossoming of the higher "I." The sensible love of the self—by creating the higher "I"—enables one to love the higher "I" of others. The broadening of drives enlarges the sphere of satisfaction. Love is not a sentimentality. It is a creative dynamism, which consists in the fusion of two beings thanks to the soul's warmth, a condition for the reciprocal sublimation of egoism. Because this is so, love is the educational force *par excellence*. The educational task—which includes the self-education of educators—is finally concentrated in the problem of the sublimation of self-love.

From the egoism of the psychically healthy child will be born the capacity to love himself and his parents in a healthy manner. Purged of sentimentality, love finds its pleasure in giving pleasure to others. The education for love—whether one wishes it or not— remains falsified unless one understands that its rooting in self-love is capable of being changed into sublime pleasure. The lack of such understanding, instead of attaining the sublimation of self-love, only succeeds in deflecting it either into sentimentality (spoiled child) or aggressivity (frustrated child). The two deformations come together in the search for egocentric pleasure. It is therefore of capital importance to make a clear distinction between perverse, harmful pleasure and sublime, salutary pleasure. True love, out of sublime egoism, wishes to procure for the other (in this case the child) only salutary pleasure and opposes his perverse pleasure. This is the very definition of love as an educative force.

The theme to be developed is that of the higher form of egoist love, starting with its biological rooting all the way to the ramifications formed by human love in its various aspects: social, conjugal, and parental.

Biological Origin of the Bond of Affection

The fact that love derives from egoism is attested to throughout all of phylogeny.

The elementary forms of the bond of affection are already found at the prehuman level, where they manifest themselves in two aspects: the lasting liaison between male and female, and care of the progeny.

Now, the female's love for her brood (a prefiguration of the educational bond) proves among animals to be more imperious than the sexual bond: the care of progeny can be observed even at a very primitive level, above all among insects (bees, ants, spiders), where it is not as yet accompanied by a lasting sexual liaison between the parent animals. Sexual mating in fact among the higher animals is reduced to a period of heat. These indications of the biological prevalence of parental love remain significant, even though the differentiation between parental and sexual feelings and their shades of love will clearly appear only at the human level.

As for sexual mating, its most elementary means of excitation, prefiguring love-tenderness, is the caress. Observed even among certain very primitive animals, for example, mollusks, it is still due only to the exigencies of approach and does not really express tender emotion. At higher levels, where the sexual act is enriched by a real caress, affection shows its egoistic character more clearly. At its origin the caress is simply a means of sexual excitation; the caressed partner is perceived as an object of pleasure. Before being sublimated and becoming the expressive sign of love, the caress presents in the most elementary fashion the feature common to all love: the tendency to give pleasure to the partner in order to obtain from him or her (by a play of excitation) the greatest possible pleasure.

The care of progeny—first sign of parental love—becomes the rule without exception among mammals, where it is required by the specific form of feeding. However, such care, enriched by affection, is observed among birds, where one sees it accompanied by the first sign of education: the initiation into flying.

Love for progeny, capable of an abnegation which often goes so far as the sacrifice of life, is on the phylogenetic plane the only expression of the surpassing of egoism in its elementary form. That is why maternal love—the highest expression of the gift of the self—on the plane of human ontogeny becomes an indispensable condition that alone can help the child to leave his primitive egoism, that is, his hereditary egocentrism (the ancestral disposition to the choice of false means of attack and defense).

Now, from its phylogenetic origin, the bond to the progeny is egoist in nature. Maternal love—because of its root—is the continuation of a physiological bond: the offspring, although detached, remain for the animal mother a part of her own body that she defends often instinctively in the case of attack as if her own life were at stake. On the human level, this physiologically egoist component is enriched by a whole gamut of feeling that can attain the highest degree of sublimity, but that also can become unnatural and tainted with exaltation and perverse inhibition.

The child's affection for the mother (for the parents) is also a sublimation or a perversion of self-love which of necessity is its root, since the newborn infant is completely turned in upon himself and egoistically experiences only his own needs. He begins to attach himself to the mother because she is the source of all his satisfactions. But he will soon love his mother because he feels loved by her. However, the feeling of being loved has for the infant only an egoistic meaning: being the center of attention and protection.

All educational errors are caused by sentimentality that sees in the child-parent relationship unconditional sublimity, instead of understanding that the beauty of the relationship resides precisely in the dynamic fact of an egoism that must be sublimated.

It would be impossible to sublimate egoism if it did not contain from its origin the source of complete sublimation: the evolutionary impulsion. On the human level, evolutionary egoism—having become superconscious instinct—impels the child to seek the condition for his healthy maturation: love, the warmth of the soul (just as the young animal needs to be protected by the warmth of the nest).

Love, the sublime satisfaction of egoism, bears within itself two inseparable aspects; received love and given love. To be able to be given, love needs to be received from an early age. The sublime aspect of love is the gift of self. But this gift demands reciprocity. Only sentimentally superheated love grants the gift gratuitously; but the underlying egoism will manifest itself soon enough: exalted love becomes charged with rancor (love-hatred). The satisfaction found in the gift of self is exhausted when it is not sustained by the satisfaction found in the gift of the other. Love is the sublime communication between *ego* and *alter*.

This reciprocity of the gift of self determines the educational relationship down to its smallest details.

In order to assure himself of protective love and finally of the parents' esteem, the child is ready to let himself be molded by the educational exigencies. His egoism begins to be sublimated: his attachment becomes capable of sacrifice. The healthily loved child renounces forbidden satisfactions and even, temporarily, the pleasure of play. But this gift is withdrawn as soon as the child does not receive the emotional compensation. Only the reciprocity of the gift, proven on the part of the parents by understanding love, can prevent the child from rebelling. In an effort to force love, he will try to place himself at the center of attention. In order to get there, he will slyly and subconsciously invent the most unexpected, most illogical means, those most contrary to his parents' demands. Thus the parents become for the child and the child for the parents a source of displeasure. Now, according to the law of egoism, all sources of pleasure incite to flight or attack. If real flight is impossible, as is the case in the family situation, it is transformed into imaginary flight, followed by attack-defense: the revenge of disobedience runs the risk of becoming increasingly principled and obsessive (in certain rather rare cases, flight, instead of remaining imaginary, ends by being carried out and the child becomes a runaway).

From the sublimated need of reciprocity of the gift of self finally comes the definition of the educational task in all its evolutionary amplitude.

Education is able to develop the child's evolutionary impulsion only to the extent to which the parents have been able to satisfy their own evolutionary impulsion. But also the parents' evolutionary impulsion is vivified to the extent to which they are able to accomplish the educational task.

In the end the meaning of the educational bond aims not only at the child's intrinsic good; it is also just as beneficial for the parents. For in the educational relationship the parents find—or should find—a second youth, a return to the evolutionary meaning of their own life, and protection against the vital danger that threatens the adult: stagnation. Revolt against the educational task is precisely—due to the continuous rancor that it engenders—a major cause of the parents' stagnation and even of their premature aging.

The evolutionary exigency of education extends to the parents. For the child, owing to his complete dependency—not only in respect to his material needs and the needs of his soul (affection), but also his judgments—remains for a long time a purely imitative being. His evolutionary impulse suffers when it is disoriented by the example of parents who are in a state of stagnation.

Love is not simply a feeling, it is also an act; and only the act of love determines the value of the feeling. It is only to the extent to which it is carried forward by the evolutionary impulsion that parental love can overcome sentimental deformation—which is nothing but pseudo-sublime verbiage—and become a fruitful act, an example.

The act of love derives from the force of acceptance. This force consists in patience toward the loved being. Only the exercise of patient and active love—difficult though it may be—can prevent the parents from lapsing into stagnation. Actively exercised toward the child, the capacity for love grows, and this amplification will necessarily extend to the relations between the parents. Their affective bond—often of too sentimental or utilitarian an origin—can thus be made tranquil and fortified so that the primitive egoism of the sexual tie is enriched by a bond of the soul that, itself, again becomes the condition for the healthy accomplishment of the educational task by creating the harmonious atmosphere necessary for the children's evolution.

The mastery of the self that parents impose on themselves out of love of the child is the opposite of the moralizing verbalism expressed in incessant scoldings. Certainly when one is in the throes of innumerable real complications, nothing is more difficult than to remain patient. But this is precisely true also for the child, and above all for the child educated by irritable and irritating parents.

The activation of love—like all ideals—is a guiding goal that can be realized only by degrees of approximation. Its realization is not facilitated but rather sabotaged by the sentimental idealization of love. The entire problem of the educability of human nature resides in this difficulty of maintaining the drive to surpass. It is precisely because of this difficulty that the problem of education becomes part of the psychology of instances. Love is the master quality that requires the mastery of the self, which is simply another term for harmony of the superconscious; it is the disharmony of the subconscious that causes impatience, irritability, the ensemble of deficient reactions.

Only mastery of the self confers the educational strength that is authority. Firmness with the child—necessary though it may be— becomes an educational danger if it is not buttressed by the parents' firmness toward themselves, thanks to which they compel themselves to grant the child as much freedom as possible so as not to irritate him. No one can endure the constant imposition of another's will. It is only through the interacting play of freedoms that prohibition, when it become inevitable, is totally accepted and freely consented to, so that the child's imagination does not even have the time to begin brooding and does not threaten to take the path—one of the most dangerous—of preferring to escape into forbidden reactions. Having as its goal not the parents' convenience but the child's essential good, patient firmness bears its just measure within itself: it avoids both accusatory nagging of the child and sentimental submissiveness to his caprices; it will also cast off the vanity-engendered vexation of the educator who is rendered impotent (and the angry and excessive sanctions that come from this) as well as the sense of guilt that induces parents to repress their educational errors and to continually repeat their falsely justified shortcomings.

The other name for this patient love is *justice*. Treated with justice, the child has no need in his turn to have recourse to false justification. Feeling himself swathed in active love, he loses the sense of insecurity that forces him to ceaselessly "palp" the degree of affection his parents have for him and thus with the help of his obstinate disobedience gain the center of attention.

Under these conditions the child ceases to be a source of inconvenience for the parents. His feelings of guilt will no longer emanate from egocentric anxiety but rather from the evolutionary impulsion: they will show him the injustices he has committed against his parents. In place of sterile remorse, salutary regret, a feeling of responsibility, will appear. Instead of leading to repression, responsible guilt—not repressed guilt—will stimulate the drive to surpass. Thus even the committed mistake, temporary disobedience, becomes the means of realizing the educational goal.

Sociability

Added to the sublimation of egoism is the other previously mentioned educational task: *the spiritualization of the unconscious.*

The path of the child's maturation leads from egoism to love, from the unconscious to the superconscious.

The stages of sublimation of egoism coincide with the stages of spiritualization of the unconscious. The two essential goals of education—sublimation and spiritualization (idealization and ideation)—interpenetrate and mutually stimulate each other. During the course of ontogeny the satisfactions promised by love are founded (or should be founded) on lucid judgments, judgments that confer their full motivating power upon healthy promises of satisfaction.

If education is a process of sublimation-spiritualization, there are two priniciples on which it can be based: love and truth. In other words: the individual example, and the generalized theory. The two principles form but one: theory can only underline the fact that education's active principle is love. Theoretical study must highlight not only the egoist root of love but also its sublimely motivating force, something that is possible only through the analysis of the calculation of satisfaction (and its phylogenetic root).

The need for theoretical understanding grows during periods when individuals, having lost their sensible orientation, no longer know how to be a living example.

Our age is characterized by anarchy in all value judgments. Societies, decomposed into egocentric individuals, are painfully searching for a new structure.

Nothing would be more out of place than to broaden the scope of the present study with a detailed critique of social life. But, on the other hand, nothing would be more inadequate than to search for the solution to the educational problem exlusively in the circumstances of family life and to neglect completely the immense influence exercised by social life. The parent-educators are egocentric individuals who comprise the disoriented society, and the generalized disorientation is essentially due to contradictions between the reigning ideologies.

Social life that lacks the affective bond is unthinkable. But when it extends over large numbers this bond cannot go beyond cordiality. Even in human beings of healthy constitution, the force of love is not intense enough to be able to spread one's sphere of satisfaction indiscriminately over all other human beings.

Such an effort would undoubtedly be the supreme guiding ideal. But the attempt to achieve its perfect realization creates only an exalted task. In accordance with the law of ambivalence, the quality of love, when it is imaginatively exalted, splits into two perverse counterpoles. On the plane of conventional moralizing these two contradictory poles are manifested in the guise of sentimentally exalted love (the altruistic ideal of abnegation) and egocentrically restricted love (the egoistic counterideal of unscrupulous social ambition). Both these counterpoles are subtended by hypocritical sentimentality, hostile blame, vanity-inspired exultation, the various means here as everywhere else of repressing guilt or projecting it onto someone else. The ideal of abnegation, exalted altruism ends by blaming the other as not being worthy of the gift of self it insists on bestowing on him; on the other hand, unscrupulous egocentric ambition enjoys exulting and taking advantage of the moralizing sentimentality of others. It runs aground in callousness where others are concerned, the sign of an excess of sentimental sensitivity toward oneself.

Only the dissolution of these falsely motivated resentments—and therefore the dissolution of the moralizing task—could restore the quality of premeditated cordiality to members of society. Moralistic exaltation vainly endeavors to suppress egocentricity by attaching itself to actions, just like false education, without paying attention to the imagination's perverse games of escape and justification. Imposed from the outside, duty-morality likes to claim that one's ethical effort is all the more meritorious when the suppression of unjust acts is achieved despite the persistence of desires for escape and of falsely justificatory motivations. The result, whether it is a banal hypocrisy that stymies the ethical effort or nervous convulsion characterized by an imaginative exuberance of good intentions, is powerless to resist the promises or imagined temptations (unless the exuberance runs aground in ascetic convulsion).

The behaviorists' experiments have demonstrated that nervous irritation arises at the animal level owing to exposure to contradictory excitations. The most profound reason for nervous irritability in man, the thinking and valuing being, lies hidden in the contradictory value judgments of the reigning morality.

Conventional morality—exalted abnegation—is a mistaken ideal, contrary to nature. Morality is merely false idealism as long as it does not refer to the evolutionary scale and therefore to the biological foundation of all of life: the search for sensible satisfaction. What could be more immoral than to conceive of the ethical effort—instead of drawing pleasure from it—as a duty only partly and half-heartedly accomplished? Surely this is to introduce into ethics perverse love, the scission into love and hate. The consequence is seen even in the sphere of elementary drives, which become half exalted, half inhibited. Inhibitive abnegation ends by exalting immeasurably the primitive attack and flight instincts of two elementary drives (nourishment and sexuality) and the hinderance of their healthy expression. Excessive inhibition due to moralizing abnegation is opposed by an unhealthy increase in the pressure of material needs and of sexual pleasures. Their enticements, invading the imagination, come to light through the explosion of attack and flight actions, which in the end distort all of social life. Confronted by this situation, the virtues of abnegation preached to each new generation are soon rejected. Their powerlessness to assure success in the social struggle elicits only mockery. Amorality prevails.

The two ambivalent poles of conventional moralizing, even as they engage in battle, reciprocally support each other. The morality of the unscrupulously ambitious could not subsist for long without its exalting complement of abnegation, the indispensable subterfuge that confers a tinge of pseudo-sublimity upon faded life.

The moralizing error of society has the most disastrous influence on the plane of education.

The educator's fundamental quality—integrity of character—demands that actions and words be in conformity. The drama of the scission of judgment begins from the moment that the child is able to observe and think. Hearing his parents preach and seeing them act, the child loses trust in both his parents and morality. He is unable to formulate his confusion, and were he able to do so, his questions—considered impertinent or embarrassing—would only arouse aggression in the form of punishment, or the flight into hypocritical evasiveness.

Without the possibility of a valid defense, the child is thus exposed both to the imperative of the morality of abnegation and the demands of unscrupulous ambition. The two imperatives merge in the boundless demands for dutiful conduct, against which the child struggles boundlessly. By means of a deluge of verbal moralizing, false education tries to make the child renounce the pleasure of play, and only succeeds in unleashing his disobedient refusal; and, conversely, false education strives to impose unscrupulously ambitious countermorality and obtains only abulic flight when faced by duty. From early childhood on, renunciation is hated as an externally imposed duty. The contradictory valuations, instead of being dissolved by education, become exalted and inhibited—and combat each other—in the child and increase proportionately as he grows up.

The adolescent under the stress of maturation will try to cut through the conflict and will simply exacerbate it. Attaching

himself to idealistic systems—religious, political, artistic, etc.—
that society prepares and proposes to him, he will experience a
series of grandiose aspirations followed by falls. Then, gripped by
material concerns, he will soon become resigned and content with
the compromises prepared by society. Unscrupulous ambition
carries him away, and the fall becomes permanent. On becoming
an adult, he will merge with the multitude of the semi-banalized.
The few regrets that may persist will be drowned again and again in
the mediocrity of false justification in its ideological and conventional form. In case of success, the unscrupulously ambitious
person will imagine that he has attained the full meaning of life.
This solution tends to the complete rejection of abnegation; however, it is rarely fully realized. More or less persistent guilt creates
infinite variations in character between the two exalting counterpoles of conventional moralism-amoralism. There exist in reality
all the gradations from excessive banalization, which seeks social
success at all costs, to nervousness which, due to excessive scruples,
leads to social defeat. An eternal adolescent, the nervous person
does not succeed in adjusting to the banalizing exigencies of social
life. Idealism continues to haunt him, the sign of an authentic
underlying drive to surpass, which, however, for lack of true
support, is cut off from realization. All impetus is fanatically frozen
in an exalted task of abdication subtended by constantly repressed
ambitious regrets. The distressing contradiction of values, and the
great burden of guilt that results from it, will incite the misguided
individual to escape into the infantilism of imaginative play. Owing
to a pseudo-spiritual ambition that is cut off from both external and
internal success, the nervous person aggravates his defeat by repressing his guilt. From the depths of the subconscious the conflict
arises again in the oneiric form of the psychopathic symptom. All
symptoms symbolically express the guilty conflict between the
morality of abnegation and the countermorality of unscrupulous
ambition.

In the individual's subconscious depths, the conflict apparently
has no way out, because it is continually supported and exacerbated
by the pressures of a disoriented society. This baneful influence is
propagated through the channel of distractions that too often are
pseudo-artistic (certain films, novels, etc.). In an imagination inclined to exaltation, the ideological conflict between moralism and
amoralism is again individualized, concretized, and goes so far as to
assume monstrous forms. Sexual and material desires, either exalted beyond measure or inhibited to excess, become the cause of
indissoluble torment.

One could admit—biologically speaking—that this repeated concentration of the social conflict in the individual psyche, this subjectively painful exaltation of the fundamental mistake, is the "will" of nature.

Only in the inner depths of suffering and reflecting individuals can the socialized error find its revision and the conflictual situation its solution. The way out can be found only to the extent in which the individual frees himself from the allurements which vainly idealize his false sublimity of abnegation and his false temptation to run wild.

True morality is not in the first place a social problem. It is above all a problem within oneself. That is why morality involves an effort at self-education that requires the most decisive courage, the courage to resist a social milieu that is imbued with falsely idealizing ideologies. Physical courage is defined by the capacity to defend oneself against the external world when it threatens the elementary need of bodily survival. Moral courage consists in the ability to defend one's essential self, one's superior ego, one's personality, and this can only be done by attacking the deforming threat in oneself: false motivation. In this regard, it is important to understand that biologically based morality—consequential egotism—culminates in the gift of the self and abnegation. But the gift has meaning only if it is given not starting from vanity-inspired impoverishment and egocentric reticence but from inner richness in full harmony with oneself. Abnegation has meaning provided it is not the self's negation but its supreme affirmation. This supremely egoistic abnegation can even lead to sacrifice of one's life; it thus reverses the elementary animal need for survival at all costs, while remaining within an extended calculation of satisfaction. The price that should not be paid for survival is betrayal of the superior self, because for the person who loves above all else the integrity of his higher self, such betrayal would be followed by an inexpiable guilty dissatisfaction. Moral courage in its fullest expression consists in renouncing life—in a circumstance that would impose this most decisive of choices—rather than letting oneself be seduced by the temptations of a lower self intent on a falsely justified compromise.

Moral courage envisages the personalization of the individual, and in its higher instances results in authenticity. Biologically explained as the healthy expansion of drives, on the level of individual morality it is defined as the harmonious flowering of desires. Far from being a constraint or a duty, morality is the ability to satisfy life so as to be satisfied by life. Moral courage in the end acquires social significance precisely because the effort of realization can only be accomplished through the individuals who make up society. To the extent to which the harmonized, balanced individual (who bears his center of gravity within himself) succeeds in becoming independent of reigning ideologies, he acquires the ability to create a bond between himself and his fellow beings by means of free-flowing positive feelings: tolerance, cordiality, friendship, love, and goodness. He is thus freed from warped entanglement with others, the result of the idealistic exaltation of self-abnegation to the advantage of others, as well as from a greedily scheming ambition whose objective is to take unscrupulous advantage of others. Conventional morality engenders the asocial attitude, nervous autism as well as banalized aggression. Only love of the self in its noble form, the love of one's higher self (the harmonizing superconscious), can lead to the love of another's higher self, to true sociability.

The individual cannot find the way out and loses himself in nervous suffering or banal euphoria. The species—owing to the fact that the way out is biologically based on the elementary need for authentic satisfaction, the driving motive of evolution—will succeed in surmounting the essential danger (the two forms of conventional antimorality). The demoralizing error justified by false ideologies can only be overcome on the slow path of elucidating spiritualization, which leads to the comprehension of subconsciously hidden motives. In spite of the obsessive character of the moralizing error (propagated by education over the generations), evolutionary adaptation to the meaning of life continues on its slow march. With a view to realizing its goals, it employs even the most senseless derangement, the pseudo-moralizing deformation of life become semiconscious. Suffering in its individual and social forms becomes the vehicle of evolution. Evil (unsurmounted suffering) exists only on the individual plane. At the level of the species, evil becomes good (surmounted suffering). In the biogenetic view, which alone conforms to the realities of life, there is no need at all to have recourse to exalting, utopian idealism. It is not moralizing good intentions but the suffering that results from their floundering which obliges life become semiconscious to grow conscious of its immanent danger—false choice and false valuation, which, taken to their ultimate consequence, are expressed in a distorted vision of morality: vacillation between the two ambivalent poles of erroneous valuation: moralism and amoralism.

The problem of education cannot find a satisfactory solution without the study of the social factor. This factor is not in the first instance of an economic and material order. It resides above all in the *economics of desires* and their promises of satisfaction. Technical inventions change the life of society only incidentally (even though they are due to a psychic factor, that is, the practical intellect in search of its satisfactions). The life of societies will remain essentially unchanged as long as another psychic factor—the blind affectivity of desires—obsessively produces the misuse of technical inventions. Thus the essential problem is of a psychological order.

Since the beginning of time few human beings have been able to attack in themselves the fundamental error that ultimately is concretized in the two conventional attitudes of flight and attack: the abandonment of self (the disintegration of the self by way of false motivation) and the aggressive affirmation of the disintegrated self, which together are the innermost causes of the deformation of individuals and societies.

The parents who form the society of adults are almost always characterized by the fact that their evolutionary force, their drive to surpass—the guarantor of healthy education—is either shattered or exalted. The inadequacy of the reality in which the educators wish to incorporate the child is determined by this condition of the adults—in short, their evolution is often *terminated* without being *achieved*. How can they possibly fulfill in an adequate manner the essentially evolutionary function that education is? The entire difficulty of a theoretical and practical order, the entire tragedy of education, is contained in this disparity between the deformation of the adults' impulsion and the imperious evolutionary need of the child, whose impulsion has the physiological strength of an irresistible forward movement, an elementary drive, a long time before becoming vision, aspiration, an ideal capable of being formulated. When the child, on the threshold of adolescence, begins to be able to formulate his vital impulse, the impulse has already become unnatural, broken or transformed into rebellion. In the course of his evolution, the child has experienced as deceptive and unjust the attempt to adapt him to the world of the adults, to familial and social demands, to an insufficient reality. He has learned to respond to this falsely justified injustice with the false justification of his own injustice.

The ambivalence of ideologies and the decomposition of the sphere of values that results from it have attained their culminating point in the present age. The social consequences of inner failure vastly overflow the family framework. The harshness of the struggle for material survival is matched by the need for escape sought in unlimited amusement at all costs and the wild unleashing of desires.

The falsification of values is commercialized by the advertising and entertainment industries, which offer adulterated nourishment both to the mind and to the imagination. Incapable of critical resistance, youth can only react with an obscure mixture of attraction and repulsion. The rebellion against the world that is his legacy and the wish to play the adult—characteristic traits of the adolescent—carry youth to extreme positions, preparing it for a life that in turn will be tainted by ambivalent demoralization. Driven by a desire for amelioration, many young people rigidly seize upon old values whose formulation is outdated; others indulge in a frenetic unleashing of desire that is mistaken for proof of virility but that in truth only prolongs the childish rebellion against parental prohibitions. Other young people, more studious, seem to fulfill their tasks and appear untouched. But making a virtue of submission, in keeping with received precepts, they lose themselves in materialist ambition. In their depersonalized minds, the pursuit of a diploma replaces the drive to surpass and the thirst for knowledge. Obviously, such distorted traits—and many others as well—have always existed. What stigmatizes our age is the generalization of these traits to the detriment of enthusiasm and authenticity. What youth grown old before its time lacks is the inspiriting faith in life and its value.

In this morass young people and adults prove to be in agreement. The projection of youth's faults on the adults and that of the adults on the young is merely a sign of impotence due to a refusal to rethink the problem, starting with each individual's responsibility. The common fault is unanimously flung back on society, regarded as an entity that supposedly exists independent of individuals and supposedly presides—like a divinity—over men's destinies. Isn't this conception, proposed by modern sociology, a new form of speculative metaphysics set up as a dogma, and all the more dangerous since it asserts itself with the authority of a science? The search for the essential, inner cause is thus considered superfluous, and this repression—in keeping with psychic law—produces the obsessive repetition of the denied and therefore falsely justified fault, which is the true cause of decadence. (Sociological research, like the work of behaviorism and many other disciplines, is indispensable. The error consists in claiming to have a theoretical base that presents this research as a means sufficient in itself for discovering the solution to the problem of life.)

It is, however, true that society is a kind of entity. It is a living organism composed of cells: families and individuals. The healthy or unhealthy functioning of an organism reverberates in its cells, while the organism itself is profoundly determined by the cells' healthy or unhealthy functioning. This is not just a comparative image drawn from biogenesis. History teaches us that at the origin of today's highly organized and therefore fragile societies stands the clan: the family and its members. The life of the family remains of paramount importance for the life of society. The inter-influences at play among society, family, and individuals become comprehensible in all their amplitude thanks to the observation that the creation of societies is a historical and evolutionary activity of the species. Like all human activity the successive creation of societies is subtended by the motives that animate individuals. In the individual's inmost depths the diversification of motives is elaborated, which in turn causes the unfolding of the historical process that replaces primitive societies by ever more highly organized societies. Why should the elucidation of motives not be able to create a remedy for the fragility of these societies? Individual motivations, in part superconscious and subconscious, valid or invalid, vitally satisfactory or unsatisfactory, condensed in the form of just or erroneous ideologies—determine at each historical stage the life of societies, their healthy or unhealthy organization. The problem of the transformation of social illness into health thus depends necessarily and above all on the elucidation of motivations, that is to say the transformation of public opinions into psychological science. The ideological excitations originating in the social milieu—the effect of motivation—become motivating causes in turn only to the extent that they are metamorphosed into an inner cause, as a result of their repercussion on the emotional plane. Social organization, by reverberating in the family milieu and therefore in its individuals, acquires in this way, and only in this way, its vital significance; it will be experienced as acceptable or unacceptable. External stimuli, insofar as they are unfavorable, provoke in the individual reactions of flight or attack: fantasies of escape and false justification. These imaginative ruminations determine the affectivity of whole peoples and codetermine the decisions of governments. In the end they unleash social conflicts: revolutions and wars. But long before these explosions take place, the imagination of dissatisfaction grumbles in the bosom of families. Fed by the consequences of social disorder (insufficient salaries, material preoccupations, lack of hygiene, lack or scarcity of housing, etc.), the rebellious imagination ravages the inner life of individuals and is discharged in the family milieu in the form of quarrels liable to destroy the affective bond and poison the atmosphere in a constant and irremediable fashion. The children's education suffers, and the evil is propagated from generation to generation.

The fate of man and the destiny of humanity is prepared in the bosom of the family.

Whatever might be the irritations deriving from social disorder, the fatiguing state of nervous agitation is first of all imputable to the insufficient responses of the individual, to his psychic disorder. The weariness of the exasperated parents can only intensify the children's irritability and provoke their wearisome disobedience. There is no remedy for the vicious circle that binds social life and family life except the parents' effort to improve themselves, difficult though it may be.

Yet nobody has the right to blame the parents excessively, for their educational inadequacy—the prolongation of the education they received—is a result of the present human condition, and no one has taught them how to overcome its consequences. A person who is conscious of his own weaknesses could only be indulgent about this. Unfortunately, life is not indulgent. Inherent justice resides precisely in cruelty: the fault implies its punishment, suffering. The irresistible evolutionary impulsion rejects all verbal excuses—which are nothing but repression—and accepts only active excuses: spiritualization of the error and sublimation of the fault. The children's suffering, cause of their underhanded rebellion, reflects upon their inadequate educators, since in the child is concentrated the meaning of their own life and hope, the source of strength. The disappointment with the children intensifies inner disorder in the adult generation, a disorder that renders oppressive the burden of one's troubles due to the social milieu.

What—in the last analysis—prevents badly educated educators from addressing themselves to the only task that will lead to release from the vicious circle—that is, to make the effort on themselves instead of hammering away at the child—is the fact that false motivations deform not only individual activities but also create erroneous ideologies. In fact, falsified educational interventions acquire a principled rigidity as a result of the generalized false justification furnished by the reigning ideologies, which are indeed the foundation of educational theories.

Conjugal Love

It is above all preconceptions on the subject of marriage and conjugal love that influence the problem of education.

Because of the importance of the family cell's healthiness or unhealthiness for the social organism in general and the education of children in particular, it is important to draw an overall sketch of the positve and negative motivations that link parents and educators.

More than any other fundamental situation, the common life of two people is threatened by permanent complications due to the false motivation intrinsic in each of the spouses. Constant friction risks creating wounds that will never heal. Hostile reactions imperil all interpersonal relations, but they never manifest themselves so frequently as in the common life of a man and a woman. The meaning of the couples' life consists precisely in their overcoming this danger.

It would certainly be absurd to claim that the goal of a couple's life lies exclusively in the fulfillment of the educational task. According to such a conception each new generation would live only in terms of the generations to come. Just as the sexual act carries within itself its full enjoyment independent of its procreative function, the educational act, when it is healthily fulfilled, also entails a premium of enjoyment that—because it is due not to the temporary coupling of bodies but to the bond of souls—becomes the joy of life.

In this sense one can say that monogamy is an evolved form of the couple's life that guarantees for both partners—at least in principle—the flowering of their human value. In polygamous societies the woman is reduced to the level of a mere chattel for sexual enjoyment; this fact, instead of favoring her evolution, has as its consequences a debasement of her human value, a debasement whose noxiousness appears not only on the educational plane but also on the path of heredity. In this regard the monogamy of the West could well be one of the reasons for its hegemony. However, in order to be lived healthily, monogamy demands from a man and woman a degree of maturity that is rarely achieved. And one would be wrong not to admit that one of the principal causes for the West's decadence is found in the family's lack of stability. Evolutionary progress, here as everywhere else, is not accomplished without hesitancy, and this implies attempts at regression and manifestations of failure. Overcome by perversion, monogamy, instead of leading to the unification of the couple, threatens to run aground in an excess of rivalry between the sexes, the destructive consequences of which strike at both parents and children. On the social plane, woman's material emancipation will undoubtedly facilitate divorce. But this easy solution will not eliminate the underlying evolutionary exigency based on the indissoluble bond between parents and children. The exceptional strength of parental feelings makes this bond—in its negative form of guilty dissatisfaction—resist divorce, or at least the guilt is likely to persist in the case of divorce with regard to the abandoned children.

If the couple in disaccord avoids divorce, often the educational situation is no less compromised. Resentments at work between the parents in the long run destroy the feeling they have for their children. It is true that in the tangle of motives and actions the badly educated child becomes in turn a cause for disaccord between the parents-educators. There are undoubtedly situations in which the childrens' reticence is exacerbated far more by a harmful extrafamilial environment than by the parents' deficiencies. Around the age of fourteen the child goes through a period of conformism that subjects him to a great extent to the influence of peers who are often warped. In an age in which all of youth finds itself in a state of rebellion against the adult generation, this danger increases. This does not change the fact that the devaluing judgments that circulate among young people can in the last analysis be charged to the same laxity of mores that too often make the adults incapable of forming healthily constituted parental couples.

It is therefore important to highlight in particular the generalized preconceptions and individual motives that lead to the disaccord of the parental couple, preconceptions and motives that constitute the principle cause of abdication as regards the educational task.

The most intense source of satisfaction is creativity. No prejudice is as baneful and vain as that which accords precedence in creation to specialized talents instead of first searching for it in the flowering of the personality through the art of living. Life's masterpiece is the human being healthily formed of flesh and soul. This creative activity extends from birth to death. It embraces the entire cycle of life in an incessant recommencing. The baneful prejudice is to believe that this creativity is devoid of originality simply because everyone, starting from a certain age and by uniting with the opposite sex, is capable of participating in the creation of life. But the most precious and rare originality lies in the creation of a healthy life, and it is above all psychic health that is determined by a constant creative effort. The couple remains responsible for the creative act and its vitally satisfying prolongation. All through life and until death, each parent is involved in a completely original and inventive creativity that aims at the supreme art: the harmonious creation of his or her character, the precondition for the home's stability and therefore the precondition for the creation of the children's healthy characters.

The creative act in its plenitude extends not only over all of life but also over its contents, over all the intensified sexual instincts that give birth to multiple desires capable of being exalted or harmonized. Evolutionary creation—the harmonization of the character—demands the struggle against exaltation with a view to the healthy accomplishment of two selective acts that create security: the choice of profession, the material basis for the foundation of the home, and the choice of a sexual partner.

The choice in its two forms, material and sexual, is indispensable for the constitution of any couple, but it does not in itself ensure the security of the home. Security is the result of the motives underlying the choice. The union of the couple, in order to become definitive, involves a constant creative activity that consists in the effort to resolve nascent resentments, destroyers of the home. But this effort of mutual edification, to be tenable—whether supported by a balanced temperament or with the brake of reason—requires mutual tolerance. Thus understood, the choice of the spouse is one of the most fundamentally important decisions, if not the most important. Also the full maturity of sexuality implies the capacity for a choice guided by an instinct of attraction that divines the affinity of characters (*anima* and *animus,* according to Jung). Instinctive attraction includes not only the will to choose the procreator of the desired child but also the hope of a mutual characterological fecundation capable of satisfying the drive to surpass. Since no choice can be ideally satisfactory, responsible choice implies acceptance of the real partner with qualities to be developed and faults that must be overcome by life in common. Acceptance is the sublimating force that renders the choice definitive by excluding fantasies of escape.

The choice is rarely definitive due to a lack of sufficient maturation on the part of the partner. The wrong choice can be due to motives of a banal and utilitarian order, or to a sentimentally exalted love that runs the risk of degenerating into love-hate and disillusionment. Instead of acceptance, ambivalence will manifest itself: resignation-rebellion.

The false calculation of satisfaction implied in such a choice will be contrasted with the factitious image of a partner endowed in dreams with illusory qualities. The dreamed-of partner—an insubstantial phantom and therefore enhanced by intense suggestive power—will divide the couple, which, although in appearance united, henceforth will live in a state of *imaginary divorce.* Imagination escapes from an ever more disappointing reality in sexual adventures that, charged with guilt, often remain pure unrealized temptation, or in the imaginary prospect of another partner able to ensure a better material base, higher social rank, or a more attractive spiritual bond. The temptation of such reveries becomes almost irresistible in the case of nervous persons because of their penchant for imaginative flight when faced by reality. The secretly cherished phantom-image is at the origin of the pathogenesis of the couple's life, because it does not rise up solely to oppose one's spouse; it soon will be projected haphazardly onto encounters with other men or women and will thus indefatigably feed the regret at being bound by the choice. The spouse is condemned to become an unbearable obstacle.

To these imaginary escapes will be added accusation of the partner and false justification of oneself. While the instances of escape remain secretly hidden, the accusations are exteriorized slyly, if only by imponderable provocation that aggravates the mutual discontent. The common fault resides in insufficient maturity, which has brought about the irresponsible choice and continues to manifest itself in incessant repetitions of the imaginary and tentacular choice, magnifying the mutual destruction of the couple's characters. Each spouse will admit to only one fault: the ghastly mistake of having been so completely swept off his or her feet as to choose the other. This avowal itself, instead of reestablishing responsibility, serves only to deny it. It contains the reproach directed at the "charmer," against his or her very existence, responsible for having made the infatuation possible. The other's entire fault is that he or she exists. Sooner or later in the accusing imagination arises the unconfessable and repressed idea of seeing the importunate one disappear, an idea that bears within it a desire for death. It is, however, necessary to understand that in the course of successive aggravations of the imaginary divorce, which is often complicated by an indissoluble sentimental tie, it is not the real death of the partner that is desired but rather abrogation of the choice. The wish for his or her death is—most of the time—not really held; it is only a screen on which is projected the haunting thought of a definitive divorce. The dreamt-of liberation is passively entrusted to the final intervention of fate. At the apogee of this process of ambivalent decomposition of sentiments into resentments, self-idealization—which imagines itself as deserving an ideal partner—is supplemented by an indulgent exacerbation of self-pity.

In order to stave off guilt, the accusation is detached from the spouse and tries to generalize itself. In the end it is fate that is accused of withholding its liberating intervention. Despair spreads over all of life, which is perceived in imagination as a dismal grayness. The death sentence pronounced on the other runs the risk of being changed into a deadly self-condemnation: from generalized despair ideas of suicide sporadically arise, though they are rarely carried out. Whatever the ostensible causes of suicide, its most unconfessed motive will always be despair about oneself. Moreover, the ostensible causes will frequently be familial or extra-familial misadventures; love misadventures which can even lead to murder. One must ask oneself whether destructive rage does not in all cases have its essential roots in the inadequacy of elementary creativity, a sign of vital impotence (exalted choice of the partner, amorous disappointments, failed marriage or cohabitation, celibacy, etc.).

In their banalizing form the dreams of escape and justification can avoid the complications and torments of imaginary divorce. False justification will serve to deprive vital creativity of its vigor and reduce this problem to the convenient solution which consists in a real break with the irresponsible choice. The rupture will be realized either in a camouflaged form (deliberate authorization for sexual adventures), or in the definitive form of divorce. But divorce—as long as the initial fault, insufficient maturity, is not rectified—will merely open the path for a dissolute life or a new disappointing choice.

It is, however, conceivable that there can exist, at least in principle, a case in which divorce is a valid solution: this is the case if one of the partners, in spite of the mistaken choice, has done his or her best during their life in common to dissolve resentments without obtaining a positive response from the other partner. This constant effort will have sufficiently sublimated the character to render a better choice possible. The motive of divorce will be valid because its intention is only to recover the creativity contained in marriage. False justification will obviously suggest that each partner be convinced of having done his or her best. But this repression of conjugal inadaquacy will continue to produce its pathogenic consequences even though it is covered by banalizing euphoria. Neither subjective conviction nor objectifying theory will be able to solve the problem in the concrete case of Family X or Y. Life itself will attest to the value or nonvalue of the solution, either by harmonizing absolution or by the dissolution of character. One must also ask whether the proof of true regained creativity resides in a change of situation or whether it resides rather in the acceptance of the situation, which in most cases is demanded by responsibility toward the children.

Divorce is an indispensable social institution because of the frequence of lack of maturity in marriage partners. On the individual plane guilt persists—or at least should persist—if only in relation to the children. This guilt can even be euphorically covered or masked by conventional justification. This will only accentuate the banalizing debasement. On the other hand, in a situation where the divorce remains imaginatively desired without the realization of the pseudo-liberating plan, the ravages of nervous irritability will take over more and more. Here the motivations—in contrast to the condition of banal cupidity—are not conventional and superficial, but insidious and secret. They bring about inconsistency of reactions because of love-hate ambivalence.

This condition deserves full analytical attention because it highlights the survival—exaggeratedly deformed—of the drive to surpass which, in its healthy form, provides a couple's life with biologically profound significance. This drive (the need for autonomous creativity), degraded into guilty obsession, creates an amorous fixation on the erstwhile imaginatively idealized partner, and the inevitable disillusionments unleash hostile fantasies and a desire for divorce. In reality, there exist all the gradations between idealizing fixation and banalizing divorce: for example, temporary separation, a kind of flight. It will have a tendency to exacerbate the obsession with the idea of returning, because in the initial choice was invested all the exuberance of a confused but tenacious impulse. Definitive divorce will be just as rare as a definitive return, which can be realized only by the dissolution of the partner's phantom image, the secret motivating cause of both overestimations and devaluations.

The spectacular intensity of hate-love varies in accordance with the idealistic derangements (religious, literary, political, etc.) that lie beneath it but also according to the social layer. The phantom of the ideal partner, if it is focused on a precise representation—which is not always the case—will be represented by a movie star, a boss in an office or factory, a political leader, or a celebrity in the art world. Erotomania finds its fuel there. Nothing prevents the illogical imagination from veering off toward an immortal figure of the past with whom no living person would be able to compete. Whatever the variation, the phenomenon has an unsuspected frequency, hidden from direct observation, like all the elements of inner motivation.

The frequency of this phenomenon demonstrates that it is an essential motive in the pathology of the couple's life and in its elementary need for creativity. Insufficient realization of this need leads to the ambivalent scission of values. Guilt, repressed by means of self-idealization, is projected onto the real partner, who, having become exceedingly inadequate, is sentimentally replaced by the fiction of a phantom partner, who alone is worthy of the cult of love. The fact that transposition of the need for creativity from a real to an imaginative plane is reversible demonstrates that it is a falsely motivated process of substitution. Thus, for example, there exists a phenomenon of physical or psychic belonging (*Hörigkeit*). The real partner, despite all disappointments, remains the object of the love cult, thus assuming the function of the fictitious partner. Adoration can be mutual and enclose the couple in a state of vanity *à deux*, where all disappointments are by common accord projected on the surrounding world, which in turn has become unreal. Conversely, it can happen that the pathological state of attachment occurs only after the death of one of the partners. Failed creativity flings the survivor into a state of inexpiable guilt, and the deceased—the object of love-hate in life—becomes, due to neurotic or even psychotic reversal, the idealized phantom.

Constituted by the complete repression of hatred, the proprietary symptom is quite rare. Habitually, the ideal phantom is not fused with the real partner, except in moments of sentimental reconciliation. Since obsessive opposition is reenacted again and again, the imaginary divorce keeps being accentuated. The exigencies of life in common will make it necessary to set aside the phantom of the ideal partner. The phantom will be set up as an idol in a secret corner of the psyche, and all the disappointments of conjugal life will be delivered to it as a sacrifice. Forced renunciation lends itself wonderfully to the idealizing hypostasis of one's self and the admiration of one's strength for abnegation. The accumulated bitterness is discharged in quarrels, permitting each of the spouses, linked by love-hate, to project the fault openly on the other, who, believing himself or herself unjustly accused, becomes doubly enraged. Sentimental reconciliations only temporarily appease an impotent rage, that explodes even more violently at the slightest incident, progressively achieving the mutual destruction of character. Reconciliation becomes rarer, and of the sentimentality *à deux* only the egoistic aspect persists: immense self-pity, even more decisively than the incidental quarrels, separates the couple into two irreconcilable antagonists. Reconciliation is no longer a sentimental outpouring but a discouraged pose, a mask of despair, which badly conceals the reciprocal lack of esteem.

So reconciliation threatens finally to be rejected. It is felt to be a shameful submission. In indignation is concentrated all the false motivation: definitively repressed guilt ends in vanity-engendered pseudo-dignity and a sentimental and accusatory conviction about the other person's unquestionable baseness. The more intense love was, the more it changes into hostile disappointment: nothing remains of the disappointing choice but the imaginary divorce, congealed at last in sulkiness and rancor. The intonations of voice continually express resentment; the faces, fixed in masks of reproach, can no longer relax, unless the arrival of a spectator makes it necessary to play the comedy of perfect accord. It can even happen that one's face will beam at the approach of anyone of the opposite sex, which in the secret imagination awakens the idea of a possible affair.

At the peak of this process of decomposition of feelings, the sexual act comes to be inhibited because of rancor. To the impotence of feelings is added organic impotence, a new cause for complications and torment. Also, the false motivations threaten to deviate into often grotesque ambivalences. So, for example, it can happen that mutual provocations are subconsciously intensified and multiplied in the hope that the torment, becoming unbearable, will finally break down the barrier of guilt and indecision that in the nervous couple stands in the way of the both desired and feared real divorce. Increasingly venomous provocations are subconsciously charged with the aim of obtaining by means of the other's aggressive response proof of his or her depravity and justification for the persistent plan of divorce. But the obsessive repetition of provocations will merely intensify the common suffering and with it each partner's sterile remorse, which in fact will render separation unrealizable.

In the case of the *banal couple,* characterized by the absence of inhibiting guilt—which facilitates the initiation of real affairs—the empty shell of the conjugal bond is often preserved for fear of scandal or the need to protect common material interests. The superimposition of intricacies of a nervous and banalizing order is the rule, and their admixture determines the degree to which feelings are decomposed and character is destroyed. Neurotic complications are frequent. They manifest themselves by the explosion of psychopathic symptoms (which symbolically express guilty dissatisfaction or unattainable satisfactions) and by recourse to substitute satisfactions, as for example drugs. One will not be far from the truth in considering conjugal misery as a frequent cause of alcoholism, above all in its dipsomaniac form. The repercussion of this state of affairs on the children's life need not be underscored.

Because guilt over the children is often the major reason for opposing divorce, the parents end by considering the children an obstacle to their liberation. Hate—though often masked as sentimental love—hounds the offspring. Finally, the children's revenge brings despair to a frenzied culmination.

Originally thought of as unbearable, the family situation finally becomes unlivable in the true sense of the word.

The variations of imaginary divorce are innumerable. One would tend to assume its complete absence in certain families that are rigidly welded by a moralism that appears impregnable. And yet the excess of moralism could merely be the consequence of the complete repression of the imaginary divorce. The damage it creates, which nevertheless persists subconsciously, is manifest only in the cold demands with which parents impose on the children their own renunciation, extending to pleasures that, however innocent, become suspect and unacceptable. Vanity-inspired satisfaction drawn from this repression replaces natural pleasures, which are radically prohibited for fear of lapsing into intemperance. This moralizing reversal has always been known; its meanings and ramifications can only be explained by starting from the calculation of motivations.

Only the harmonizing dissolution of the imaginary escapes does away with the tendency to justification, even if it is moralizing. The dissolution of convulsive ambivalence frees one from the morbid conflict. It liberates perversely sequestered energy from anguished suffocation, and thus installs what one could accurately call the "respiratory rhythm": a harmonious alternation between concentration and relaxation, duty and pleasure. Duty itself—in the case in point, fidelity to one's choice—becomes a pleasure. It is no longer fidelity to the other so much as fidelity to oneself, strength to resist fantasies, formative self-discipline. The humiliating sense of yielding to an alien imposition loses its *raison d'être*. The reference to the higher satisfaction of self-harmonization is in itself a sufficiently strong motive to overcome the self-reproach of giving in out of weakness and submissiveness, instead of defending oneself with a counterattack as proof of one's courage! Guilty anguish is replaced by a taste for dissolving resentment with the help of daily mental hygiene. All the aesthetic elements—harmony, rhythm, taste—are united in the liberating effort. But taste can only be formed by means of the just valuation of the promises of satisfaction. What is the constant revaluation of the *raison d'être* of one's definitive

choice, if not strength of mind? A couple's life cannot be constituted healthily and realize its creativity, which culminates in the
educational task, without a constant spiritualization-sublimation
that imparts profound meaning even to material duties (household
and professional work).

Built on biological foundations (the search for satisfaction and
voluntary choice, the appanage of human life and its responsibility), healthily achieved marriage is far from being conventional and
the effort to become bourgeois. Its profound significance resides in
the fact that it provides an ideal basis for the effort at harmonization
that restores creative power to the couple. In no other situation
does the need for self-discipline manifest itself in such an imperious
and constant manner.

But it is precisely this effort to achieve that becomes the central
reason for the error that brings harm to the life of the couple and
that of their children. Instead of spiritualization-sublimation, the
error—here, as always, condensed in an ideological counterideal—
proposes the devaluation that justifies perversion. In order to escape
the torments of imaginary divorce and the coldness of rigid moralism, false justification seeks to find the liberating remedy in libertinage. The erroneous ideal is all the more seductive since it
presents itself in the guise of a false aestheticism that, searching for
virile strength not in the drive to surpass but in regression to
elementary instincts, is pleased to pose as both male and female
Banalized sexuality is inscribed in the false calculation of satisfaction. It mocks family life and sees in it only the bourgeois side,
which in fact becomes reality when the difficulties to be surmounted and the vacillations to be overcome are lived as a conventional and unpleasant duty.

To make of banalized sexuality the pole of attraction is no longer
vacillation but a decisive disorientation in the contrary direction,
which exerts its destructive influence on the sphere of activity and
the life of the person, the family, and society. By opposing the
evolutionary expansion of sexual life, whose place of fulfillment is
the home, the erroneous ideal unceasingly feeds the fantasy of
escape and is at the origin of the destruction of the family. It is the
major cause of real as well as imaginary divorce.

Here, as everywhere else, moralism is powerless to combat the
seduction of amoralism, for both are only the two counterpoles of
unhealthy ambivalence. Nothing can better help to overcome these
two contradictory and complementary deviations than knowledge
of the laws of harmony and ambivalence that preside over imma-

nent reward (psychic health) and immanent punishment (pathogeny) and thereby govern human life in all its forms and, above all, family life and its educational task.

The noxious effect of real divorce on the children is well known. But is sufficient attention paid to the damages of imaginary divorce? Nothing is more harmful for a child than to live in the asphyxiating atmosphere of a family in a constant process of decomposition.

Sulky silences, as well as the quarrels that are vented in a child's presence, shatter his biological need for security. Instead of being able to control themselves in the children's presence, the parents tend to exaggerate their mutual accusations. Without realizing it, they make the child the witness-arbiter of their discord. The children side with one or the other parent, and the hope of obtaining their favorable opinion is profoundly inscribed in the secret motivation of the parents' puerilism.

Convinced that the infringement of his or her absolute rights is perfectly clear to everyone, each parent firmly believes that the child is on his or her side. Both theatrically accentuate their morbid attitudes in order to obtain more definitely from the child—or the children—a feeling of pity and the condemnation of the culprit. Feeling himself appointed as judge, imitating the aggressive intonations of the voices that endlessly pierce his eardrums, the child becomes insolent or sinks into the apathy of despair. Whether the rebellion is expressed by apathetic mutism or verbal impertinence—after all, the two are not mutually exclusive—the child in turn enters the infernal round of provocations and outrages; and the offense becomes his own. Starting as the judge, he ends up as chief defendant. The parents can agree on nothing but to turn on the child, who has become the scapegoat. But the parents' mutual recriminations will soon start again. They will tend to appeal again to the child's arbitration by reproaching each other before him for their educational errors. At this point the child will in turn set up in a secret corner of his soul the specter of flawless parents, an image of escape and a constant source of resentments and increased disobedience. In families with several children the situation becomes more complicated, because the struggle between the parents and their subconscious appeal to the children's arbitration provokes the taking of positions that are particularly liable to exacerbate the struggles among the siblings. However, whether there is only one child or several, what varies is the constellation of motivations.

Their degree of distortion will depend—at least in great part—on the intensity of discord between the parents.

Children bow to authority, even severe authority, if it is just, and the first condition of justice is the example set by the parents. Inadequate education tends to replace example by moralizing remonstrances or exemplary sanctions. Instead of the parents demonstrating severity toward themselves—which, precisely in the disunited family, would reestablish justice—severity is only practiced toward the children. Authority is then merely external: it consists in humbling the child, training it instead of educating it. Just like animal training, which alternates the use of the whip with lumps of sugar, exasperated punishments alternate with promises of rewards. The attempt to buy obedience is all the more marked and unfortunate as the promises—whose fulfillment is generally placed in a more or less distant future—almost always concern satisfactions of a material order that often, in order to increase their stimulating force, go beyond common sense and the parents' budgetary means. The situation is further complicated by the fact that the child who is treated too severely and is deprived of love tends to exaggerate his material demands, which are magnified by their symbolical significance as a proof of love. On the one hand, the child egocentrically exalts his material desires instead of learning to sublimate them; on the other hand, anguished by the idea of not being sufficiently cherished by his parents, the child torments them in order to procure new promises, eager to obtain proof that his parents will at least consent to what costs them a lot. As a result, the parents see themselves forced to wait for the opportunity not to have to keep their promises. Under the pretext—a pretext always easy to find—that the child has not kept his promises, the promised rewards are replaced by new punishments, whose severity often increases as the parents, ill at ease at applying such a method, will tend to conceal their injustice by accusatory and angry false justifications. This very frequent form of education in the end resorts to only exemplary punishments—too often corporeal—that are aggravated by the psychic punishment of constant disappointment, which not only involves the refusal of gifts but which (and this is much more serious) extends to the symbolic significance with which the promises have been invested. Disappointed again and again in his avid need for affection, which he can no longer express in a symbolic manner, the child is subconsciously driven to express his disappointment symbolically. The revenge of disobedience, in the obsessive search for satisfaction, no longer retreats before any punishment. The vicious circle closes and is renewed.

One can imagine that such a method—showing the sugar and using the whip—would be quite ineffective if applied to animal training; it would only succeed in irritating the animal until it was made dangerously vicious. All the more reason then that this method can only prove dangerous as a means of human education, where all interpersonal relations are determined by extra-conscious motivations. The revenge of disobedience is nothing else than acquired viciousness, too often mistaken—as are all other character traits—for an ineradicable hereditary given. On the other hand, the hereditary factor will play its codetermining role in the form of a generalized irritability often accompanied by organic spasmophilia. On the psychic plane this predetermination will manifest itself as a tendency toward emotional convulsion, which is simply a proclivity for ambivalent decomposition, convulsive because of the contradictory tug-of-war between excitation and inhibition. The deformed character traits of the child will come into being, starting with hereditary convulsiveness. Their specific nuances will be due to the irritating educational method that varies from family to family, a method that itself will be codetermined by the education the parents have received.

Due to the fact that educational deficiency—like all other inadequacies—is subject to the law of ambivalence, it follows that the falsely authoritative method must correspond to a method devoid of all authority. The complete lack of effectiveness of the false authoritative method can cause disoriented education to fall into its diametrically opposed fault. In place of severe accusations, sentimentally exaggerated love makes its appearance. We have seen that in the case of the blackmail exercised by means of material promises, the essential condition of a satisfying parent-child relationship—the bond of love—when deprived of its profound responsibility, is sabotaged at the level of tender affection, and symbolically transposed onto the monetary level. The pose of authority is supplanted by excessive sentimentality to the extent to which the symbolically materialized form of blackmail is overtly replaced by a purely affective blackmail that utilizes the promises of love, which are in turn overly exaggerated. The system of rewards that have remained vain promises and ended in excessive punishment is replaced by an educational method whereby rewards are freely granted and gifts offered even before they are desired, while punishments, rarely promised, are even more rarely inflicted. The parents' affective expansiveness is no less harmful than the method of deprivation; because the spoiled child responds to any and all calls to order by endless sulking, if not by fits of tears and rage. The helpless parents give way when faced by the emotional fits which the child inevitably escalates into a rage in order to obtain the satisfaction of his slightest whims. The situation is turned around. The parents now live under the unceasing threat of punishment inflicted by the children.

These two forms of inadequate education are susceptible to innumerable variations and combinations. An only child will often be spoiled, while in familes with several children one will find preferences unjustly granted to the oldest or youngest, the girls or the boys. One of the most frequent situations is that one parent tends to spoil and the other to frustrate. But just as often both parents will spoil the favorite child and frustrate the others. Thus in the bosom of the home alliances are created that are unadmitted and for that very fact extremely tenacious, and these divide the family members into adverse groups that battle each other continually in an insidious manner. Only an understanding of the functioning of extraconscious instances can succeed in clarifying the variations by precisely connecting character deformation to the underlying falsified motivations.

In truth, the connections of false motivations are too complex and the variations of warped behavior too multiform to allow one to hope that their psychological elucidation can succeed in becoming common knowledge to the point of eliminating the source of educational inadequacies at their very source—in the bosom of the families. Yet the knowledge of subconscious contents and their reactive expression is not only of theoretical interest. It offers a possibility of remedying the consequences of educational errors, at least in cases where the children's psychic deformation occurs so strikingly and becomes so unbearable for the parents that they decide to seek out and accept curative intervention.

The theory of education attains its full fruitfulness to the extent that it gives birth to a technique and practice of re-education.

PART TWO

RE-EDUCATION

PART THREE
RE-EDUCATION

3

THE ORIGINS OF
RE-EDUCATIONAL TECHNIQUE

So long as the theory of education does not find its fundamental principle—the biological basis and moral goal that has just been described—the technique of re-education will remain flawed by imprecision. It will be either too empirical or too speculative.

The principles of education developed up to this point give rise to a re-educational technique that is radically different from all the methods habitually employed.

Before presenting in detail this re-educational technique and its method of application, it is indispensable to formulate more clearly than we have done so far the reasons for our opposition to orthodox methods. However, it is appropriate to emphasize that the study of extraconscious motives—the essential determinants of psychopathic behavior—is possible only by starting with the works of Freud, Adler, and Jung, and the renewal they have brought about. In their theories we already find—though in a scattered fashion—the elements for the study of motivations. Should these elements be considered the essentially veracious results of their attempts at explaining the ensemble of psychic functioning by pathogenic causes? It will be important to demonstrate this by separating the essential elements from their doctrinal swathing. To do so obviously requires a polemical stance. A critique of the entire body of work by these authors would go beyond the scope of the present study. But since they are the first to have envisaged certain aspects of the extraconscious motives that underlie family relations—the central theme of this study—it is indispensable to take into account the results of their investigations, at least as regards the child-parent relationship. Limiting the psychological problem in general to the theme of education obliges us here to neglect the contribution of C.-G. Jung and other authors whose investigations did not have a preponderant influence on the technique of child re-educating.

It should be mentioned that an interesting attempt at educating pupils in groups is under experimentation in the active schools founded by Montessori, Dewey, Decroly, Ferriere, and other innovators, whose ideas were introduced in France by R. Cousinet. In these cases it is rather a matter of the reorganization of teaching. However, the re-educational influence exercised upon the character of the child participating in such groups can be considerable.

Certain methods of re-education, applied in groups or individually, have already been in use for a long time in the case of children affected by organic handicaps (idiotism and cretinism). These methods can expect only a very limited re-education of intellect or character because their set goal is sensorial and motor education rather than re-education of the psychic system.

The methodical re-education of children who are not handicapped but affected by character disorders that are often accompanied by mental retardation has been recognized as a problem only since the advent of depth pyschology. This discipline made it possible to discern the functional nature of the disorder and, by ceasing to explain the disorder exclusively by heredity, began to envisage treatments based on a study of the workings of the psychic system. This does not negate the fact that these disorders are codetermined by physiological causes, such as endocrinal imbalance.

The general line of this renewal is traced by the doctrines of Freud, Adler, and Jung. The feature that is without doubt the most essentially characteristic—and that in any case is held in common by all these doctrines—resides in the absence of a phylogenetic foundation, the indispensable support of ontogeny and the study of the successive maturation of psychic qualites. The three doctrines neglect the phenomenon of essential differentiation between animal life and human life: the expansion of instinctual drives. This results in an inadequate formulation of the evolutionary goal and a lack of comprehension of its coincidence with the educational task. The confusing divergence of these doctrines is first of all the result of the instability of their foundations. In this regard it is interesting to note that each of the three doctrines has striven to grant predominance respectively to one of the three instinctual drives in their unexpanded form. Thus Freudian psychoanalysis opts for the sexual drive and bases its theory on primitive instinct; Adler's individual psychology is founded on the vicissitudes of the material struggle, explained by an instinct for social domination, itself merely a vague allusion to the broadening of the nutritive instinct. And, lastly, Jung's theory is filled with the preoccupation of granting predominance to the evolutionary drive. But this is conceived only as beginning on the human level where, having become prescient, it coincides with the effort at spiritualization. Cut off from its phylogenetic root, spirituality appears as idealism, badly defined in both its origin and goal.

In accordance with what has been said about the phylogeny of psychic functions, it is appropriate to emphasize that on the human level, the true problem of behavior originally resides neither in sexuality nor materiality but in their motivating valuation. Psychic conflicts arise from the struggle between vitally just or erroneous valuations. These conflicts, when they prove insoluble, become the essential cause of the unhealthy deformation of the psychic system. Valuation being a function of the intellect and its need for prescient adaptation, all psychic deformations—even if they are manifested on the sexual or material plane—are *maladies of the spirit.*

If it is true that just valuation is the remedy that nature opposes to the danger of psychic deformation, the theory and technique of re-education must uncover and combat erroneous valuations, the source of false motivations.

In studying the psychopathic states of adults (all the way to the oneiric explosion of symptoms), Freud has demonstrated that the symptoms of adults spring from a history that can be retrospectively traced back to early childhood. The oneiric explosion of the subconscious is, according to Freud, the final consequence of an earlier repression of sexual desires, a repression in force since childhood.

The entire Freudian theory is based on this triple movement: *guilty desire—repression—oneiric reappearance.*

The great discovery of this reversal (repression-reappearance) is flawed by the preconceived idea that only sexual desires are subject to repression since childhood, a mistake that dictated to Freud his sexualizing theory of instances and their maturation. In searching for the origin of the guilty desire, he thought he had found it in the Oedipal situation. As the desires of Oedipus were parricidal and incestuous, Freud felt obliged to conclude that the child wanted to have intercourse with the parent of the opposite sex and hoped for the death of the other parent. The support sought in the Oedipus myth is nonexistent: Oedipus the child did not know his parents.

Moreover, Freud himself in the end declared that his theory of instances (which is summed up in the appearance of the pseudoethical instance: the superego) was only a crude first hypothesis, subject to revision. If this is so, is it not evident that his entire theory of the successive stages (oral, anal, phallic) of ontogenetic maturation should also be subject to revision?

On the other hand, when it comes to the Freudian discovery of the inner functioning of the pathogenic reappearance of repressed guilt, it is important to realize its great significance as a whole. Once purged of its sexualizing systematization, it opens the door to an entirely new orientation of re-educational psychology.

With his discovery of the repressive process, Freud demonstrated that all conscious thought is often—unknowingly—submerged by illogical elements because of the uncontrolled resurgence of the subconscious pathogenic "contents." Since the goal of thought is the control of motivating affectivity with a view to achieving a mode of activity reasonably adapted to the demands of reality, the uncontrolled upsurge of "illogical thought" runs the risk of creating a falsified valuation capable of deflecting activity from its sensible goal. There is no remedy for this pathogenic danger but a movement that is the reverse of repression: the release of the subconscious motivation. The release of repression elucidates the motivation hidden from consciousness and submits it to the control of reason. This recognition of subconscious motivation (in which illogicality can reach the point of oneiric symbolization) creates a new instrument for reason, a new *way of thinking* that consists in the possibility of translating the most intimate secrets of the psychic system into conscious language.

Freud himself had a glimpse of this conclusion, which is ineluctably included in his discovery. He spoke of the existence of a *false rationalization*. However, his theory of the Oedipus complex deflected him from a detailed study of this phenomenon. False rationalization can only involve motives and can only consist in the fact that reason, falsely employed, illogically deformed, attempts to graft onto guilty, unavowed, and repressed motives lying and falsely justifying pseudomotives.

By exaggeratedly sexualizing the language of the subconscious because of his Oedipal conception, Freud even deformed his own discovery and prevented the new way of thinking opened up by him from developing in all its fruitfulness.

However, if one is content to see in it just a symbol and not a reality, the Oedipus complex can be used to express the resentments that really exist in the neurotic family. It symbolizes love exalted into incestuous desire, and hate exalted into parricidal desire. It has in fact become common to present the complex now as a symbol, now as reality. The sexualized terminology is thus utilized to perform a sleight-of-hand trick. Under such conditions it is easy to contend that the context can be experimentally observed because love-hate can be found in any form of analysis, and in analysis employed according to the Freudian method the interpretation will always be sexual.

The reduction of the Oedipus complex to a symbol might at first glance seem to be in full accord with Freud's teaching, which consists precisely in the discovery of extraconscious symbolization. But this is not the case; the accord is illusory. Freud most specifically insisted that desires defined as Oedipal, which he thought to have discovered in the child, should not be considered symbols but reality. And for good reason. If the basis of his theory of instances and of the stages of maturation were merely a symbol, the entire edifice would have only a symbolic significance. In contradiction with his discovery of subconscious symbolism, Freud was obliged, *nolens volens*, in order to establish his system, to consider the Oedipal image—a symbol, because borrowed from a myth—as a reality, and thus to elevate the pseudomyth of the Oedipus complex to the rank of a dogma.

Now the Oedipus complex regarded as reality is a physiological impossibility.

That is what a physiologist, a disciple of Selye, whose discoveries opened a new era in psychosomatic medicine, says of the subject:

> At birth there exist in the testicles only perfectly constituted interstitial cells and still almost rectilinear, semiparietal canicules that must undergo transformation before secreting spermatazoa.
>
> When one knows that the organ creates the function and all the emotions attached to it, one asks oneself how psychoanalysts could possibly speak of a sexual instinct in the child, since observation of animals has already demonstrated to us that the interstitial is opposed to reproduction. Under these circumstances one fails to understand how psychoanalysts continue to ignore embryological and histological fact in order to speak of the sexual instinct in the child when it is born. It can happen that one makes a mistake from the scientific point of view, but to persist in the mistake in order to be able to preserve one's incorrect conceptions is a lack of probity that cannot be excused. [Dr. Jean Gautier, *L'interstitielle, Le génie médical,* December 1951]

This being so, it follows, with all the evidence one can wish for, that the causes of ontogenetic formation and the pathological deformation of the child's psychic system do not reside in an innate Oedipal sexuality that decides the status of maturation (the new-born child is not polymorphously perverse).

The prime task of a re-educative psychology therefore consists in searching for another principle capable of serving as support for the theory of ontogeny. Where can one find it if not in the factors of phylogeny? Life is a continuous evolution, and the causes of its evolutionary genesis traverse it from its origins to its presently attained level. As the most characteristic trait of human life is the capacity of choice, *the stages of the child's maturation can consist only in the successive development of the valuing intellect, the instrument of lucid choice as regards satisfactions.* The knowledge of evolutionary direction and its stages of maturation are indispensable for the understanding of the problems of childhood. It is therefore of first importance to counterpose to the Freudian hypothesis of an Oedipal ontogenesis an overall view of *the maturation of the intellect.* As for the details of the deployment of the valuing function with regard to the diverse modalities of its progression from stage to stage, nothing prevents us from taking them—as they will be presented here—for an additional hypothesis subject to verification and amplification. Yet it might be even more just to see them as a brief sketch that in order to be enlarged would require a very specific study that goes far beyond the scope of the present work.

This polemical section of our work will be as brief as possible. It is inevitable, because it is dictated by a concern for unification. The re-educational technique founded on knowledge of the categories of false motivation would be deprived of its foundation without a preliminary outline of the maturation of the valuing intellect and the deviation it suffers due to educational errors. The deployment of the categories of false motivation is the consequence of deviation. The valuing intellect is degraded into overvaluation of the self (vanity), undervaluation of the self (exalted and repressed guilt), undervaluation of others (accusation) and overvaluation of others (sentimentality).

FREUD'S DOCTRINE RECTIFIED BY THE THEORY OF THE VALUING INTELLECT'S MATURATION

According to Freud's doctrine, suckling would be the first indication of Oedipal desires, constituting the oral phase of infant sexuality.

To make the theory acceptable, it would be necessary to furnish proof that already in the case of mammals suckling is an act of sexual rather than nutritive importance. In the absence of such phylogenetic proof, psychoanalysis should offer a sufficient reason according to which, beginning at the evolutionary level attained by the being become conscious, the act of suckling is charged with such sexual importance that this new meaning can become the support of ontogeny. In view of the physiological impossibility—already emphasized—of such a supposition, it is immediately obvious that here it is a matter merely of a projection upon the child of desires deduced from adult sexuality. Thus the child is considered a miniature adult.

The nursing baby cannot have sexual desires, because no desire can be formed within him beyond his need for loving protection, the psychic bond that, after birth, replaces the complete physical union that protects the life of the fetus.

But the nursing baby already emotionally evaluates his vital needs (in which the physical and psychic are still insufficiently differentiated), because he experiences satisfaction and dissatisfaction.

Excitable and overexcitable emotivity contain the need for autonomous pacification, an energy potential that, by gradually acquiring the capacity for active choice, will subsequently deploy the germ of innate hereditary intellect. The emotional valuation of the infant is the germ of the calculation of satisfaction that in the end motivates adult behavior.

Since the beginning of life, the need for loving protection involves not only the satisfaction provided by the mother but also the possible dissatisfactions arising from the objective environment in which the infant is incorporated and in which he must gradually learn to orient himself.

In the beginning persons and objects are merely affections subjectively perceived in the form of a chaos of excitations; from this point gradually crystallizes both temporal continuity and spatial simultaneity. The real universe emerges from the chaos of excitations, thanks to a successively dawning consciousness due to satisfying and dissatisfying experiences.

In the infant's experience the instinctual drives are inseparably united but still undifferentiated. But the instinctual drives that present themselves in the course of maturation will create the multiplicity of desires that incite the adult to an incessant search for satisfactions. The ontogenetic deployment of psychic qualities is in the first place characterized by propulsion toward the valuing intellect, whose path to maturity goes through successive stages of sensorial recognition (gustative, tactile, auditory, and visual) and cognitive recognition (imagination, intellect, and spirit). Full maturity—often unattained—is achieved when the mind becomes able to healthily value (dominate and harmonize) the multiple desires that arise from the expanded bodily drives (materiality and sexuality).

Nursing as a *nutritional act* is certainly accompanied by a nuance of *presexual sensuality;* but it also contains the germ of *object orientation;* the infant puts into his mouth the objects of which he wants to become cognizant. But also, even the first acts of oral recognition are accompanied by an attempt at tactile exploration.

The first object that the infant encounters—except for the mother's breast—is his own body.

As soon as he is unswaddled and above all after weaning, the infant addresses his needs for tenderness and recognition to his own body. Still living in his chaos of excitation he needs above all to create for himself a bodily pattern that will help him to incorporate himself into the object-filled space, a stage that he will attain only after he has acquired the ability to move through space and to go to meet the multiple objects that surround him.

As a result of his first attempts to explore his body, the infant will expose himself to the first parental prohibitions. In playing with his limbs in search of his bodily figure, the infant meets the sexual zones which already at this point are more sensitized than the others, but are also hypersensitized by the mother's caresses and thus surcharged with affectionate significance. From earliest childhood on, affection has been received not only in the form of care but also in the form of caresses that have by no means avoided the sexual zones. These organs demand hygienic attentions that the nursing infant cannot distinguish from caresses. Such contacts are inevitable, but it must be emphasized that patting the buttocks, a frequent sign of affection, is one of the major causes for hypersensitization of infantile pseudosexuality. It is not superfluous to observe that the skin's softness surely gives the mother a sensual sensation which is added to her need to express her affection, so that the child's pseudosexuality is, if not created, at least hypersensitized by the adult's sensuality.

The child should stop playing with his organs at the end of the period of bodily exploration. He would not remain fixed on it if a significance with an obsessive nuance were often not added to it. To the extent to which not only the caress to which he is accustomed, but even the indispensable affection is denied him, the growing child will tend to grant himself sentimental self-consolation. He will remain fixed on these physical contacts, trying to procure for himself the affection experienced intensely in the past, in the longed-for form of a bodily caress concentrated on his most sensitive organs. Starting from their own sensuality, adults incorrectly interpret the infant's pseudosexual manifestations that they have often unwittingly provoked. To these habits, which are considered suspect, they oppose exaggerated and impatient prohibitions, which are experienced by the baby as new refusals of affection. And the baby responds with an obstinacy that can end by rendering obsessive and incorrigible the pseudosexual habits acquired in this way.

Similar complications run the risk of being repeated several times during the course of the child's ontogenetic evolution. Provoked by the adults' erroneous interpretation, they will increasingly fix the child's curiosity on the sexual organs. The excessive prohibitions resulting from this will cause the child's magnified irritability and thereby prevent him from evolving healthily. Remaining affectively frozen at this badly negotiated stage, the child will clumsily approach the next stage. Moreover, the pseudosexual curiosity thus awakened will end by being transformed into real, prematurely awakened sexual practices. Consolatory pseudomasturbation will become a very frequent solitary vice in childhood. Its underlying significance will remain the self-consolation of deviated affectivity. Empirical interpretation takes the anomaly as the evolutive norm. Sexual hypocrisy, extremely intense at the beginning of the century, wanted to conceal the problem: Freud dared to raise it. But oblivious to the many other causes of the child's affective deviation, he accorded exclusive importance to sexuality and thus turned an empirical anomaly into the explanatory principle of life and its meaning.

The *anal phase* of Freudian theory coincides with the period of education in cleanliness. The infant, who until now has freely received loving protection, for the first time encounters indispensable demands to which he is expected to adapt himself by a willed effort in order to deserve love and praise. If the child comes out of the preceding phase insufficiently prepared, his resistance will be transferred to the new stage. The obstinate child denies his mother the "gift"—as Freud says—of his excrement. He becomes ungenerous with it or distributes it at the most inopportune moments. Instead of praise, the child receives recriminations that are taken for a new denial of affection, especially if, on the first occasion, they have the tone of prolonged scolding. The reproach has as its consequence the birth of guilt, and it will set in motion the innate tendency to get rid of it by repression (during this period one can also observe the first appearance of symptoms with symbolical significance, among which bed-wetting is one of the most frequent). In a more general manner at this stage of the child's education in cleanliness appears the first indication of a split in the need for satisfaction, which thus begins to be perverted into ambivalent calculation. Satisfaction is no longer sought solely in obedience, which up to this point was the child's only guide. It is equally sought in a new form of disobedient obstinacy, subconsciously subtended by a shade of triumph, a maliciousness that is still partly innocent.

However, this triumphant disobedience threatens to gradually become charged with sly aggressiveness due to the fact that the education in cleanliness coincides with a new stage of inquiry, and this considerably complicates the situation. Having become able to walk, the child begins to explore the spatial environment and to move toward his encounter with objects. He appropriates or destroys them in keeping with a nascent will that, still full of egocentricity, tries to affirm itself. The child collides with an avalanche of prohibitions whose vehemence, hitherto unknown to him, becomes the cause of his growing obstinacy. It is true that the child is surrounded by dangers that demand almost incessant intervention: he falls, makes objects fall, is bent on experimental destruction, burns himself, etc. The mother's patience is sorely tried, and the father, a formidable personage, begins to emerge from his passivity, something that does not always improve matters. During this period the child works at acquiring the notions of *allowed* and *not allowed,* but also those of *mine* and *yours.* In the bosom of the nervous family his nascent will beomes obstinate to the extent to which his need for exploration and appropriation too violently encounters angry prohibitions and shouts, which are bound to traumatize his fragile nervous system.

This period—because of its coincidence with the education in cleanliness—is called "anal" by Freudian psychoanalysis. It should come to an end around the age of two. But in the obstinate child it will be prolonged and thus end by being confused with the period of *accentuated independence,* which is natural and transitional around the age of three, a period that even the docile child is not exempt from passing through. At this age, spatial exploration—having normally served to prepare the blossoming of will—should give way to a new form of exploration. This concerns the inner world, which little by little emerges from the primitive chaos of excitations. The ego, which is being formed, begins to differentiate itself no longer only from the objective environment but from the person of another. The distinction between *me* and *you* begins to be established. It is expressed even in the docile child by an attitude of opposition, which serves to affirm his nascent self, an attitude that should normally lead to a more or less idealizing identification with one of the parents, the evolved basis of obedience. This first stage of becoming aware of oneself prepares the formation of the affectively autonomous ego, which therefore should become able to establish affectively satisfying relationships with the egos of others, which in turn will be recognized as autonomous to the extent in which the intellect takes its rough initial shape.

But if the succession of stages is disrupted too severely, the "layers" of developing affectivity are superimposed on one another and become entangled. The child, insufficiently freed from his affectly chaotic, primitive egocentricity, will fall into a stubborn exaggeration of his need for self-affirmation and risk not finding a way out of it. His stubborn opposition, angry and underhanded, is transformed into an insufficiently disciplined need for appropriation as well as a persistent resistance against the education in cleanliness.

Pathologically persistent character traits can be caused by this. They risk influencing all of future life, provided, however, that the tendency to stubbornness, normally temporary, is subsequently elevated—at the awakening of intellectual valuation—to the rank of a guiding principle. With this qualification, it can be admitted that the exalted need for appropriation, secretly subtended by nostalgic laments for unsatisfied affection, may through subconscious inversion be transformed into a need for self-protection that is at all costs appropriative, and which—as the Freudian theory of the anal phase emphasizes—will search through all of life for material security at the expense of others and by means of an unscrupulous aggressiveness.

As for disobedient holding-back, unresolved as regards the infant's cleanliness, it will have a certain tendency to remain fixed on the functioning of the organs. The affective cluster of resentments, born at this stage of maturation, can end by creating psychopathic habits with an organic basis and a symbolic significance. These first oneiric expressions, such as bed-wetting, will be utilized as a subconscious expression of protest. Yet these organic symptoms (refusal of cleanliness) will rarely go beyond the age of thirteen or fourteen, when they will be replaced by other symptoms. (This replacement is subconsciously demanded by the calculation of satisfaction, because puerile symptoms—like bed-wetting—symbolizing a triumphant protest addressed to the mother, finally clash with the shame and torment of inferiority vis-à-vis one's peers.)

The Freudian school, beginning with its theory of fixation and regression, associates with this "anal" period, when it is improperly overcome, morbid traits in the adult character, such as avarice, obstinacy, and aggressiveness. One cannot repeat too often that such fixations can actually come into being as the result of a deep wounding of the need for affection, but that they become obsessive only because of a false valuation of principle, because of false motivation, which is added to them and which, as an essential support, underlies them without the subject's knowledge. The egocentric traits that constitute the supposedly anal character are in reality the consequences of an inadequate detachment from the period of egotistic obstinancy that, when normally overcome, should lead the child toward a healthy unfolding of his ego. What a mistake it is to claim—as does the theory of the anal character—that the child sets his refusal against the education in cleanliness because the sliding of excrement down his rectum offers him a satisfaction analogous to that of the sexual act, an enjoyment whose pleasure he would like somehow to prolong. This example demonstrates in the most instructive manner to what lengths of speculative waywardness one can be led by the tendency to neglect the path of a simple, natural explanation in order to claim that one is exploring the subconscious with the help of a sexualizing and stereotyped symbolization that ends by seeing a vagina in every crevice and a penis in every oblong object.

Yet penis and vagina will in fact take on exaggerated importance when children encounter the problem of the difference between the sexes, which they will be obliged to tackle without the help of the parents and with their own still very rudimentary means of explanation.

Having acquired language, the child—from the age of five on—enters a phase of prelogical reflection, which Henri Wallon calls the period of syncretism and globalism. The child begins to elaborate an objectification of his linguistic concepts, whose contents at this age are still completely subjective, imaginative and affective, confused and global. Emotional choice begins to be exercised, beginning with a world that is not only immediately perceived but mediated and conceptualized. But the concepts transmitted by adults are for the child, at the beginning, as chaotic as his perceptions originally were. This is a new stage of inquiry into the world and himself (into himself because the child begins to differentiate himself from the world as an autonomous subject only to the extent that the world, detached from his simple sensorial "presentation," becomes an objective representation. The world represented in the form of images will become the object of a comprehension that attempts to move from imaginative to cognitive.) Because of the diversity of the representative images, there begins even at this age, a diversification of emotional choice in individualized options. These options are still only guided by affect. The multiple and still completely infantile affects determine the bizarre imaginative quality of the child's naive reflections and of his valuations, still completely devoid of criticism.

This is the moment to observe, parenthetically, that in the case of most adults thought remains partly imaginative and affectively weak. The phenomenon can be observed chiefly at the level of the exploration of one's inner world and its motivations. This deficiency is of capital importance for human behavior in general, especially where interpersonal relations are concerned.

The child, still naturally sunk in his affective and imaginative thought, even in regard to the external world, needs to be guided by the adults' explanations, and does not fail to manifest by his tireless questions this vital need for investigation. His incessant "whys" can end by exhausting the parents' patience. Excessive impatience, interpreted by the child as a denial of affection and esteem, can have serious consequences. Wounded in his need to understand, the child can remain forever intimidated. He will no longer even dare to ask questions, either of himself or of his parents, and he will be inhibited in his evolution toward autonomous reasoning. Once he is an adult, he will tend to repress them, even those regarding his vital problems, or be content with conventional, prefabricated solutions.

Here, as always, the consequences of the psychic lesion vary in keeping with the law of ambivalence. They can become equally manifest in the reverse form of a tendency to opposition that can go so far as negativism. The subject will be content with any response suggested by his undisciplined imagination, and he will set it against any argument one may present him with. But since each perversion has a corresponding possibility of spiritualization—no longer through ambivalence but through antithesis—it is not excluded that in rare cases a positive overcompensation may occur. If the lucidity of the mind is great enough to be able to discipline the affective imagination, the opposition to base, prefabricated ideologies can lead to the blossoming forth of an intellect avid for investigation. One must also bear in mind that the determination is never so unilateral as this development might lead one to believe. This qualification concerning the blossoming of positive or negative qualities is of capital importance for the present polemic, because this qualification allows us to foresee the inadequacy, perhaps the most central one, of a re-education founded on the Freudian method that links every present deficiency too interpretatively and too unilaterally to a past trauma. The method would be inadequate even if the trauma, which is considered determinant, were not sought exclusively in the repertory of presumed infantile sexuality.

Among all the questions that the child in this phase of his maturation may ask himself or his parents, the questions regarded by the adult as of a sexual nature are those which generally meet with a radical refusal of explanation. At least this is how it was at the time that Freud elaborated his doctrine. Now, precisely during the phase of global and syncretic thought, the child is faced by problems which, in the adult perspective, are of a sexual nature: the difference between the sexes and the arrival of a new baby. The refusal of an explanation exasperates the child's disoriented curiosity and forces him to search by himself for an interpretation which can only be syncretic and global, infused with affective and imaginative elements.

The adult speaks of a difference between the sexes because he knows that the organs which differentiate boys and girls in the most obvious manner are used for the sexual act. The child knows nothing about all this. For him the penis is the "faucet," and the ambition of boys comes down to their vanity of being able to urinate farther than girls. Boys are frequently favored by their parents; this intensifies their feeling of superiority tied to the organ that girls don't have, and in girls it can create feelings of inferiority and a wish to possess the organ capable of such feats. There is a traumatizing element in this, but one that is based on triumphant or frustrated vanity rather than on sexual superiority or inferiority. It can happen that the naiveté of these games of pseudosexual competition is tainted by a vague suspicion that the organ is destined for a further task, a supposition that is due to the magical prestige of the forbidden created by the adults' hypocrisy. Nothing allows us to reach the conclusion of a castration complex in the Freudian sense, even if it were true that the girls' imagination might be haunted by the idea that the virile organ has been amputated from them, and that the boys, because of the vanity connected with the organ, may fear that it will be punitively cut off. Such fears—if they were the rule—would not concern the sexual potency of the organ. Normally the child at this phase of maturation knows nothing about that. This excludes the possibility that he might attach to it—even subconsciously—the idea of a punishment related to presumed incestuous desires. If it is true that the Oedipus complex (in its sexualized form) does not exist and cannot exist, it is necessarily also true that the castration complex in the Freudian sense is nonexistent. The boy does not fear punitive castration on the part of his father because he supposedly wanted to have intercourse with his mother. Such theoretical, pseudomythical, and pseudosexual suppositions are no less imaginative than the children's fearful interpretations. The theory of sexual complexes only proves the persistence in adults of a syncretic and global speculation in regard to the factors of inner life and motivations.

As for the problem of the newborn baby, this too is not of sexual origin. It thrusts itself on children long before they are able to trace it back along the chain of events all the way to the sexual act. The child is first interested in birth, not in conception. To forget this means to introduce here again the adult perspective. The problem of the new baby is by all evidence dictated to children by the persistent need to rest in their parents' love. The new child is a threat to the soul of the nervous child who is emotionally hungry for affection. But the arrival of the newborn also imposes on the child's explanation-hungry mind a problem of the greatest importance. The origin of life presents itself as a problem around which all his curiosity, already latent, tends to focus. Where does the newly born baby come from? The problem is due not to sexual curiosity—not chiefly, at least—but to a vital interest of a much deeper and natural origin: it is the spiritual problem in its unfathomable and magically awesome aspect, the mystery of life and its origin, that presents itself for the first time to the intellect of the child who is eager to understand. The explanations given by the parents (the fable of the cabbage, the rose, or the stork) are sooner or later rejected, and the explanations that the children invent—such as, for example, the stick stirred around in the mother's belly—clearly demonstrate that their attempts at explanation are infiltrated by fragments of a comprehension which begin to go back all the way to conception; but these suppositions—far from being the result of Oedipal fascination—instead fill the childish soul with a magical horror because of the natural modesty imposed by the prepubescent condition of the organs. These pseudosexual problems are bandied about by the children, and even those who

are not personally haunted by them are finally touched by conta-
gion. In the end all the grievances against parents and adults cluster
around this problem. A vital mistrust awakens, starting with the
practices which the children suspect are connected with the act of
conception. There is no doubt: children and adults devote themselves to a shameful and horrible matter. But even more serious is
the refusal to give any explanation about a mysterious and vital
problem. The childish imagination is deeply stirred by this problem which is suspected of being shameful. The child's idealism, his
vital impulse, is in danger of being wounded by it; the child is
disappointed in his parents, disappointed by a life in which such
vaguely presumed, impure things occur. All false motivation is
brought to an unhealthy pitch around this accusation, and pseudosexuality really becomes traumatizing. The true cause of the trauma
is not prepubescent horror confronted by sexuality, because this
horror would disappear quite naturally in the course of maturation
if it were not overwrought by the wounded need for affection and
explanations. The persistence of this wound will cause the child to
enter the stage of puberty psychically traumatized—overwrought
and inhibited—just when the problem of sexuality will begin to
present itself to him in its real aspect.

In order to avoid imaginative exaltation of a pseudosexual nature
and its later transformation into a trauma of real sexuality, would it
not be sufficient to diminish childish curiosity by an explanation?
Sooner or later, a prudent initiation, metaphorical or rational
depending on the child's age, is demanded. In our time it has
moreover become a frequent rule. But explanatory initiation by
itself is ineffective. The child needs not so much a logical as a
psychological initiation, and this initiation consists in satisfying the
needs of his body, his soul, and his mind.

The ensemble of these needs tends to guide maturation toward
its rarely attained goal: the autonomy of the mind capable of
choosing sensible and harmonious satisfactions. Although susceptible to delays and deviations as a result of false educational interventions, maturation continues indefatigably without truce or respite
on its ascending path. But Freud, by placing the goal in sexual
development, finds himself obliged to allow for a period of latency
which supposedly begins around the age of seven. It is appropriate
to point out that for Freud the latency of sexual evolution is not an
interruption of maturation, since according to him this period is
subconsciously utilized with a view to repressing the Oedipal
complex, from which would appear to spring the conflict between

instinctual pleasure and social duty that would further establish the
too rigid superego. Here again Freud has intuited a truth; but one
whose formulation remains inexact. The "phase of latency" is in
fact a stage of the greatest importance for the maturation not indeed
of sexuality but of the mind's valuing function.

Toward the age of seven, the child begins in fact to detach
himself from his pseudosexual problems and his quest for prelogical explanations. Thought prepares itself to acquire its usefully
prescient logical structure. The child's interest focuses on the daily
exigencies that, because of his attendance at school, assail him from
all sides. Whereas until this point the child has encountered duty
only in the form of sporadic prohibitions, from now on duty
becomes a constant imposition, a demand for work that comes into
conflict with the exclusivity of pleasure hitherto found in play. For
the child this conflict, fundamental for all of human life, centers on
two groups of problems: the companions and one's collective play;
the teacher and one's schoolwork. The coordination of play and
work, of pleasure and duty, becomes childhood's central problem.
The solution that the child finds for this problem will be of decisive
importance for his entire future life. For life to be sensible, the taste
for work alleviates duty and must alternate with the pleasure found
in distracting play, which is also controlled and refined by taste.

Whereas up to now the child has yielded to prohibitions, the
foretaste of duty, in hopes of a reward of affection and praise, the
advent of logic and prescient reflection must teach him to seek and
find a more *long-term* satisfaction in well performed work, and not
exclusively in loving affection and pleasant play. This evolutionary
step brings about a radical change: obedience to the parents'
demands must give way to obedience to the demands of work. The
hitherto passive obedience imposed by others should be replaced
by active self-discipline if duty-work is to become pleasure-work,
and if satisfaction is to extend to all the activities of life.

The calculation of satisfaction thus acquires a new dimension of
autonomous valuation: starting as affective, it becomes intellectually prescient. It thus prepares for its ultimate blossoming, which
will no longer concern external work but the intrapsychic work of
bringing order to the desires: ethical harmonization.

But intellectual autonomy will only gradually free itself from the
persistent need for tender affection and dependence on others. The
child remains dependent on the encouragement sought in praise.
He will submit to the exigencies of work in a spirit of competition
with his peers, competition which, if over-wrought, will seek
vanity-inspired triumph. Which is the same as saying that to the

extent to which early childhood is deprived of understanding love, perverted motivations will continue to underlie the calculation of satisfaction. The hungry need for affection and the vanity-inspired search for praise will prevent the child from healthily overcoming this crucial stage.

The difficulties will prove all the more insurmountable as the affectively wounded child risks being also deprived of the complementary source of satisfaction typical of this age that resides in collective play and the esteem accorded by his peers. The wounding of affectivity and the hypersensitivity that arises therefrom make the child incapable of incorporating himself in the collectivity. Brooding too easily and by that very fact excluding himself from common play, the child will have a tendency to withdraw into his spiteful feelings and the isolation of his imaginative play. The unhealthy exaltation of the imagination will retard not only the maturation of his understanding of reality (adaptation to reality) but also the healthy deployment of his scholarly intelligence. Even though excessively hungry for praise, the affectively retarded child receives only punishments from his teachers, doubled by the incessant scoldings—not to mention additional punishments—inflicted on him by his increasingly disappointed and helpless parents. Homework becomes a constant imposition, all the more unbearable as the calls to order degenerate into sermons about a threatened future, the constant preoccupation of parents with their proud dreams of a brilliant career, which has no appeal for the child still completely incapable of such long-term perspectives. To hear talk only about duties becomes an intolerable torture for the child. Since the pleasure of play has been taken away from him, whether by punishments or by his own sulking inhibition, the child sees himself cut off from all normal outlets. During this decisive phase in which the evolution to healthy autonomy should solidify, helpless young people fall into a state of pseudo-autonomous rebellion. Unless they become exceedingly indifferent, they are driven to seek refuge in sulky autism, another perverse form of independence. (Autism has a tendency to persist and become an ambivalently manifest character trait, either in its vainly insolent form, where arrogance is only a mask for guilty shame, or in the emotional form of timid submission beneath which is hidden a secret tendency to malevolent accusation.)

The flight into autism is one of the major causes for the maladroit (exalted and inhibited) approach to the pubescent phase, which Freud called "phallic," a phase that begins around the age of thirteen or fourteen. Disturbed in his relations with his peers, the nervous pubescent child does not succeed in healthily transferring his affectivity in accordance with the natural exigencies of this stage. On the plane of deep-seated emotion, puberty is character-ized by an interest directed toward the opposite sex. The interest is colored by a nuance of affection that is all the more overwrought and inhibited since the child has previously been frustrated with his parents. Not having received affection, he will not be able to offer any: his timidity or his arrogance are merely the caricature of his inhibition. He will suffer cruelly because of his inability to exterior-ize it.

On the external, more spectacularly visible plane puberty is characterized by transformations of a physiological order, prelude to the maturation of the sexual organs. However, it is only a matter of the full development of the genital apparatus, the preparatory phase during which the secondary sexual traits are accentuated above all. The genital organ is prepared for its procreative function, but it is still far from functional maturity. Not only the full development of the appartus but its mature and healthy functioning will only be accomplished at the command of the imagination. In this regard, it is debatable whether to call this stage "phallic," because exactly at this stage the imagination, still filled with modesty, certainly does not stray in the direction of sexual prom-ises; at least it will not do so in the case of normal development.

Nature itself seems to want to protect the organ in its state of gestation by means of modesty, the inhibiting presentiment of future relations that will be established quite naturally once the imagination will be healthily sexualized.

But to the extent to which the need for affection has been troubled since early childhood—and this is rather the norm—the imagination will become sexualized prematurely. However, at this still childish period there will only be pseudosexualization, which is not due to a real organic impulsion but to the collective enthusiasm of a young generation in need of healthy maturation. The more there are young people who enter puberty in a state of affective regression, the stronger is their tendency to play at being adults. They smoke, drink, and pose as all too knowing. Sexual practices are considered the ultimate sign of virility. This is a vanity with a pseudosexual nuance that is not without danger for the maturation of the organ's healthy function, a danger evident above all for the pubescent with a nervous character, whose exaltation continues to conceal inhibitions very much disposed to express themselves in organic language. Gradual impotence in achieving full sexual plea-sure is the most widespread organic symptom; it is the consequence of the tendency to imitate adults, a tendency that is very freqent in the period of pubescence.

The need for affection, overwrought to the extent to which it has been frustrated—breaking the barrier of modesty—rushes toward a new promise of loving satisfaction and its pseudoadult enjoyment. Imaginative projection is transformed into precocious activity in search of group practices or the self-consolation of solitary vice, depending on whether the case is one of inhibition or unhealthy exaltation. Modesty, precisely because it has been prematurely violated, threatens to change either into a false modesty that resists practices felt as shameful, the most frequent attitude among nervous youngsters, or into an immodest display of would-be virility, a tendency that on the contrary affects the banalized. One or the other of these solutions will be chosen by the pubescent youth not only as a result of his own perversion, but also under the influence of the value judgments reigning in the adult world. Conversely, however, adults are determined to prize sexuality in a puerile— hypocritical or cynical—manner because they cling to the obsessive memory of their own precocious experiences and their prematurely acquired, vitiated attitude. The hypocrisy that reigned in the adult world in the past epoch compelled youth to bow to it, whereas the present valuation of adults instead is the sort bound to make young people more uncontrolled and wild.

Freud, in his time, had above all the opportunity to analyze the psychopathic consequences of hypocritically repressed sexuality, and his conclusions (leading him to his pansexual theory) have played—against his true intentions—a considerable role in preparing the terrain for the present acceptance of untrammeled permissiveness, a psychopathic symptom ambivalently tied to the old hypocrisy. Unleashed or hypocritically repressed, sexuality will be falsely overvalued because in the two types of mistaken solution natural pleasure is replaced by a problematic sexuality. Cut off from its healthy satisfaction, in the end sexuality imposes itself as an obsessive problem. By losing its naiveté, the search for satisfaction becomes doctrinal, and the nuance of obsession compels people to make sexuality the central problem of life.

One cannot emphasize enough the possible errors of clinical observation, above all in analytical psychology, where the facts to be observed are the fluctuations of affectivity. Error can be avoided only on the condition of knowing the laws that govern psychic functioning. These laws involve the typical paths of just or false valuation, and these typical and lawful paths are none other than the instances. Not understanding these lawful paths led Freud to an erroneous interpretation of the sexual problem, and his error culminated in his false conception of the superconscious instance, whose blossoming characterizes the period of adolescence.

The entire error of the Oedipal concept—the result of a hypocritically undervalued sexuality and overvalued pseudovirility—finally explodes in the confusion between the "superego" of Freudian theory and the authentic superconscious.

According to Freudian theory, the Oedipus complex is ultimately dispersed because of the guilt aroused by incestuous and parricidal desires. From the wreckage of the Oedipus complex there supposedly arises a moralizing instance: the too rigid superego, in which parental prohibitions are preserved by way of introjection because of submission or rebellion.

The Freudian superego thus understood is an unsatisfactory compromise between the debris of the Oedipus complex and the parents' educational interventions. The superego is rigid because of the tug-of-war between pleasure (instinctively sought by the Oedipal desires) and the demands of social reality imposed since childhood by the parents. Thus the "pleasure principle" is supposedly transformed at the time of adolescence into the "reality principle," from which would derive the unpleasant and rigidly observed "moral principle." The Freudian superego imposes a duty-morality.

Insofar as it tends to become established in adolescence, the superconscious has a completely different structure. One can never emphasize this enough. It is the instance of authentic valuation, the sign of full maturity. The brake of valuing reason, the reasonable brake of instinctive pleasure (sexual and material), the superconscious *is not the product of a domestication of instinctiveness but, on the contrary, the precondition of its healthy and harmonious flowering.* It is true that the flowering of the superconscious instinct—precisely because it is the evolutionary ideal of the species (whose realization requires long-term evolutionary periods)—remains a rather rare phenomenon. In this regard, individuals endowed with an intense desire to surpass can be considered positive variations of the species that indicate the evolutionary direction. To confuse the authentic superconscious with the rigid superego means not to recognize the whole tragedy of adolescence—its enthusiasm and its danger of going under.

However, the instance that Freud called the "superego" does exist. But in actuality it is an underego. It is not the authentic superconscious but the subconscious, in which are preserved puerile resentments with their ambivalent motivations and their unhealthy, convulsive or banalizing tensions.

The erroneous conclusion of the ontogenetic theory is the inevitable consequence of the Freudian doctrine's insufficient phylogenetic foundation. This results in a false conception not only of adolescence but of the meaning of life in general. Knowing only the subconscious, Freud saw himself obliged to draw from it the explanation for superior functions whose blossoming is nowhere prepared for in his doctrine. The sphere of guiding values—and with it human culture in general—thus appear as a by-product of repressed sexuality, domesticated to the advantage of social conventions.

The true superconscious does not issue from parental punishments, nor from a presumed infantile sexuality. Its origin will be traced not to conventional morality but to the ineluctable evolutionary thrust. That is why the superconscious instance aspires to surpassing the norms attained by the human species (society's "rules of the game," transmitted by one's parents). The drive to surpass is the ethic, the joyful morality, based on the principle of autonomous satisfaction. The drive, in search of autonomy, strives to attain the harmonious flowering (and not the repression) of sexual and material desires. This flowering can only take place through the dissolution of sexual and material desires to the extent to which they are falsely overvalued, and which—because exalted or inhibited—are the source of all dissatisfactions. The drive to surpass and to blossom is superconscious, because from the most profound depths of himself, and unknown to himself, every human being aspires to essential satisfaction. This can only be found in the dissolution of intimate discord, which is the cause of guilty dissatisfaction. The ethos of the superconscious is diametrically opposed to the rigid and obsessive superego, and also to its submission to the conventional moralism transmitted by parents and adults, who after having gone through adolescence and come to grips with the difficulties of life, have ended up by renouncing authentic surpassing.

The final goal of ontogeny cannot consist in an unhealthy fixation on the past and on whims of conventionalized educators. Its goal can only be the acquisition of a comportment that no longer needs to be guided by one's parents, and whose search for autonomy will tend towards an adult maturity of which adolescence is merely the prelude. True maturity demands the surpassing of parental influence. It does not show itself by an external detachment but by the dissolution of residual resentments. This drive to surpass awakens at the time of adolescence because it is the essential force that animates the infant, that which has caused it to grow physically and evolve psychically. The original drive for authenticity, gradually suffocated by educational errors, has continued to smolder, and it is at the time of adolescence that it finally bursts forth, even though generally the flame has an ephemeral duration and is insufficiently purifying.

It is then that we witness the spectacle of a youth yearning for maturation, rebelling against its parents and the world inherited from the adults. The excessive accusation of the adolescent is matched by exalted idealism, the fugitive manifestation of a mind that strives for autonomy but indulges in illusory plans of amelioration of the self, or, more frequently, of the world; having sprung from resentment, such plans are themselves merely sentimental and vain, fated most of the time to remain without a future. This idealist form of rebellion against the adults' hypocritical moralism is matched by its ambivalent counter-form: banalizing rebellion. The insufficiently matured adolescent, vain about his finally acquired freedom, will confuse liberty with libertinage. He will rush toward pleasures and unleash his sexual and material desires, until now the target of interdictions. The idealism displayed in verbiage is thus opposed by the explosion of egocentricity insufficiently dissolved during the course of childhood because it was deprived of understanding affection. The rebellion against hypocritical moralism degenerates into a frenzied imitation of license, the privilege envied in the adults. It is precisely through these two forms of ambivalent rebellion, both contaminated with hypocritical resentments, that each generation of adolescents prepares to create a new generation of regressed adults and deficient parents.

However, these spectacular manifestations of adolescence striving for maturity must not lead one to forget the essential dynamism that underlies them. The survival of the evolutionary thrust is expressed in its healthy form in those persons in whom the drive to surpass, instead of being degraded, demands its realization through all of life's vicissitudes. It is through them that the superconscious instance tries to perform its function, which tends to the establishment of a healthily ripened personality, capable of surpassing conventions by authentic valuation, the highest function of the mind.

In fact, the personality is constituted only thanks to an authentic valuation capable of freeing itself from the duty-morality (the Freudian superego) and acceding to pleasure morality, the ethos that achieves satisfaction thanks to the dissolution of the ambivalent motivations of the subconscious. The superconscious, guide to authentic valuation, is the *conscience,* the more-than-conscious knowledge of ethical values. This superconscience of values inspires a hesitant and deliberate valuation of the consciousness, and causes its determination to freely adhere to the ethical exigency, even rejoicing in it, because it leads to harmonious autonomy. Harmonious autonomy cannot be established except by a constant effort at elucidation in regard to the subconscious motives that underlie an unsatisfactory lack of harmony. The effort at elucidation (spiritualization) feeds the essential desire and confers on it the strength to attain self-mastery (sublimation). In the effort toward spiritualization-sublimation virile maturity is summed up. But maturity will never be definitively acquired. Its virility resides precisely in the endless struggle against assailing desires that, since they are badly educated, have remained egocentrically puerile.

Having reached the end of the ontogenetic history of the mind's maturation and the causes of regression, a final reflection is required, in which both error and truth are summed up.

If psychic deformation (going so far as to produce oneiric symptoms) were the consequence of a deviation of sexuality already noticeable in the child, it could no longer be imputed to false or incorrect education. Infantile sexuality would be an irreducible fact, the consequence of biological predominance of this instinctual drive, and its deviation would be the result of influences of an ancestral and irresistible nature (Freud, *Totem and Taboo*). The child as well as the educator would be in the throes of a perversion, unassailable because endowed with a natural character (the child would be—as Freud says—a polymorphous pervert). Education would then be reduced to a matter of training that has for its goal the suppression of instinctiveness and its submission to social convention. Education would merely be an attempt at domestication.

In truth, far from being only domestication, education has a significance that surpasses even the maturation of the individual's mind. From the highest point of view, each individual is nature's attempt to progress in life's evolutionary direction. This progression is realized thanks to one's autonomous liberation as regards the ascendancy of the subconscious, whose pseudosatisfying and deforming temptations govern the ensemble of individuals, that is, society. From this perspective, it is not an exaggeration to say that the drive to surpass envisages the evolution of the species.

Thus understood, the surpassing drive is the evolved form of the elementary evolutionary instinct and its spiritualizing advance toward lucid adaptation. The evolutionary thrust is transformed into the attraction exercised by the superconscious ideal and its promise for the ultimate satisfaction of sensible desires, healthily selected and harmoniously brought together. Ontogeny is a means for the advancement of phylogeny. Their common goal is the genesis of the valuing mind, a form evolved starting from the primitive capacity for choice.

Healthily guided by education, ontogeny is the prolongation of phylogenetic evolution. The common guiding line, by tying together the stages of maturation on the human level, leads to the blossoming of the guiding instance.

The superconscious guides human life toward the realization of the only ideal that is not unhealthy exaltation. The superconscious directs the elementary search for satisfaction toward liberation in respect to the subconscious and its temptations of false motivation, the source of psychopathic deformation and essential cause of all dissatisfactions. *The ideal aimed at by the superconscious is psychic health*.

The goal of re-education—the re-establishment of psychic health—coincides with the ethical ideal. Only from the elucidation of the immanent *raison d'être* of the ethos comes a truly satisfactory method of re-education.

Adler's Theory and the Study of Motives

The mistake of Freudian theory, which claims that it is sexual desires—if not exclusively, at least as a matter of preference—that are subject to repression, soon inspired a dissenting reaction: Adler's individual psychology.

In combatting what he called Freud's sexual jargon, Alfred Adler was led to entertain a theory that accords dominance to the nutritive instinct and the need for security, which on the human level are assured by incorporation in the social exigencies. His re-educational principle consists in readapting the individual to the conventions of society, bringing him back to "common sense," to adhering to the community's rules of the game (*Gemeinschaftsgefühl*).

The need for incorporation into society is moreover already found in a certain sense at the basis of the Freudian theory that opposes the pleasure principle to the reality principle. Pleasure is supposedly reserved exclusively for the instinctive satisfaction of sexuality for to which reality is opposed, conceived uniquely as the social environment with its conventional requirements of discipline and duty. In Freud as well as in Adler the essential aspect of psychic health is neglected: the adaptation to the evolutionary meaning of life, the ultimate principle wherein pleasure and duty (essential satisfaction and ethical imperative) are perfectly united.

While Freud prefers to study the parent–child relationship, Adler is mainly interested in the conflict between brothers and sisters. The need for prestige (the need to be loved and esteemed) when it is exacerbated by vanity leads children into a struggle for domination. Not the least of Adler's achievements is the discovery of the constant rule according to which the obedient submissiveness of one child—when he manages to triumph and assures himself the position of favorite in the eyes of parents and teachers—unleashes the rebellious disobedience of another, even leading the child to scholastic defeat and, from there, all the way to becoming a maladjusted social failure. Thus, setting out from the study of the motives that determine the underhanded antagonisms among children, a new perspective opens up. It allows us to glimpse a whole network of motivations, knowledge of which is indispensable for an explanation of children's behavior. The explanations offered by Adler are necessarily totally different in nature from those attempted by Freud, because it is clear that the Oedipus complex cannot explain resentments arising among siblings, unless one claims that the child is jealous of his brothers and sisters because they prevent him from mating with the parent of the opposite sex. The truth is, however, that morbid resentments—acquired through the relationship with the parents or the relationship with the siblings—are of one and the same nature if looked at from the point of view of a calculation of satisfaction subject to falsification. The parents' resentments, like those against brothers and sisters, are deployed in accordance with the categories of false motivation.

As for Adler's domination instinct, it too is prefigured in Freudian theory under the term *aggression instinct*. The divergence lies not in the psychic phenomenon but in its interpretation.

According to an almost generalized habit in psychology, every ill-defined function is called an "instinct." By this term are confused under the same heading also the elementary drives of unconscious origin (sexuality and nourishment) as well as the perverse attitudes of subconscious origin, as is precisely the case in overbearing aggression. Far from being an indefinable instinct, a prime factor able to serve as the basis for a theory, overbearing aggressiveness as it is manifested on the human level is an involutive effect of deficient psychic functioning. It belongs to the domain of false motivation and, thus understood, is nothing but the tendency to accusation.

In accordance with Freud, the "aggression instinct" does not belong to the unconscious as does the sexual "instinct," but rather to tendencies of the "ego." Now, the ego is the conscious instance opposed to instinctive life. It is impossible to see how what is conscious could give birth to an instinct. But one can easily understand how Freud saw himself compelled to introduce aggressiveness as a prime factor, in view of the fact that the complexities of the struggle for material subsistence (which occupies a great part of human life) would have been insufficiently explained if one regarded sexual libido as the sole source of vital energy. It is this very reason that led Adler to complete—and even replace—the so-called sexual "instinct" with the so-called domination "instinct." What is true is that adaptation to social reality is characterized on the human level by the aggressiveness evoked by the struggle for material goods and that it thus belongs to the expanded sphere of nourishment. But unlike the *instinctive aggressiveness of the animal, which only threatens individuals of other species, human aggressiveness is directed against its own kind.* Indeed, this is the trait of perversion that proves that the analogy with animal aggressiveness, which might make one conclude it is an instinct, is blatantly mistaken. In reality, we have an ensemble of very complex motives aimed at long-term power and dominance. Overbearing aggressiveness appears in childhood and becomes diversified in the multiple forms whose common "politics of prestige" define the life of societies and the conflicts between societies. When it is overwrought, the struggle for prestige and security can be ascribed to a false calculation of satisfaction that destroys the affective bond. Since it is perverse exaltation, human aggressiveness is subject to the law of ambivalence; it is opposed by an ideal of love rendered powerless because of its unreal exaltation. Just as all ambivalent manifestations transform natural emotions into morbid resentments, human aggressiveness is an activity that can be explained by starting from the categories of false motivation. It is a guilty activity due to vanity-inspired ambitions, hateful accusations and sentimental self-pity.

Freud rounded out the theory he originally based on sexual instinct by introducing the coexistence of an instinct of aggression directed no longer only against others but also against oneself. In his eyes, there supposedly exists a "death instinct" that takes one beyond the pleasure principle. This is a new attempt to turn a factor of perverse motivation into a principle that explains life in general.

In fact, the death wish, directed not only against others but against oneself, does appear in the unhealthily deformed psyche, which is often haunted by the idea of suicide. But these desires do not have an instinctual origin. They are the consequence of perversion and its guilty torment. If one understands secret motives and their calculation of satisfaction, it becomes evident that the perverted individual can very well—and without transgressing the pleasure principle—seek an absurd satisfaction in the decisive flight from life. His flight into death is a symptom that expresses his emotional despair and his vanity-inspired triumph. He believes that he is imposing on the alleged offenders an endless remorse by seeking refuge in death so as to escape definitively from an environment he accuses of being unlivable.

Freud and Adler undertook the study of the inner functioning of the psychic system. In order to penetrate into this virgin territory, they each chose a different point of departure. The paths they marked out are not without detours and deviations, and this prevented them from advancing to the central point where they could have met and joined forces. The distinctive but also unifying feature of their theories appears most clearly as soon as one envisages these two attempts as setting forth from the central point of the problem, from which all paths of exploration branch out. This central point is a biologically fundamental phenomenon: the search for satisfaction.

In a certain sense, Adler was closer to the discovery of the calculation of satisfaction and its subconscious complications. These complications were perceived by Freud under the concept of "false rationalization" and were foreseen by Adler under the formulation of "prestige politics." With this formulation the secret cause of all subconscious complications is announced: the deep, vanity-inspired nature of the false calculation of satisfaction.

What allowed Adler to foresee the vain, calculating nature of the false rationalization discerned by Freud was precisely the fact that he studied the resentments that arise among siblings. Between brothers and sisters, the need for vanity-inspired triumph manifests itself in a far less disguised manner than in the relations between children and parents. (The vanity that deforms this relationship was nevertheless already pointed out by Freud. Rather than describing it he conjectured it, using the pseudomythical and sexualizing term *narcissism*.)

Convinced of his point of view and in order to emphasize his opposition to his predecessor, Adler was forced to reject even what is still valid in Freud's initial discovery: the explanation of the subconscious genesis of the psychopathic symptom (the repression of guilty desire and its oneirically disguised reappearance). Thus Adler saw himself obliged to search for a new explanation of the symptom's genesis, an explanation that—though it is only complementary—is nevertheless no less important and fruitful.

The fact is that the child's desires, repressed by prohibitions (or overwrought by their absence, which in the end gives rise to the unsurmountable obstacle, the cause of repression) result not only in the oneiric symptom studied by Freud in adults but also the multiple traits of character deficiency. This deficiency—the first degree of morbidity—is in itself therefore much more frequent than the explosion of symptoms. Adler observes that the diverse traits of the deformed character are finally organized in a morbid system of defense and attack. The insufficiently adapted child, in an unfavorable position vis-à-vis his siblings and peers, utilizes his deficiency with a view to taking advantage of it. He imaginatively transforms his inferiority into superiority. This advantage is too tempting and too easy to obtain for the deficient child to be able to renounce vanity-inspired triumph. *The more deficient the child is, the more vain he will be.* He will try to dominate his close relations by underhanded submissiveness or aggressive rebellion. A defeat of this subconscious plan will in the end bring about the more or less marked appearance of abulic traits that are inseparable from the neurotic character. The advantage of imaginary superiority turns against the child and only serves to reinforce his real inferiority.

Since "prestige politics" are subconsciously obsessive, the plan to profit from them, starting in childhood, threatens to encompass all of one's future life.

By opposing to the *functional cause* discovered by Freud (the oneiric reappearance of repressed desire) the *finalist cause* (the plan to derive advantage from it), Adler was tempted to speak of a *plan for life,* which underlies the chain of morbid productions in the adult and is supposedly elaborated since childhood, while its irreducible persistence is allegedly the sole cause of morbidity.

The truth is that the finalist cause—the search for a mistaken advantage—supplies a precious determinant for the explanation of the mindless tenacity of unhealthy adaptation; but by itself it still does not sufficiently explain psychopathic effects. The plan for life is itself a psychopathic phenomenon that needs to be explained. This plan is not conscious. It eludes control, it acts obsessively from the depths of the subconscious, and therefore its observation does not authorize one to contest the discovery of the subconscious and its repressive function.

Neither the functional cause discovered by Freud nor the finalist cause advanced by Adler is, taken each on its own, capable of explaining the process of deformation. The two causes complete each other and are both equally at the origin of the malady of the spirit in all of its phases. The common root of the two series of causes resides in the vanity-inspired blinding of the mind, which leads to the false calculations of satisfaction.

The vanity-inspired falsified calculation of satisfaction is the true cause of psychic deformation, for in this calculation are implicated the two constitutive factors studied separately by Freud and Adler—repression and finality. The calculation is falsified by the search for vanity-inspired satisfactions (the acquisition of prestige foreseen by Adler) and the vanity-inspired blinding, and by depriving the conscious of its calculation of illusory gain results in oneiric expression (the repression studied by Freud).

An overly radical opposition to Freud's discovery induced Adler to explain the oneiric symptom exclusively with the help of the finalist cause. Adler saw himself obliged to consider this cause—the plan of life—as an irreducible entity that operates rigidly and without any possibility of revision throughout life. The fact is that the "plan," an unhealthy attempt at adaptation, necessarily leads to defeat. For Adler, the oneiric symptom is only an attempt to protect the "plan" against the revision suggested by one's failures. This is true. But how can one fail to see that Adler's explanation is based precisely on repression? What is repressed is the need to revise the subconscious "plan." (The symptom is a protection against the guilty anxiety connected with the defeat. It absorbs the anxiety and expresses it symbolically. This fact was already observed by Freud.) Therefore the irreducibility of the plan is not an original factor, but an effect of the pathological process.

In the course of life, every new suffering regarded as insurmountable because of guilty inadequacy runs the risk of activating the repressive function. But as the symptom is the substitute for a revision, how can one deny that traumatizing defeat is capable of producing, instead of a symptom, the revision of one's plan of life? And in place of repression, the lifting of repression.

The turmoil due to actual failure forces the psyche to reconstitute itself either in regression or evolution. The revision can have either a negative or positive character. The symptom itself is the product of a negative revision, and instead of the symptom there may take place another form of negative revision of the subconscious plan: its reconstitution not being oneirically disguised but active in character, the product of new morbid means of attack and defense. On the other hand, the possibility of a releasing revision ensures re-education its chance. The precise aim of the curative turmoil is to prevent the character's new reconstitution from being infiltrated by the old plans of false satisfaction. *The aim of re-education is to dissolve the subconsciously pre-established plan in order to replace it with a reasonable "plan," whose valuations are controlled by the mind.* Now, the most reasonable plan of life—and therapeutically the most effective—should be in conformity with the evolutionary impulsion, a plan that surpasses by far the adaptation to social conventions foreseen by Adler.

Infrequently and in certain cases sensible revision can take place without therapeutic intervention, and this proves in the most incontrovertible manner that the subconscious plan is not an irreducible plan of life. This sensible revision will take place if on the one hand the subject makes use of a certain amount of energy that has remained lucid, and if, on the other, he is exposed to exceptionally intense suffering, which only leaves him the choice between definitive destruction of the psychic system or a sensible revaluation of his means of defense.

The plan of life is not definitively fixed beginning in childhood. To claim that this is so would be the same as saying that only the child is capable of the act of valuing. It is true that the child's prelogical and affective valuation tends to persist, to remain uncorrected and to become automatic. And this despite the fact that the plan of life, supposedly fixed, is the dynamic result of a falsified act of valuation whose judgments, automatically renewed continually, are transformed into constant motives. What Adler calls the "plan of life" (an incorrigible plan for action) is not the cause of morbidity but rather the effect of an incessant false valuation that has remained prelogical and is incapable of relinquishing the infantile oneiricism through which it has gone astray.

Since false valuation (the repression of guilty satisfaction and the search for vanity-inspired pseudosatisfactions) is by its very nature ambivalent, it produces relative instability in the subconscious plan of life. The principled rigidity of the neurotic character is counteracted by an excessive changeability. *The nervous person—as indeed the maladjusted child—does not have a single character; he tries out a number of characters* that appear alternately depending on the situation and the people encountered. The nervous person is now timid, now arrogant; now generous, now parsimonious, etc. He is always dependent on the opinion of others, and his attitudes change (within the framework of false motivation), depending on whether he thinks he can elicit the kindness and esteem he has coveted greedily since childhood. The inadequate means of defense, the attempts to try out many characters—ranging from submissive to rebellious—are even more pronounced in childhood when character formation is in full gestation.

Children exposed to a deficient education alternately traverse periods when they try to adjust now by submission, now by rebellion, before becoming fixed in one of these two typical attitudes. Even the child who in the end gets stranded in rebellious disobedience has gone through periods full of tormented regret and exalted good intentions before having recourse to a more or less complete repression of his unbearable guilt, and this results in fixation on an antagonistic character.

If it were not superfluous to insist on an obvious fact, one might recall that the fluctuations and modifications accompanying the elaboration of the "plan of life" stretch from childhood to an often very advanced age, if not to all of life. The child who does not find in his parents an edifying example avidly searches for it around him, and the instability of his character exposes him to the positive or negative influence of peers and teachers. But the search for an example occurs in the most decisive and prolonged way under the suggestive influence of reading, capable of producing a veritable magical spell because it acts most directly on the overwrought imagination. The unstable character of the nervous person is incessantly decomposed and recomposed under the influence of models met by chance in books or in artistic or pseudoartistic spectacles. The favorite imitated model is often diametrically opposed to the plan of life acquired in childhood. Aspirations are concretized in the guiding image. Often the image will be represented by a purely imaginary hero, a current star in any sphere, or a personage dead for centuries. This is how the elevated task is formed, incompatible with the exigencies of surrounding reality and the subject's intrinsic talents. From these successive influences, amalgamated by false motivations, finally comes a plan of life at times both rigid and vacillating, a mosaic character composed of debris, which at the slightest unforeseen shock threatens to shatter and collapse in disarray.

What remains incorrigible in the deformed character is not the rigid plan acquired in childhood, but the false motivation that underlies all the multiple sketches of character. The adult's pathological deformation is the result of continually falsified intrapsychic work whose constant effort at adaptation proves insufficient and morbid. The pathological situation consists in the fact that this effort is not directed by the needs of a lucidly evaluated reality but by deceptive imagination. It is this indeed that incites the child to want to take advantage of his deficiency, even to exaggerate it, in order to be able to use it as a reproach and punishment directed against the milieu, which is judged guilty, and to impose himself on it as a victim, setting himself at the center of attention with the help of his deficiency (as Adler quite rightly observed). But the vain advantage sought in this way remains illusory. The irritated milieu responds to the provocation, which in the long run is unbearable, by having recourse to its own deformed means of defense and attack. The anticipated advantage is inevitably transformed into an unbearable disillusionment that reinforces the rancor. Going from provocation to provocation, the deficiency ends by mobilizing the tendency to repress one's fault, the true cause of a further explosion of symptoms.

Thus the finalist plan to take advantage of the deficiency becomes in fact, as Adler had foreseen, an indispensable condition of the pathogenetic process, subject to becoming more and more serious until the symptom explodes. It makes no difference that the functional cause remains the process presented by Freud: the oneirically disguised reappearance of the repressed fault. Whereas repression of one's deficiency determines the subconscious work, indispensable for elaboration of the symptom, the other cause—the search for a senseless advantage—determines the specific form taken by the character deformations and symptoms, depending on the diversity of the inciting situations.

The apparently contradictory Freudian and Adlerian explanations are not incompatible if one keeps in mind the fact that the child's healthy maturation and his unhealthy backwardness are conditioned neither by the sexual instinct nor by the domination instinct. Aggressive resentments appear only as a result of the vanity-inspired advantage sought in repression of the fault. Fault and punishment are one and the same thing. The fault that evokes its punishment consists in the ambivalent decomposition of the natural intrapersonal bond that bears its advantage of satisfaction within itself (love and esteem).

Is one fully aware of the distortion introduced by a psychology that, oblivious to the natural and self-evident bond, presents love exclusively in its deformed aspect, debased by jealousy (a debasement that hides behind the presumed need of Oedipal intercourse as well as behind the struggle for domination)? If unhealthy deformation is made the explanatory principle, nothing but hostile aggressiveness seems to survive in human motives.

Understanding of the true significance of the discoveries of Freud and Adler permits us to entertain the possibility of the unification of apparently contradictory theories. The common denominator is *love-hate,* described by Freud as the child's unassuaged need to mate with his parents, and described by Adler as envy of prestige and material security. (The need for love and the need for security are originally equivalent, because the infant feels secure only when it is surrounded by the parents' affection.) The link between infant inadequacy and adult deformation cannot be attributed to the repression of a sexual complex that would result in a rigid superego, nor is this link formed by a rigid plan of life that the child already allegedly sets against its educators and that would persist unchanged throughout life. This link is constituted by deformation of the mind: by a valuation that lacks lucidity, creating on the one hand the repressive constellation of the subconscious and, on the other, the plan for its senseless utilization.

Vanity-inspired valuation (Freud's "false rationalization," Adler's "prestige politics") is essentially false and faulty. Vanity-inspired valuation is false because it falsifies the elements of deliberate calculation by falsely rationalizing the motives; it is faulty because instead of reaching a satisfactory solution of the problem of life, it only leads to the deformation of life and the degradation of the mind.

The prestige politics discovered by Adler foresees the false calculation of satisfaction in an empirical and fragmentary manner. Thus light is shed on certain details of subconscious calculation. But they remain isolated facts, as long as they are not linked to the underlying motivations that are subject to ambivalent decomposition. Calculating motivation and its search for advantage (empirically observed by Adler) ties together all the apparently isolated details of manifest activity in a structured whole, which, in turn, is differentiated in accordance with the specific path of erroneous calculation. Comprehension of the faulty error and its legitimate structure permits us to reconstruct the aberrant paths of subconscious calculation and leads to exposure of its antithetic bond with sensible calculation. It thus becomes possible to equate the problems of life and find their equitable solution by psychologically lucid calculation, which is capable of determining the "unknowns" of motivation in keeping with their real value.

Only the methodical knowledge of this calculation in search of its advantage—the calculation of satisfactions—assures a solid foundation to the re-educational intervention.

4

THE TECHNIQUE OF
RE-EDUCATION

Beginning with Freud's and Adler's discoveries, re-education has become possible. The assistance given the parents is of public interest, and therefore re-education has become a kind of institution, appreciated by some, questioned by others. To the extent to which the basic theories contain truths, even if flawed by errors, their re-educational application and its technical procedure can be improved.

It will be possible to attain improvement only through an understanding of the educational goal and its laws, as set forth in the preceding pages. However, re-educational technique remains—in spite of its practical utilization—of secondary importance. The essential is to understand the guiding principles that govern not only re-education but all the factors of practical life. Once these principles are established, it is no longer necessary to present the technique of re-educational application in all of its details. It is enough to trace its guiding lines in order to complete the present study.

The fact that inner motivations were discovered in some measure by Freudian and Adlerian analysis obliges us to use those systems in an effort at synthesis. The unknown can only be reconstituted by departing from the known, which tries to organize itself in an harmonious whole. In depth psychology the unknown is the repressed, the known is what is released from repression. In order to advance a methodical and scientific release from repression, it is important to begin each time afresh—without fear of repetition—from details previously released, even if they were discovered by predecessors known to everyone.

This method is obligatory in theoretical research, and it also guides practical re-education. Only its use will put an end in the life sciences to false, vanity-inspired research, to the temptation of pseudo-originality, which incites each research worker to invent a new terminology that often conceals the use of already discovered truths but often also deflects the synthesis toward baseless speculations. Psychology and its practical application—re-educational technique—would thus become like all other sciences, the work of teams of researchers who would relay their findings from generation to generation in a common search for truth.

In this sketch of the re-educational technique will be found not only repetitions but also gaps. The principled foundation of the technique—the knowledge of the calculation of satisfaction—is regarded as acquired. This calculation, founded on the laws of harmony and ambivalence, has been described throughout this book. One will find it also described in my other publications, notably in *The Psychology of Motivation*. Once the principles are established, it is no longer a matter of dwelling on the sketch of the re-educational process and its underlying foundation. The sketch will therefore be confined largely to exposition of the external measures to be taken in order to establish a propitious terrain for the common work that reunites educator, parents, and children.

However, this book is not addressed only to future re-educators, who, however, should not recoil from the effort of a profounder inquiry.

It is therefore appropriate—before beginning to sketch the details—to sum up in all their simplicity the guiding principles of re-educational progression:

From birth the child clamors for the satisfaction of his needs. His maturation resides in the deployment of the functions that permit the acquisition of autonomy in the search for sensible satisfactions (material, sexual, spiritual).

In search of satisfaction, desires become linked with an imagination subject to affective exaltation (the cause of unhealthy deformation) or are clarified and become intellectual prescience and, finally, spiritual clairvoyance (the goal of healthy formation.)

Therefore the re-educational effort must concentrate on the exalted imagination (in its forms of escape and justification) in order to obtain the revision of erroneous motives, which by impeding healthy maturation become the cause of affective backwardness (obstinate disobedience) and of intellectual backwardness (scholastic deficiency).

The re-educational measures (instead of being empirically dispersed and remaining random and sometimes even contradictory) must be dictated as a whole and in detail by anticipation of the paths of deviation and by knowledge of their main features (subconscious motivations) and ramifications (deficient behavior fixed in character traits).

Knowledge of the laws that govern the calculation of motivations frees the re-educational technique from two redoubtable obstacles: fragmentary empiricism and random interpretation. In this sense, one might say that the study of motivation puts at the re-educator's disposal a tool of analysis that is profoundly different from that advocated by the schools of Freud and Adler.

The Re-educator

If treatment calls for concentrating attention on the calculation of falsified motivations, the re-educator would be wrong to neglect the study of the *family milieu*. Such an error would be no less serious than the usual neglect of secret motives. Deep-seated motivations and manifest behavior complement each other and create the social situation—or rather, here, the family situation—that the re-educator proposes to correct.

The imaginative ruminations that decompose emotions into ambivalent resentments are unleashed by external and interpersonal provocations, the false reactions of children and parents. But also— and conversely—the falsified reactions are incessantly suggested by each person's inner ruminations.

In the disunited family, parents and children, setting out from their solitary ruminations, are provoked provocateurs.

This observation determines the very progress of the re-educational technique.

The secret motive of mutual provocation resides in frustrated vanity, which tries to transform itself into triumphant vanity.

Effective disentanglement is only possible through analysis of the double entanglement: the first is the *active intrigue* sustained by mutual provocations. It is strikingly manifest and finds itself indulgently expressed by the parents' complaints. The other—the *entanglement of motives*, fueled by each person's secret ruminations—is jealously hidden in each person's inner depth. That is what must be tracked down. This tracking is possible because the entanglement of motives has the same nature in both children and parents. Acquired by the parents during their own childhood, it is affective infantilism. The tendency to false justification uncontrolled by consciousness has persisted independently of time and events. True enough, it is fed by events. But they will not change its essential structure, which is imperturbably deployed in false motivation, in excessive justification-incrimination of oneself and others. In this sense, it is right to say that the intimate entanglement of resentment is not subject to historical development but only to the law of ambivalence. This is essential and legitimate.

Reactive entanglement, on the contrary, is accidental and historical. It has a history susceptible of being recounted, which permits us to pursue it from childhood to adulthood. It is composed of perturbing events: interfamilial and interpersonal provocations. The chain of unendurable events is fixed in character traits. But the perturbing events could not be constituted in a deficient character unless the subject, beginning in childhood, responded to suffered provocation by hypersensitized rumination. Within the framework of secret false motivations are thus gradually formed—covering it and causing it to disappear—habitual falsified reactions, one's character traits.

If he overlooks the framework underlying motivations, the re-educator will be tempted to simplify his task. He will endeavor to establish an explanatory link between such and such a character deficiency and such and such a past trauma. Past events, often forgotten, can be associatively revealed. All the techniques at present in use are based on the associative method. (Except for existential analysis, which is more philosophical than psychological in origin, the method remains—for lack of an exact study of motivations—flawed by empiricism and random interpretations.) Far from resulting in simplification, negligence in regard to the essential becomes the cause of excessive complication.

The drawbacks of the associative method have already been emphasized. We should insist here not so much on objections of a theoretical order as on complications of a technical and practical nature.

The method of association is retrospective rather than introspective. But such retrospection, owing to the fact that the entanglement of motives remains uncontrolled, runs the risk of being subjected to their deforming influence.

The danger becomes great when the analysand subconsciously uses the associative path as a means of retrospectively heightening his fantasies of escape and justification. Escape into the past threatens to become a habit, obsessive even outside the analytical sessions. The overwrought evocation of injustices irrevocably suffered, or considered as such, lends itself perfectly to feelings of self-pity, the vanity-inspired justification of present deficiencies, and the excessive incrimination of old familial or extrafamilial situations. The imaginatively produced associations risk being only a screen destined to hide—and even aggravate—the present swarm of false motivations.

It certainly would be foolish to claim that past events are without importance. But it can never be emphasized enough that they are not responsible for the deformation of character in itself, but solely for its accidental constellation, which is different for each individual (timidity or impertinence, abulia or turbulence, etc.).

It is easier to remove this or that accidental trait of the provocative attitude than to dissolve its essential common cause: the morbid terrain (the tendency to imaginative exaltation). Certain traits can be removed easily—above all in the child whose character has not yet assumed a definitive stance when faced by the events or circumstances that can arise in a treatment situation or even outside treatment (dependency on the opinion of others, the persuasive influence by or imitation of an example, change of milieu, sentimental attachment to certain companions, certain teachers, or even the re-educator, etc.). The curative shock is particularly apt to produce such changes, which are quite temporary and easily assumed to be the result of the analysis and a decisive improvement.

The re-educator who has been able to remove a child's character trait of which the parents complain would be wrong to think that he had achieved a lasting success unless he has been careful beforehand to deal effectively with the secret entanglement of motivations on the part of both the child and its parents.

So long as the family atmosphere does not change, the provocative situation will be re-established after a more or less brief interval. The removed character trait will reappear, unless it has been replaced by an equivalent or ambivalent deficiency. True, in certain cases (for example: the thieving child), it is desirable to transform the heinous trait into a socially less dangerous one. But it is also true that in other cases the persistence of false motivations can lead, as the result of inadequate educative intervention, to an undesirable transformation of the perverse character constellation.

Only the harmonizing dissolution of the ambivalent entanglement of motives can be considered a true improvement.

A clear distinction between the two forms of entanglement that interlace in the bosom of families—false motivation and false provocatory reactions—is indispensable to re-educational work.

It is in the nature of things that the family has always been considered the most propitious place for the child's blossoming. No one, it would seem, can love the child as much as his own parents. That is true, provided that the capacity for love is not split into love-hate. And here lies the original discovery of depth psychology. Hate can mask itself as love, and overwrought love is subtended by hate. This is, in germ, proof of the existence of false motivation and its law of ambivalence. It is on this discovery that depth psychology must base its investigations and conclusions instead of studying only incidental intrigue, which has led to a too exclusive incrimination of the parents.

It is true that parents, by their educational faults, bring about the entanglement of false actions; they provoke the incidental intrigue. But this observation, if one were to rely on it alone, would in the end deprive re-educative work of its efficacy and even of its *raison d'être*. *The omission of the essential fault held in common by parents and children has as its unforeseen consequence the recognition of generalized irresponsibility.* The parents were irresponsible children, and the children, judged irresponsible, become parents who have the right to cast the fault back on their own parents. Without knowledge of the laws that govern love and its decomposition, the fault would remain ungraspable. The educational error seems no longer an accident—empirically corrigible by re-educative work—but something that, subject to ineluctable historical development, will infallibly provoke the hatred of generations.

Excessive incrimination of the generation of parents and its ambivalent complement, vanity-inspired self-exoneration, actually constitute at the present time the most prominent distinctive trait of a youth that behaves like irresponsible children while playing the part of adults. Would it be unjust to point out that this deplorable state of affairs can in large part be imputed to the advent of depth psychology, which has too exclusively emphasized the parents' educational failings? By stressing hypocrisy without searching for its true cause—the inner lie—it has, against its own intentions, magnified in these young people the motives for rebellion and supplied them with an extremely ambivalent, falsely justifying pretext: the wide spread of cynicism.

Faced by the malaise of the age, the re-educator will be powerless if he refuses to delve to the very bottom of the problem.

The essential failing—the tendency to false justification—is not the exclusive property of children or parents. It is innate in human nature.

The re-educator, to be in a position to assume his conciliatory role, must maintain an attitude of objectivity that will prevent him from accusing or excusing too exclusively either parents or children. The indispensable condition for objectivity lies in the realization of the existence of this essential fault common to human nature.

Whether he wishes it or not, the re-educator himself is included in this fault that must be discovered, even if his own tendency to false motivation does not attain the degree of intensity that causes psychopathy. The demarcation between normal and pathological, imposed by social exigencies, becomes a mistake when faced by the essential problem. Included as he is in the common fault, the re-educator must include himself in the analysis instead of following the easy way out, which resorts to self-justification, even if it is doctrinal.

In order to acquire the ability to analyze others, the re-educator must subject himself to prior analysis. But it can never be emphasized enough that the goal of didactic analysis does not consist—at least not in the first place—in dissolving infantile complexes and past traumas. It is a profound mistake to believe that a review of the past can be enough to confer an unshakable state of psychic health. In psychic functioning nothing is static, except the laws that govern the incessant fluctuation of motives. Only knowledge of these laws permits us to understand the dynamics of motives and their ever-present tendency to falsification. The goal of didactic analysis is to make us lucid in regard to this fault that is common to human nature, so as to make the future re-educator fit to grapple with it in himself and thus cure himself of the presumption that he has been forever cured by a static review of the past. Such a presumption could only lead to a pseudocure, a stabilization in error. The wisdom of the language expresses this error by a whole series of terms whose common root is the semblance of being, the para-being (para-être: par-estre): to parade, to appear. The goal of didactic analysis is precisely that of making the re-educator able to avoid inauthentic "appearing" and to incorporate it in the curative dynamism thanks to the acquisition of a method of self-control in the face of the fluctuations of present-day life.

The common fault—stagnation in the over-wrought exaltation of self-love—is the cause of a lack of objectivity. By successively objectifying the fault, the re-educator progressively delivers himself from it. In the end he understands the main circumstances (the motives) and the details (the false reactions fixed in character traits).

The fault being common to human nature, its objectifying release from repression brings the re-educator not only to a relative knowledge of himself but also to an objectified knowledge of others (children and parents). To the extent that the re-educator succeeds in freeing himself from the lack of objectivity due to false motivations, to the very same extent he has the right to hope that parents and children, thanks to his help, will in turn be able to free themselves of false reactions, the mutual provocation of which they complain.

To help another person to see clearly into himself, to guide him to live healthily, is an exceptional undertaking. Re-education is also and above all a vocation, and it can only secondarily become a profession transmissible by the paths of didactic analysis. Hence it is important to differentiate between analyst and counselor. Since this work has to do with a calculation whose elements are the motives, the necessity for the distinction is explained by comparision with the domain of mathematics. The enrichment of knowledge is here reserved to men who perfectly possess a talent for mathematical analysis, while the mass of professionals in possession of acquired algorithm are perfectly capable of solving the practical problems connected with technical applications. In the same way, the dynamic process of the psychic calculation of satisfaction needs to be brought to light more and more, with a view to constituting a fund of knowledge available to professionals. Armed with this pre-established knowledge, counselor/re-educators will no longer proceed according to empirical directives and even less—at the height of ineffectiveness—on the basis of a persuasion that, under the pretext of analysis, would rely on doctrinal speculations, if not on bluntly conventional valuations.

An alert counselor, the re-educator will be in a position to arrive at the entanglement of secret motives, setting out from the blatantly manifest intrigue. He will listen to the parents' complaints; he will even provoke them with the help of a precise line of questioning, but he will consider the answers only as the givens of a problem to be solved by analytical reduction. The nature of the accusations presented by the parents is—precisely because of the provocative entanglement—revelatory to the highest degree of the educational fault. However, the re-educator will avoid accusing the parents, and he will resist the frequent temptation to establish his contact with the child by emotional means. The contact will have the curative value to the extent that it will be based on a confidence inspired by the *objectivity of the investigation and the precision of the explanations*. Confidence based on esteem is a sufficiently profound bond; any other sentiment is the sign of a re-educational fault. A too affective attachment on the part of the re-educator would reveal a lack of impartiality, which induces him to use sympathetic complicity as a surrogate for his explanatory incompetence. Impartiality implies love of his profession and through it true attachment to the patients: interest in their difficulties and the desire to help them. Children need sensible orientation as much as well-pondered love. The re-educator's task is to help the child come out of his anxious confusion. He cannot assume his task by offering the child the love he lacks but only by revealing with precision the motives that make the child unlovable in his parents' eyes. The re-educator will not fulfill his task if, instead of reconciling the child with his parents, he allows himself to be tempted to become sentimentally competitive with the parents on the plane of love.

In re-education centers, the limited time given for consultations certainly does not allow one to undertake a long-term analysis. Re-educators are relatively few in relation to the number of families that need to be helped. Children overburdened with homework can only report once or twice a week for a session of limited duration. As for the parents who attend the consultation, since they are generally unaware of their responsibilities, they have a tendency to be satisfied with the initial results, which are often quite striking but rarely sufficiently consolidated in depth. Almost always they themselves would need to be analyzed, and this unfortunately is impossible under the given conditions. These drawbacks could only be combatted by a large-scale social organization.

Therefore the situation demands that the available time be employed effectively. Aware of the motivating calculation, the re-educator knows from the very first by what the parents and children are affected. He knows that the parents—whether they tend to spoil or to frustrate the child—will complain about his disobedience and his failures in school. As for the child, he will be abulic and apparently submissive, or agitated and openly rebellious. Of course these stereotyped ambivalences are subject to innumerable incidental variations. The attitudes of children and parents, and their responses to the questions put to them, will bring these to the fore. Knowing that in any case he will not be able to obtain a complete cure, the re-educator will be content to uncover straight off the crucial traits of the family intrigue, features upon which he will have to act by explaining motives and their circumstances and details, in order to obtain not only an accidental but an essentially founded improvement.

The explanation of motives would be a purely theoretical proceeding without any curative effect if it did not have the power to act upon the calculation of satisfaction. The re-educator must be in a position to demonstrate in detail how the motives—until now subconscious—are the cause of the provocative acts by which parents and children suffer to the point of seeking a remedy at all costs.

Parents and children are capable of recognizing the noxious connection between the secretly motivating cause and the provocative effect because they have experienced this form of suffering. The explanation is liberating, because it transforms the false valuations, the causes of the suffering, into just valuations. Even before treatment, parents and children have repeatedly tried to overcome their suffering. But these attempts have remained ineffective because of their blindness to the secret motivating link. Their good intentions were nothing but imaginative attempts, useless desires, fated to crumble. The cure assures a real foundation for the desire for improvement by attacking the motivating causes, instead of combatting only their active, provocative effects.

The re-educator's explanations are not advice in the ordinary sense of the word. The explanatory advice is not addressed to the good intentions of the parents and children, and they are not good intentions on the part of the re-educator. As the result of his elucidation of motives, the advice has an explicable value because it draws upon the capital of knowledge concerning the allurement and pernicious effects of false motivation. The explanatory advice is analytic advice. It makes explicit the implications of motives and behavior. The re-educator will be satisfied with this explanation while he waits for the desire to overcome suffering to suggest to the analysands how to change their behavior, even including the intentions on which it is based.

Among all the explanations that must be developed there is one that is generally found to be valid and whose urgency can be foreseen even before the details of the family situation are known.

We can never emphasize enough the fact that in all disunited families (a rule without exception) the atmosphere is constantly poisoned by the member's underlying tone of voice. This is typical of parents whose only conversation with the children is a scolding. Ever present in their voices is the rancor accumulated by all past disappointments. Their ordinary way of speaking follows the tonal pitch of constant complaint whose explosions into open argument are simply temporary exacerbations. These incessant tonal accusations, although seemingly imperceptible, are experienced by the child as repeated shocks, each of which is prolonged by a wave of irritation deep within that, even before it settles, is disturbed and stirred up again by the influx of new shocks, prolonged in their turn by more waves of irritation. The psychic disorder—pathogenic rumination and its discharge in vengeful disobedience—is the consequence of this endless flow of shocks and their prolongation in waves of irritation and indignation. In certain apparently united families there reign rigid principles that impose good manners. Quarrels are banned, and even the manner of speech is subjected to the control of conventional politeness; but the underlying intonations will only be more glacial and asphyxiating because of it. Even though the cadence is not that of an argument, the tonal pitch of discord is therefore no less audible.

The alert re-educator will know that the constant rancor betrayed by the voice, whatever the cadence and the pitch—and no matter how negligible this clue may seem—is in truth *the most crucial feature of the discord,* the feature on which he will have to act first of all and preferably at the first contact. It is no exaggeration to say that he will have accomplished his task as soon as he succeeds in getting the voices to become calm. But he will also know that the calm will not last long, since each member's indignation is continually stimulated by the provocation of the others and by their own ruminations. Thus, he will see himself again sent back to the analysis of motivation.

In the family's affective intonations—now ironical, now aggrieved, now aggressive—are concentrated, and in the most unexpected manner, both the entanglement of motives and the provocative intrigue. The underlying intonations have an irresistible provocative power for two conjoined reasons. On the one hand, they betray all the accumulated hate and even despair at having to put up with the antagonist. (In parents as well as in children, the intonations express either accusation or the sentimental complaint of a frustrated vanity that dares not award itself the triumph of vengeful aggression, for fear of the response.) On the other hand, the person under attack perfectly understands from the intonation the intentions because he too harbors the same intentions in himself. He understands them through affective introspection. He feels—without a word being said—that he is the object of despair, and this irresistibly provokes the upsurge of his aggressive self-justification. This also applies to certain gestures and facial expressions—shrugging one's shoulders, rolling the eyes, pursing the lips in disdain, etc.

The slightest occurrence, when it is emphasized by underlying intonations, gestures, and facial expressions (prepared by one's ruminations), is liable to provoke family quarrels that reach unforeseeable proportions.

Here is an example where a slight incident—a fork forgotten by the child when setting the table—has set off an avalanche of quarrels. The parents have come to the appointment, arranged after the examination of the child, a thirteen-year-old girl who is docile at home but unable to do her work in high school, although, on the basis of tests, her intelligence is found to be higher than average. Throughout the treatment, the parents have shown themselves to be quite understanding. However, the first interview takes place under the shadow of the evening before, on the subject of the badly laid table. From the moment they come in, their faces are distraught, their expressions fixed. The father (a stationmaster) lets his wife speak but continually gives signs of disapproval. Every time he tries to put in a word, his wife, without even looking at him or interrupting her account, makes an impatient gesture, telling him to keep quiet. Finally, at the end of his patience, he seizes the imperative hand of his wife, who immediately falls silent. They stare at each other for a moment with angry looks on their faces. I am careful not to interrupt the quarrel that explodes, and listen attentively. The reproaches they address to each other begin with calls to order. Each advises the other to keep quiet and to think of the impression they might make on me. Soon they join in a common effort at justification, trying to get me to understand the reasons for their loss of control. I then hear about the incident of the evening before, which the husband tries to tell in detail, undoubtedly seeing in it the proof of his innocence. "Wasn't I entitled to ask for a forgotten piece of silverware? How could I help jumping in anger when a fork was thrown at me? Sloppiness all the time, never any order!" His voice is choked with rage.

Parents rarely come to a consultation in such a pronounced stage of indignation. In order to prevent the scene from degenerating, it was necessary to interrupt the wife's retorts, which proved to be general accusations with little informative value. Once calm had been restored, it turned out that the fight of the evening before had had further repercussions. The child, who had gone off late to bed in tears, had stayed in bed the next morning instead of going to school. More reciprocal reproaches, and quarrels that went on into the afternoon until it was time for the appointment.

The story, in itself banal, is instructive because it reveals how a very small incident (a forgotten fork) can unleash a whole series of quarrels that continued during the session and from the start revealed the emotional climate. In the accounts that one commonly receives, the incident that sets it off is almost always forogtten. One can ask all one wants for a faithful account of the events that caused the trouble; the request is never strictly satisfied. The descriptions given are prudent rearrangements rather than a spontaneous expression of the felt resentments.

It is therefore important for the good conduct of the analysis that one clearly distinguishes the three phases common to all affective perturbation, which have been emphasized on the preceding example: *the incident that set it off, provocative attitudes* (intonation, gesture, facial expressions), and *motivating resentments*.

Incidents become traumatizing only because of one's provocative attitudes and underlying motivations. In the entanglement of causes and effects, effects again become causes, and this creates a vicious circle.

Now incidents are easily forgotten, attitudes are imponderables, and motivations are repressed. As a whole the circle thus eludes conscious control and hence tends to close again and again obsessively.

In order to cut through the knot of these vicious circles analytically, the re-educator must know their structure and must be able to explain it in detail to parents and children in terms suited to their ability to understand. However, it would be a wasted effort to complicate the analysis by a meticulous search for the infinitely variable incidents, since they only present the accidental side of the intrigue: the exterior causes. The essential point is to concentrate the analysis on the inner motives (the resentments) and the explosive reaction (the provocations). The essential point is to try to obtain by analytical reduction a lessening of the resentments that confer their provocative virulence and traumatizing power on often minimal incidents.

In order to do this, it is well to concentrate analytical attention on the often imponderable attitudes that accompany the provocations and are the most condensed expression of the underlying motivations of escape and justification.

Anger, the cause-effect of mutual provocations, is, in its inwardly experienced form, a state of indignation (impotent rage); it is, in its exteriorized form, provocatory attack taken to its extreme, an attempt to justify oneself by shifting the fault onto the other, who in turn shifts it back. The anger that grows in the course of quarrels is the expression of impotence confronted by the other's exculpatory response and by the rejection of the accusation. Thus in both adversaries despair accumulates because of the feeling that no revision of motives, no reconciliation, no improvement of the situation is possible. Anger becomes more intense because of its being incessantly cast back, from which arises the tit-for-tat of accusatory replies with which the adversaries riddle each other. The words, gestures, and grimaces become more and more menacing in order to intimidate and thereby put a halt to the accusations. But each of the antagonists tries to prove that he will not let himself be intimidated, and so the mounting rage, instead of being expressed only verbally, ends by being expressed physically.

But these provocations to quarrel would not come about if they were not prepared for in advance by the mental ruminations that take place in each person's secret heart in the form of an imaginary quarrel with the partner-adversary's ghost. Each person carries within him the distorted image of the partner, a defenseless ghost that is offered up to one's mercy. The rancorous ruminations continue in the form of a monologue somehow turned into a dialogue with the partner-ghost, the target of incessant triumphant accusations that obsessively suggest their future outcome ("I'll give him a piece of my mind"). During the ruminations, the accumulated self-justifications do not suffer accusatory replies and so become certainties as vain as they are sentimental. ("I would never do such a thing," "Everybody is against me!", "The world is bad," etc.) In the face of the real partner's counteraccusations the defense can only become harsher. The dialogued monologues with the ghostly partner disintegrate the affective bond, converting it into hate and feeding the desires for escape. In a situation where the other's excessive accusation proves to be impossible—and this is above all the case when a child faces an adult—the quarrel condenses into a frigid anger that gradually extinguishes any warm feelings.

The re-educator can bring about a suspension of the open quarrels that poison the family atmosphere only if he deals with each partner's dialogued monologues. It is his task to introduce himself into the monologue, taking the place of the accused ghost, so as to assume his defense in a calm and well-pondered manner. This interiorization can be achieved only with the help of an explanation of the false motives for rancor. The task of introducing himself into these inner monologues would be unpleasant and even dangerous—the re-educator, by finally assuming the personified function of "the brake of reason" in the patient's ruminative imagination, risks concentrating all accusations on himself, and in the end this could endanger the contact—if he did not have a technique that permits him to arm himself with objective patience and scientific clarity. Only knowledge of all the byways and detours of accusatory motivation will allow him gradually to dismantle the anger born in the imagination of parents and children and obtain their reconciliation.

The first measure that must be taken is the explanation of the
hurtfulness of imponderable provocations and above all of one's
intonation of voice. This explanation, which is of a general order—
but nevertheless is applied to each case in support of the preliminary findings—serves to *establish contact*, not in a superficial manner
but in depth. The parents understand very easily that the re-
educator is not offering them some vague advice, but that he is
making them face the essential cause of their suffering. They are
thus freed from the anguish of disorientation, and this bolsters their
confidence and hope.

On the strength of the acquired trust, the re-educator proposes to
the parents a *pact* at the very first session, even before having seen
the child. The pact will consist in inviting the parents to slacken the
reins. It is above all a matter of putting an end to the provocation,
so that gradually the ruminations calm down and the parents stop
pursuing the child with irritated reproaches. By dint of repetition
these are no longer even perceived literally: they no longer reach
the child except through the cacophony of their affective intonations. Their sole result is to irritate him further and provoke his
disobedient rebellion. The parents accept the re-educative intervention that is addressed to them as well as to the child. They
subsequently present their complaints to the re-educator, who—
with his explanation of falsified motives—appeases the parents'
indignation and obtains the child's agreement to the pact and to his
active collaboration.

The pact has as its goal the most rapid possible improvement of
the child's situation so that, even from the first session the re-
educator can offer him a promise of relief, which is also bound to
arouse confidence and hope in the child.

Very often at the beginning the pact will be observed—both by
parents and children—only in a very approximate manner. Nevertheless, it will serve to avoid a certain number of provocative
squabbles and to clear the ground with a view to constructive work
and the disentanglement of motives.

This initial situation having once been established, re-educational
success will depend on the precision of the analysis of the motives,
a precision without which the contact—if it is not broken—threatens to flag and to end in an interminable treatment without tangible
results.

In this regard, an image comes to mind: in order to obtain
electric light, it is necessary to flick the switch; simply groping
around is of no use, no matter how close to the contact one may

come. The same applies to lighting up the psyche. In order to
utilize the established contact effectively, it is necessary to touch the
sensitive points. On the other hand, there is no need for the re-
educator to convey all the details of analytic illumination in the
form of explanations. The essential is that he himself clearly
understands the situation, and this will permit him to condense the
treatment—when it seems appropriate to him—in clear advice.
Contrary to what one might be tempted to think, the analysis of
details is addressed mainly to the child, and the advice is addressed
to the parents. And this is because of the very different nature of the
contacts that the re-educator has to maintain with the parents on
the one hand and the children on the other.

THE PARENTS

From the beginning of re-educative treatment, contact with the
parents runs into a difficulty whose importance must be emphasized.

Generally the parents come to the consultation with a preconceived notion that the entire fault is the child's. No explanations,
however precise, can dissuade the parents of this falsely justifying
idea since they are based on the ambivalences to which all false
motivations are subject.

It is obvious that long before having sought re-educative help,
the failure of their method of education must have put the parents
repeatedly in a state of vague guilt from which they have tried to
free themselves from by pinning it on each other. Quarrels about
what educational method should be used are among the most
frequent type. Yet, in the background of these mutual accusations
lies a glimmer of understanding of the true nature of the fault, at
least insofar as it was imputed to the other, because in fact what the
parents are reproaching each other for is being too strict or too
compliant with the child (struggle for influence).

But beyond these revelatory quarrels, the common need for
exculpation has brought them to agree on the idea that the fault
resides in the child's unfortunate nature. The generalized need for
such pseudoconsolation—the projection of the fault on heredity—
forcefully proves the all-inclusiveness of the tendency toward
repression. For this supposition—even though partially legitimate—is bound to put an end to all hope. By abolishing responsibility, such exculpation merely serves to transfer the fault onto a
plane where it seems irremediable. Once it is projected onto the
plane of heredity, the parents' sense of guilt is alleviated, but their

disappointment over the child is aggravated. As a result, it often happens that parents do not hesitate to blame each other for the hereditary fault that has been transmitted to the child.

The entire hope for the success of re-education rests in the fact that revelation of the existence of a possible educational error contains in itself the remedy for any nascent resistance: the idea of a possibility for improvement arouses hope. Moreover, it would be a mistake not to emphasize the fact that faced by the realization of responsibility one or the other parent spontaneously confesses that he or she has for a long time been doubtful about his claim to innocence. This docility is increased to the extent that a vague sense of guilt becomes precise. Why shouldn't each of the parents be relieved on learning that the fault is not exclusively his, the spouse's, or the child's? Instead of vexed vanity, which compels one to reject the fault completely, there comes into being at first a feeling of reconciliation based on the prospect of a common effort.

The pact proposed to the parents initiates them in an experience that demands their active participation with a view to relaxing the tense family atmosphere. The success of the treatment depends to a large degree on the parents' collaboration. The contact obtained during the first session is a basis that can be consolidated and expanded to the extent where the parents' contribution creates the favorable conditions for a common experience in which not only the parents are united but also the re-educator and the child are brought together. The parents' promise to adhere to the rules of the experience will be strengthened or disintegrated depending on their active participation or their sabotage. It would be imprudent not to take into account the possibility of sabotage because, from the moment they enter the treatment, the parents' motivations, as has just been emphasized, will vacillate more or less between a sense of guilt and vexed vanity. Complete sabotage is rare. It could only be the consequence of an excessive need for self-justification, which may be due to unrestrainable vanity, or a perverse servitude that is imperiously opposed to the experience of reconciliation (alcoholism, adultery, etc.). In such a case, the tendency to more or less conscious devaluation possibly may prevail over the impression produced by the analytical explanation of responsibility.

Subconsciously ambivalent sabotage is more frequent. The parents would like the treatment to be successful, and at the same time they hope for its failure. They refuse to accept the idea that a stranger may succeed where they, the parents, who know their child so much better, have failed. The sabotage will permit them to conclude that the proposed experience is unrealizable and that the re-educator was wrong in appealing to their responsibility. It must be taken into account that, in the common experience, the role of the re-educator is in a certain sense easier than that of the parents, whose self-love is put to a severe test. Outside the sessions, they see themselves exposed to the attacks of the child, whose unruliness at the beginning remains insufficiently checked. The thoughtful consideration that the parents try to impose on themselves will seem an unbearable humiliation, a surrender to the child's whims. It may even be true that they are not completely wrong in suspecting the child of taking advantage of the situation and defying them more or less consciously. If they control their aggressive intonations, their facial signals will betray their underlying indignation. This will provoke the child's maliciousness, and even his need for triumph, which will possibly lead him to being abusive. The re-educative pact would soon collapse if the love parents and children have for each other were not at bottom a more powerful sentiment than the resentments that separate them. If one must not neglect the obsessive power of false motivations, one must not imagine them to be all-powerful either.

The tendency to subconscious sabotage is present in the children as well as in the parents. The triangular experience developed among re-educator, parents, and child can only succeed if, on the one hand, the parents understand even in their inner motivation the necessity for controlling the resentments, as much for their own good as for the child's, and if, on the other hand, the re-educator manages as rapidly as possible to prevent the child from taking advantage of the new situation. Thus he will help the parents to avoid sinking deeper into their feeling of humiliation.

Any sign of impatience on the part of the re-educator risks aggravating the parents' humiliation and transforming it into vexation. It would be a mistake to try to ward off this danger by taking an attitude of emotional indulgence; it would only help to intensify the parents' self-justification. Both of these attitudes in regard to the parents would set off their resistance which, sooner or later, would be transformed into sabotage.

The parents' situation in respect to the treatment is thus characterized by two forms of humiliation from which they must be freed; pain over their educational failure, and vexation at having to submit to the educational demands. The first existed before the treatment; the second is occasioned by the treatment and inspires sabotage. The latter is merely a vexation of self-love, while the pre-existent humiliation has deep roots in the biological demands of parental love. By that very fact it becomes the best prop for the treatment in its fight against sabotage. In order to mobilize it to the treatment's advantage, one must understand its general circumstances and details. It is therefore important to fully discern in all of its depth the humiliation that the parents—confronted by their educational failure—have long suffered before seeking re-educational help. The meaning of the parents' life is prolonged in the life of the child. Parental love plunges its roots into the drive to surpass. The parents hope that the child will continue the effort of their life and that it will surpass them because of its success. To the degree that the parents fulfill the meaning of their life—the educative task included—the hoped-for surpassing will go hand in hand with the flowering of the child's own life.

For nervous parents, the child is not a being who has the right to his own life and the flowering of his own qualities. They project on the child their unrealized desire for surpassing, concentrated in an exalted task that has transcended their own abilities. They will demand an achievement from the child that threatens to be beyond his abilities. This vanity-inspired projection of the parents' sense of guilt results in the fact that for them the child from whom they demand this perfect achievement is simply a final means of self-justification. The overwrought love for the child is degraded into a subconscious obsession that remains egocentric and will decay into a sentimental and accusatory form. As the repository of the parents' exalted hopes, the child will be coddled as if he were the most exceptional being, or harassed so that he will become, in spite of himself, the most exceptional being. But in the end the spoiled child, just like the harassed child, will disappoint his parents.

There are cases in which the most blatant disappointments will not awaken the parents from the beatific hope they have placed in the child, and this clearly attests to the subconscious basis of such projected admiration. Here the fault is never the child's but always that of the uncomprehending world. Seeing himself justified on all occasions, the child cannot fail to become a self-justifier deprived of all possibility of pinpointing the error. More often, however, the hope placed in the child is diametrically reversed and becomes overwrought despair. Falsely justifying admiration is transformed into abusive incriminatiion. The parents' repressed feeling of guilt in regard to their own deficiencies is exteriorized and activated, transferred to the child in the form of punishment. Because of the transference, the punishment goes beyond all real and logical justification. In order to protect himself from these excessive accusations and punishments, the child has recourse to exculpatory lies. Soon he becomes accustomed to denying any fault, not only in front of others but to himself.

It is not surprising that this transference of an exalted task is observed most frequently in the case of an only child. Here the transference is not the result of a preference that can choose among several children, it is unilateral and spectacular. In families with several children complications arise that are liable to disguise the phenomenon. Transference in the form of hope and overwrought disappointment will become the secretly hidden motive of favoritism. Each of the parents will fix his or her transference—according to the nature of the secret overexalted task—on the child who seems the most likely to realize it. The fixation does not need to be definitive. It can be shifted from one child to another, if, for example, the favorite child adopts, due to the struggle among the siblings, an attitude of resignation and abulia. The constellations are greatly diverse, and motives of a secondary order but spectacularly manifest will not fail to affect the choice of the favorite child.

One of the most frequent reasons for this change of direction is caused by the fact that in the nervous family the father or mother often prefers the child of the opposite sex. Ambitious exaltations and idealistic aspirations have different nuances in man and woman, hence the supposition that normally the boy should seem more suited to the father and the girl more suited to the mother as regards the realization of the imposed task and the hopes that cling to it. But because of the love-hate that reigns between the parents and also provokes their imaginary divorce, sexuality—often in part unsatisfied—has a pronounced tendency to deviate toward surrogate consolations. The subconscious path of the deviation leads more frequently then one suspects—above all when the banal outlet to sexual adventure is blocked by a sense of guilt—toward a consolatory fixation, the overwrought love for the child of the opposite sex. The imaginative exaltation in search of an ideal sexual partner tends to become confused with the idealization of the child, heir to the exalted task. The subconscious confusion of these two forms of vanity-inspired projection is prepared by the fact that they are both the result of a repressed sense of guilt. The state of confusion, which leads to the exaggerated preference of a child of the opposite sex, can sweep the parents into expressions of love which go far beyond parental affection in its natural form. Such expressions, even while they trouble the child, are nevertheless experienced as an invitation to complicity, an invitation that the child, hungry for esteem and love, will be unable to resist. The complicity to which he lends himself definitively destroys the parents' authority. Between the child and the parent who attempts to win him over will be established a triumphant conspiracy directed against the other members of the family. The child will try to take advantage of the docility of the accomplice parent and obtain from him or her justification for his infringements of discipline, and this will only provoke the siblings' spiteful rebellion and the angry interventions of the parent excluded from the conspiracy, who moreover is generally the protector and accomplice of another child.

In the case of an only child, the frustrating attitude of one of the parents is often provoked by the other parent who has been able to win over the child. Very often the two parents, struggling over the child, come to be dependent on his good opinion and the favors he may condescend to grant them. Preferential choice is exercised not only by the parents but also by the child. The child alternately grants his favors and endeavors to widen the gap between the parents in order to manipulate them better. He will try to obtain in turn from one of the other parent submissive protection and the justification of his faults.

But transference of the exalted task is not diverted only in the direction of a sexually nuanced preferential choice. Perverse derangement is equally manifest on the material plane.

Preoccupation over the child's future social position is certainly justified since it involves the basis of material security. But in the end exacerbation of this preoccupation and excessive demands regarding duties—the most frequent cause for complaints and reproaches, expanded into interminable sermons—is merely an unhealthy obsession, the indubitable sign of its deep rooting. It is in the subconscious of the parents that vanity-inspired idealistic aspirations are transformed into purely material ambitions. This degradation of vital impulse is most frequent among adults. Nervous parents, often suffering from relative social defeat, will tend to play the role of disinterested idealists, while all the while projecting onto the child their deranged impulse, degraded into secretly exalted ambition. This projection is expressed not like sexual deviation in an amorous and sentimental form but rather in the form of aggressive accusation if the child does not live up to the exalted hopes placed in him. Exalted aggression is often linked—in an unconfessed and unconfessable manner—to the parents' material preoccupations (grounded in fact or imaginatively overwrought) and to the hope of overcoming them or being relieved of them by the child's material success. The disappointment will be exacerbated because the degradation of the parents' vital impulse provokes the collapse of the child's vital impulse; this is the most profound cause of the degradation of his love into unavowable hate. Hate for the parents that cannot be admitted is transferred to the duties that the parents impose.

The parents' suffering is much deeper than one thinks, because it is linked to the worst but also the best in themselves, to the drive to surpass that has remained unsatisfied and subject to deviations, a drive that is projected upon the children.

Since the parents' resistances are rooted in what is worst in them, it would be imprudent to neglect the possibility of sabotage. But at the same time: since the child's recovery corresponds to what is the best in his parents—to their vital impulse insofar as it has remained intact—the contact once established will in most cases lead to a sufficient collaboration.

It is evidently a matter of not revealing to the parents the profound enrootment of their sufferings. Such a revelation would only produce difficulties that would be impossible to deal with during the very limited time that can be devoted to parents during a treatment of children in a re-education center. But precisely because of this limitation, the re-educator—in order not to lose himself in arbitrary interpretations—must know the overwrought currents of hope and disappointment that are produced in nervous families, and must at the same time be able to distinguish them from the dramatic screen of deviations of a sexual or material nature. He must know that the parents' complaints and reproaches are in the last analysis rooted in their vanity and their sense of guilt.

Knowledge of the true causes of the parents' troubles allows one to proceed economically both in the precision of the inquiries as well as in the doling out of explanations and advice. This is all the more indispensable since, taken up by their occupations, the parents—above all the father—are usually unable to come regularly to the consultations. Of course, the lack of time may be only an excuse. Abstention—whatever the reason may be—compels one to be satisfied with the exchange of reports on conduct or telephone calls that signify, lacking anything better, a certain degree of the parents' collaboration and their opinion on the child's behavior. Even where the reason for abstention is to avoid such consultations, the parents' attitude has often changed a great deal on the basis of past interviews, so as not to endanger decisively the continuance of re-educative work with the child. A minimum of the parents' collaboration is indispensable. Without an improvement in their provocative attitude, the child will not give up his obstinacy, which may even finally extend to the re-educator.

The risk is not however the same for all children. It varies in intensity according to the case and age. It lessens from thirteen to fourteen years and becomes almost negligible in adolescents. The capacity for understanding and independence with regard to the parents has by then been acquired to a degree sufficient to permit an in-depth analysis similar to that of the adults.

This does not exclude the fact that—whatever the children's age may be—the contact between re-educator and the family milieu is always desirable. It is indispensable to emphasize the difficulties encountered by re-education and to acknowledge that they are created mainly by the parents. But it is also right to observe that such difficulties can almost always be overcome, and that in truth, in the majority of cases, parents lend themselves with much application and understanding to the re-educational task, which demands a common effort.

It is of capital importance to add that the analysis of motivations can avail itself of a tool that—to the greatest extent possible—renders it independent of any verbal or written communications supplied by the parents concerning the progress achieved by the children under treatment.

This precious tool is the analysis of dreams.

Parents play a preponderant role not only in the dreams of the children but also in those of the adults.

The problem consists in knowing whether these parental images are symbols with a hidden meaning and revelatory as to the nature of the inner conflict. If this is the case, it is clear that the re-educational technique, in order to be complete, should be in a position to disclose the revelatory significance of the parental images as well as that of all other symbols appearing in the dream. The purpose of the present work is to report on an educational experience based on the study of motivations. The fact is that in this experience the translation of dreams occupies a prominent place. It is, therefore, necessary to sum up—as briefly as possible—the contribution of the study of motives to the problem of the interpretation of dreams and, more specifically, the meaning of the parental images.

Considered from the point of view of the study of motives, the dream is a continuation of diurnal deliberation. The psychic system, when it is attacked by contradictory motivations, cannot successfully elaborate the liberating decision. The conflict of motives continues to agitate the psyche, and this state of emotion extends into nocturnal sleep. During sleep the conflict can express itself only oneirically. Often, after awakening, the subject retains the memory of images that appeared to him in his dream, and his account contains the nocturnal deliberation expressed in images. The dream images therefore form a facade which has a hidden meaning; they are symbols. Because of this, the methodical interpretation of dreams is possible. The method consists in replacing the images with their hidden meaning: the calculation of satisfaction, the conflict of motivations.

In the present hypothesis, parental images symbolize the often deforming influence that the real parents have exerted on the dreamer's inner motivations. But to this meaning, which is of incidental importance, is added another, more profound meaning. The parent-educators should have guided the child toward sensible accomplishment. Now this accomplishment consists in harmonizing desires, in surmounting the conflict between the guiding intellect and sexual and material desires (matter: *mater terra*). The parental images thus acquire a mythically profound significance; they symbolize the ideal of harmonization by means of the couple "Father Spirit"—"Mother Earth."

In the parental images is thus condensed the false motivation symbolized by the real parents, and the just motivation symbolized by the mythical parents.

When the dreamer is undergoing treatment, the significance of the parental images is amplified. The re-educational shock imparted to motivations echoes in depth and manifests itself even in one's nocturnal deliberations. The parental images serve to symbolize acceptance of or resistance to the treatment, the vision—be it negative or positive—that the analysand has of psychology, as personified by the psychologist. The therapist takes the place of the educative function that the real parents should have assumed, and thus fulfills the function of guide toward the mind. The result of this is that the dreamer identifies the re-educator now with his real parents, who inhibit his desires, now with the mythical parents, symbols of the aspiration to a harmonious and healthy flowering.

One example will help us to better discern this process of the oneiric personification of just and false motivations.

In an analysand's dream, the re-educator is seen in the guise of a day laborer. His intervention is accused of being the same as that of the real parents who have "belabored" (scolded, crushed) the child. Furthermore, the image contains an allusion to the fact that the dreamer's parents when he was a child have (belabored, cut down) his vital impulse with their excessive prohibitions that have merely succeeded in exalting-inhibiting his earthly desires. The dreamer feels that he is being pushed into the ground: earth to earth). Now, the images "dragged through the dirt," "stuck in the mud," etc. (by extension, for example, "trapped in the muddy or swampy ground"), are frequent in myth to symbolize the spiritual sloth that opposes the effort at elevation. But the day laborer is also "a builder of roads." The re-educator is thus recognized as a person who fills the function of the mythical father. He is the personification of the guiding mind. He guides the analytical intellect through extraconscious paths (superconscious and subconscious). He builds roads of comprehension and thus reconstructs the vital impulse which has been dragged through the dirt.

While it is impossible to go deeper into the matter, one observation is absolutely necessary: the re-educative technique cannot be presented without talking about the symbolic personification of motives in action, as found in dreams. A special study of the relationship between extraconscious motivations and the symbolism of dreams remains to be carried out. But symbolic images are often identical in nocturnal dreams and mythical dreams. It must therefore be emphasized that more abundant information on the subject will be found in my work *Symbolism in Greek Mythology*. In myths, parental images have one peculiarity: they have been hypostatized into helpful or hostile divinities. However, this peculiarity is not exclusive. Just like the nocturnal dream, the mythical dream—in order to symbolize the conflict of motivations—uses the parental images represented by the real parents. With regard to this, see above all my interpretation of the Oedipus myth in *Symbolism in Greek Mythology*.

The fact that the image of the real parents appears as a symbol of distortion even in the dreams of nervous adults demonstrates how great the influence of educational error is on the motives of children.

THE CHILDREN

The essential effort of re-education is concentrated on work with the child.

The success of the treatment depends on the contact that the re-educator is able to establish with the child so as to obtain his collaboration in the common experience.

In order to prevent the collapse of the pact made with the parents, it is important to put an end as quickly as possible to the child's underhanded provocations.

The most precious time would be wasted if in his work with the child the re-educator were to deal first of all with the badly adapted behavior revealed by the parents' complaints. Seen from the point of view of behavior, this poor adaptation appears as an incoherent crumbling of character traits. The essential thing is to be able to reduce the scattered traits to their common motivating cause in order to attack them effectively and economically.

Starting with the whole gamut of deficient motives, each child develops the distinctive traits that allow him to adapt well or badly to the unhealthy situation. Since false motives are divided into four ambivalent groups, each deficient character trait belongs to one of the categories.

Vanity is manifested through these character traits: need for triumph, irritability, impertinence, smugness, arrogance, fatuousness, pretensions, egotism, spirit of contradiction, illusory ambitions, boastful lies, etc. *Repressed guilt* is manifested by exculpatory lies, timidity, scrupulousness, meticulousness, loss of vital impulse, etiolation, laziness, anxiety at being judged, condemned, punished, etc. *Accusation* is manifested by reactions of aggressiveness: outbursts of irritation, indignation, angry explosions, spiteful rumination, slanderous lies, wickedness, principled disobedience, need for revenge, playing the clown or the dunce, rejection of contact, plans of escape, flight, etc. *Sentimentality* becomes manifest through an attitude of submission, hypocrisy and cowardice, pity for oneself and others, the need for protection and to play the protector's role, renunciation of play with peers in order to be praised and loved by the parents, exclusive devotion to duty, the need to be exemplary, talebearing, playing the baby or sick child, etc.

To the multitude of character traits are added the symbolic expressions of false motivation, tics and obsessive attitudes, as for example: bed wetting (protest against frustration), somnambulism (subconscious search for affection), nail biting (guilt and impotent rage), obsessive stealing in order to buy sweets, which symbolize the withheld affection, or to buy the esteem of one's peers with gifts, etc. (However, the explanations outlined here are insufficient, because these illogical traits of character are the result of a condensation of vanity, guiltiness, accusation and sentimentality.)

What a waste of time it is to attack one by one the obvious traits of bad adaptation instead of analyzing the multiform ensemble starting with the common roots in the calculation of satisfaction.

It must be emphasized that precision of explanation, even if it finds support in the categorized table of motives, achieves excellence thanks to flexibility. Manifest bad adaptation whose secret motive must be found is characterized by its rigidity as much as by its instability. Handled without flexibility, the categorized distinction would run the risk of becoming arbitrary. It would already be somewhat arbitrary to place too exclusively and definitively this or that character trait in this or that category of motives. The categories are not static but dynamic and tirelessly change into each other: vanity in its triumphant and vexed forms already contains the accusatory devaluation of others and thereby infallibly leads to sentimental grievance, the expression of guilty impotence.

The possibility of the treatment's success resides in the fact that the transforming dynamics not only function according to the law of ambivalence that governs the perversions. Behind the screen of perversions stands the quality that is distorted by exaltation and inhibition. Vanity is the unhealthy exaltation of the drive to surpass, and this exaltation corresponds to guilty inhibition; accusation is an unhealthy surpassing of the need for justice that, as a result of excitation, deviates into aggrieved inhibition. Deprived of justice, the child plunges into the supreme fault, false justification. The exalted need for justice is transformed into an unjust provocation condensed in character traits.

The basis of the technique—knowledge of the inner tangle of motives and the inter-reactive intrigue resulting from it—is a condition for the effectiveness of every treatment, whatever the children's age. This knowledge dictates the method's variation.

With children under twelve, the contact is preferably established with the help of drawing, clay modeling, etc., which offer the opportunity to discover deficiencies and whims, from which point the explanation of motives can be presented in a still impersonal manner. For example, the educator will tell the story of children with an analogous deficiency, taking care to give prominence (not too markedly, however) to the ambivalences of the secret motivation and to provocations directed at parents, brothers, sisters, and peers. Narrative precision will be most easily obtained by choosing examples from among previously treated cases, and this will permit one to demonstrate how the child chosen as an example has slowly freed himself from his perturbations and sufferings. A sufficient knowledge of the secret motives and the resulting provocations will even permit the reconstruction of the history of the child under treatment, through projecting it on a fictional "hero." In all cases, it is a matter of working with fine successive touches that gradually come together in a history as the child begins to ask questions about the fate of the fictitious little hero, the sign that he is beginning to identify with him, and this will introduce the beginning of reflective introspection into his imaginative ruminations.

Ruminations can be combatted only by a clarifying explanation suited to the child's degree of mature comprehension. Precisely for this reason, the explanation is fully effective when its content of truth can be transmitted in a condensed manner and without narrative disguise. This is generally possible starting at the age of twelve.

The purpose of the explanation is to introduce new determinants in deliberation. Only purified self-determination will result in the purification of false habitual reactions condensed in character traits.

It is a profound error to believe that the child is not capable of listening and understanding. On the contrary, he listens with the most concentrated attention. Generally he is more capable than the adult of understanding his errors and faults, because his false justifications are not yet solidified in a rigid system. The child is eager to understand, provided however that his faults are not revealed to him as reproaches, but with a view to giving him friendly asssistance. Can one imagine the ineffable confusion of the child who, without being able to explain to himself what is happening to him, feels that he is becoming more and more lost in the labyrinth of intimate entanglements and the vicious circle of provocations? The explanatory lifting of repression interests him to the highest degree because it frees him from his anguished disorientation.

However, one must not overlook the child's often very deep distrust, the consequence of his disorientation.

In order to establish contact with the child as quickly as possible, it is important to tell him from the first session of the change in the situation, a change brought about by the pact between re-educator and parents. The child will understand that this pact gives him a capital of trust that he must not waste.

Establishing contact with the child is a much more delicate task than the approach to the parents. For the parents, re-education is a profession that they cannot fail to respect. As ambivalent as their attitude may be, it will be difficult for them not to admit the re-educator's professional competence at the first approach. Nothing of the sort is true with the child. For him the re-educator is merely a strange and intimidating adult on whom he will tend to project all the distrust acquired with his parents as educators and sermonizers.

The child's motives are much more slyly hidden than those of the parents. His bad intentions, his false calculations are masked by sentimentality and are not exteriorized as accusations. There are exceptions. But the rule is that the child does not complain about his parents. Instead he projects them against the stranger. The child is prevented from accusing them overtly, much less by fear of punishment than by the love that despite everything he has for his parents. His wounded love is not strong enough to suppress the outburst of his rebellious disobedience, but it still remains strong enough to fill him with a profound guilt that—in contrast to his parents—prevents him from complaining and confiding in the re-educator.

Thus it is important from the first moment of contact to overcome the child's distrust and protect oneself against his slyness. Now, it is precisely the child's guilty distrust, even though it renders approach difficult, that makes it possible to establish the in-depth contact. The child's guilt is in a sense more authentic than that of the parents. It is not imaginative willfulness but true suffering. The child is much less skillful than the adult in manipulating false vanity-inspired justifications and accusatory projections. But above all the child's guilt is not yet—like that of the nervous adults—the capricious residue of an exalted task that has remained unfulfilled. The child's disappointment, unlike that of his parents, concerns not past life but the world that is waiting for him, the life he is entering. He has hoped it would be beautiful and pure, and he collides with its mean-spirited aspects. Undoubtedly that is merely one of life's aspects; but in an affectively disunited family it is the only aspect the child encounters. His hope is transformed into inadmissable and inexpressible turmoil.

The invitation to participate in the pact made with the parents offers the child the opportunity to come out of his turmoil and free himself from a sense of guilt.

But the child will not admit his faults or remedy them unless he is sure that his parents will show him a way and an example. The child knows perfectly what it is he has suffered. He knows, yet without being able to formulate it, that his suffering comes from the sum of scoldings to which he has been exposed, and from the sense of guilt at having provoked them.

It would, however, be imprudent to reveal explicitly his parents' fault to the child.

Now, the pact made with the parents implicitly contains the admission of their fault (the sermons that have become unbearable to the child for lack of an edifying example) and the promise to remedy it. The child understands the implicit promise, and impulse rewakens in the hope that his effort will meet with that of his parents. It is essential that the efforts come together: *that they begin at the same time on the part of the child as well as of the parents*, and that they are sustained by the re-educational assistance.

In the triangular pact are thus united all the conditions necessary for a renewal, conditions indispensable to rewaken the child's vital impulse and to found the contact on the desire for liberation from his sense of guilt.

The pact makes it possible to urge the child to revise his own faults without it being necessary to trouble him with the explanation of the parents' fault. The child understands the underlying admissions, and this is enough to overcome his reticence and prepare him to listen attentively to the revelation of his own deficiencies and their motivations. Without this preparation, which consists in the explanation of the unique opportunity offered him, the risk would be great that the child would only lend a distracted ear to the re-educator and confuse all that is said to him with the sermons to which for a long time now he has become accustomed *not* to listen.

The invitation to participate actively in the pact offers the child an unhoped-for promise of satisfaction that—a capital point—*appears to him realizable sooner or later thanks to his own efforts* and which is addressed to what he holds dear above all else: reconciliation with his parents. With all his reanimated impulse, the child understands the opportunity offered to free himself from the torment of his sense of guilt and at the same time from the unbearable regime of inculpation.

It is indispensable to make available to the child from the beginning through his inclusion in the pact a source of deserved and realizable satisfactions—to the extent of his efforts—that occur in the near future, because the entire familial and scholastic situation of the maladjusted child is characterized by the conflict between short-term and long-term satisfactions: play and work. As a result of their being opposed too radically, these satisfactions become static and contradictory instead of being dynamic and complementary. *Satisfactions are degraded into dissatisfactions: play is infiltrated by a sense of guilt, and work simply takes on the aspect of hated duty.*

This profound disruption of the dynamic process of maturation has already been mentioned. But it is of great importance that we return to it because the entire re-educative technique rests on understanding it. For the in-depth contact to take place it is indispensable that from the first approach the re-educator be able to communicate to the child the feeling that he is offered help to free himself from his most secretly hidden turmoil. This turmoil resides in the deviation of the calculation of satisfaction, because of the pleasure–duty opposition. Step by step, this deviation extends from early childhood to an adult age. It successively affects all inter-human relationships: familial, scholastic, sexual, professional. *The conflict between immediate satisfactions and distant satisfactions runs through all ages. It is the cause of all character deformations.* Whatever the child's age, the comprehension of this common cause of maladaptation guides the treatment. It dictates the variation of explanations liable to be understood and prescribes the measures to be taken not only to improve the family atmosphere but also to alleviate the child's situation vis-à-vis his peers and teachers.

The child's calculation of satisfaction does not as yet concern the choice between sensible and senseless, healthy and unhealthy. Obedience includes the renunciation of immediate but temporary satisfactions, even if they are sensible, in favor of a later and durable satisfaction. Obedience thus prefigures ethical conduct. In the child, this aspect involves the mobilization of energy for school work. But all through life the performance of work—independent of the external success it envisages—implies a voluntarily assumed discipline and thereby an inner success of ethical significance. The prize of satisfaction consists in work well done. It concerns not only the final success but also the organization of the stages, the concentration of effort, the pleasure of the harmonious functioning of the faculties throughout the effort.

These qualities should develop during childhood; their deploy-ment is one of the conditions of maturity. At an early age the child sees only immediate satisfactions: pleasure and play, and protection through the love of his parents. The child will at one time renounce the satisfaction he finds in play in favor of the satisfaction of being praised, and he will at another time prefer the dissatisfaction of being blamed to the dissatisfaction of renouncing play. It is only at school age that the feeling of duty becomes well defined. School work demands a repeated and prolonged renunciation of the plea-sure of play. At the beginning of school activity, the motives that prompt the child to work will still be determined by his love for his parents, the purveyors of praise and blame. The pleasure of work is the discovery the child will be able to make only on the condition that he healthily negotiates the stages of maturation that will progressively lead him toward an equilibrium between the satisfac-tions found in limited play and accomplished duty. These balanced satisfactions will gradually detach him from the infantile regime of praise and blame. The child remains maladjusted to the extent in which he fails to find immediate pleasure in the accomplishment of orderly and organized work. Play and work do not achieve a balance. The principal cause of maladjustment resides in affective backwardness provoked by parents who do not cease hounding the child with their praise and blame. The child remains fixed on forms of stimulation pertaining to an earlier age. Concerned with their own satisfaction, which they can see only in the child's distant social position, the parents, incapable of granting praise and blame with an even hand, use them as a means of pressure to harness the child to work and steer it away from play. Praise becomes rare and blame degenerates into sermons and phrases such as: "What will become of you?" Trying to stimulate a love for work by speaking to the child of a distant utilitarian and professional future is to commit a serious mistake: it means to perturb his calculation of satisfaction. By neglecting the immediate satisfactions which for the child reside in the alternation of play and organized work, and which will dynamically lead him toward a long-term, satisfactory result, the parents, too impatient, only obtain immediate defeat. For the child, the professional future has very little appeal; he lives in the present. The devaluation of play and the praises of work will cause him to see only work's forbidding aspect, duty imposed without love. Cut off from the love of work and the love of his parents, the child will pour all of his vital impulse into the love of play. In vain the parents will try to prevent the child from taking the only path of immediate satisfaction left to him. Threats of sanctions may result in his becoming harnessed to his work-duty. But it will only make him detest it even more and, deprived of real play, *he will stray into imaginative play.* Drowning in escapist and justificatory fantasies, the child will not evolve: he will become affectively backward.

The whole tragedy of childhood resides in this relationship of derangement that exists among forbidden real play—imposed work—wandering off in imagination. The innumerable complications that often lead to catastrophe are only derivatives of this. It is most important to shed light on this central knot, in order to deduce from it with all desirable clarity the re-educational remedy. This consists in recovering the vital impulse badly invested in imaginary play and properly distributing it over the entire gamut of healthy and immediate satisfactions: the love of real play, love of work well done, love of the parents. Thanks to a sensible organization of the child's work and play, his reconciliation with the parents will be accomplished.

The first measure to be taken in order to consolidate the contact with the child consists therefore in getting the parents to organize play and sports. As for the organization of the child's work, this will be the goal of the re-educator, who will pursue it during the interviews once rapport with the child is well established. Of course this goal consists not in teaching a method of adaptation to the scholastic program—at least not at first—but rather in eliminating the secret motives and character traits that cause the child to see only detested duty in work. It is a matter of combatting imaginative reveries—the escape into play (or the flight from play)—and rancorous self-justifications, the causes of obsessive disobedience. What prevents the child from healthily concentrating either on play or work is his profound dissatisfaction: the splotch of his sense of guilt. When he plays, he feels guilty about neglecting his work, and when he wants to work he is overcome by guilt because, lacking concentration as he does, his memory and his intelligence refuse to perform properly.

True satisfaction—both immediate and long-term—can consist for the child only in harmony between play and work. Thanks to it, there will be established an exchange of healthy satisfactions between child and parents: the child will be satisfied with his parents because they are not excessively opposed to his play, and the parents will be satisfied with the child because he is not necessarily opposed to the duties that they must exact from him.

After contact is established, the re-educative sessions follow that are destined to lead the child out of his affective floundering and confusion and adapt him again to reality.

Re-adaptation would be impossible without the creation of a new reality, more promising in satisfactions than the old regime under which the child lived. The re-educator will exhaust himself to no avail whatsoever if he does not succeed at the very start in awakening the child's vital impulse through the creation of a new situation whose two indispensable conditions—it is not superfluous to repeat this—consist in blocking off the insidious provocations and organizing the child's leisure time.

It is rare that a single session will suffice to establish adequately this indispensable basis for treatment, for often there are resistances to overcome in the parents as well as in the child.

Accustomed to granting leisure only as a reward for work performed (and this is precisely the cause of the vicious circle, composed of naggings and the refusal to work), the parents believe that the child already plays too much and that he does not work enough to have the right to amuse himself. They often give proof of a certain lack of good will as regards the organization of entertainment; it is also true that they often lack the time to deal with it. As for the child too lost in play, he will hesitate to abandon the company of the peers who drag him along, whom he wishes to follow, while the abulic child will claim that he does not care for collective games since he is afraid of appearing clumsy and ridiculous in them. It is very important to free the former from the baneful allurement with his peers, and to lead the latter preferably toward collective, organized games (scout troops, sports, etc.). These initial reticences will gradually give way when faced by the explanation of their underlying motives.

The fact is that affectively backward children are badly adapted not only to work but also to play. This is true for the turbulent and rebellious child as well as for the apparently docile and submissive child. The first child seems better adapted to play, the second seems to prefer work. These are only appearances.

The *dunce*, for example, enjoys terrorizing his peers, especially if he is physically stronger. Excluded from collective play, he gets together with one or more other children of his ilk. Excluded from the esteem of their parents, their companions and teachers, the dunces are all the more eager to gain the esteem of their peers whom they mutually incite to surpass each other by feats of unruliness which are merely boastful and too dearly paid for by punishments. Although repressed by provocative jauntiness, the underlying regret is often immense. In a good many cases, the child can be restored to health provided the central circumstances and details of his false calculation of satisfaction are uncovered and he is helped to successfully overcome the barriers that enclose him in his deviation to such a point that without therapeutic help he would no longer even dare to consider the possibility of recovery. The fact is that among such types of backward children one finds the cases most difficult to treat. Some of these subjects are brutal and not very intelligent, which does not favor adaptation to disciplined play or to the discipline of work.

Another type of backward child, frantic for amusement and yet ill-adapted to play, is the *clown*. He does not terrorize his companions, but he is the teacher's terror. Living under a regime of exemplary sanctions inflicted by teachers who dread him, he is furthermore deprived of the affection of his disappointed parents, who add their punishments to those of the teachers, hoping thus to force him to get down to work. They only manage to plunge him deeper into escapist play, and this makes him unfit for any prolonged effort at concentration. His need for distraction is unleashed at school, where he cannot sit quietly for hours on end and follow the lessons attentively. His inability to concentrate joins with the senseless calculation of obtaining the love and esteem of his peers by offering them a distraciton with his clowning. But this perverse calculation does not lead to the expected satisfactions. By his obstinate submission to his peers' good opinion, the clown, far from obtaining esteem, only collects the contempt of the class. His companions encourage him to perservere in his absurd intention to amuse them. But they will not fail to betray him by underlining his misdeeds with exaggerated laughter or by other means attracting the attention of the teacher, whose punitive intervention will prolong the desired amusement. The vain culprit will see in the attitude of the class the sought-for tribute of admiration. Alone in vainly overestimating himself, he will persist in his senseless behavior, not knowing how to connect causes with effects, the central circumstances (false motives) to the ramified details (downpour of sanctions and everyone's contempt).

In contrast to these types of rebellious children, there are the different types of submissive children. Besides, the two groups are not radically separate. They are linked by successive gradations. Bad adaptation is almost always due to a mixture of rebellious and submissive traits. For example, the clown is subjected to his peers by his eagerness for play, and he rebels against his parents and teachers, who impose duties. The opposite type is the *vanity-inspired exemplary child*. Submissive to parents and teachers and anxious for their esteem, he withdraws from his peers. His renunciation with regard to collective play can go so far as pronounced hostility. Avoiding his companions, the child is riveted to his desk. Not having acquired the reflexes that would permit him to enter into competition on the plane of play, he accuses his companions of brutality. His vexed vanity will seek triumph on the plane of scholastic competition. He can be successful in this by cultivating more and more a bookish intelligence at the expense of the impulse for flowering. A bad companion, he will always avoid collective punishment; he does not want to be the "scapegoat" for others. Only his notebooks count. The contempt his companions have for him continues to grow and pushes him further and further toward the solitary satisfaction sought in exemplary behavior, a path that would ultimately seem arid to him if the parents and teachers' continuous compliments did not encourage him to perservere and vainly go astray on it. The frustration of play and the stifling of the feeling of humanity—which should have been exercised in his relations with companions—will mark him forever. Eager for esteem, throughout his life he will try to find it in titles and honors. He is apt to become a man with a dessicated soul, submissive to every convention. In adulthood, this affectively backward type can be found on all the rungs of social success. During the re-educative consultations, one never meets this type of child. It is nevertheless indispensable to present his diagnosis here because the re-educator will often enough have dealings with parents who were in the past exemplary children. Whether men or women, they supply the most dangerous type of frustrating parent. One might say that they wish to avenge themselves on their children for their own frustrated childhood. Their battle cry: "Duty comes first," makes them crushing for their children. By the rebellion they provoke they harvest the belated sanction of their conventional exemplary behavior. The mixture of moralism and unscrupulous ambition that characterizes such parents results in their being comfortably installed in common opinion and public approval. The vanity of a success obtained at the price of renunciations of which they are proud blinds them to their defeat on the human plane. Walled in on all sides, they prove reticent and hostile to re-educative help, even though they have been compelled to have recourse to it.

What is more, this infantile deviation of submission to duty and the renunciation of play is likely to result in an inversion that will become explosively manifest in adolescence as an irresistible frenzy for amusement and distraction. Nervous inhibition is replaced by the banalizing lack of inhibition. Rebellion wins out over submission. This ambivalent reversal is too well known for us to dwell on it. This unrestrained seesaw will, however, remain a rather rare and isolated attitude, except during a period in which certain deviations of public opinion favor it due to the destruction of the sphere of values and their ambivalent split into moralism and amoralism.

But at all times there has been another pathogenic form—a much more frequent one—of the conflict between play and duty that, instead of leading toward social success, threatens to end in abulic surrender. The *abulic child* is characterized by the fact that attachment to duty and a frenzy for play are not manifested sequentially but simultaneously. The child suffering from this common form of abulia is unable to separate the need for work from the craze for play. Even while working he escapes into play. He plays while he works, and as he plays he feels guilty about the sabotaged work. In order to preserve the esteem of parents and teachers, he makes an effort to do his homework, but he does it very badly. The parents confiscate his toys; he escapes into imaginative play, into obsessive reveries that hamper concentration. His output—even if it is obtained despite a considerable waste of energy and time—remains insufficient. His vital impulse becomes etiolated. The fatigue that results from the interminable work and the intellectual regression due to floundering in imaginative play brings with it a permanent loss of concentration and ends by progressively accentuating the etiolation.

In its most advanced state, abulic etiolation can lead to the collapse of all faculties. The child becomes unable to follow the lessons in school. Affectively and intellectually backward, he is bereft of all volition. His work lacks real results and escapist play no longer condenses in clear, precise images. The child no longer works and no longer daydreams: he is disoriented and as though drowned in fog. Whether riveted to his desk at home or on the school bench, the child is in a constant state of absent-mindedness from which he can no longer tear himself away. There are cases in which hebetude freezes the face in a mask of debility. But this flight into pseudo-idiotism is merely a form of self-protection, an attempt at avoiding all incriminations and all responsibility. It is an avowal of surrender. Hidden behind the mask is a nameless turmoil over being swallowed by the void. The child is its terrified spectator and impotent victim. A helping hand held out to him, understanding assistance could perhaps still save him from torpor. The child does not understand what is happening to him, and, alone with his incommunicable fear, he will let himself slip into lethargy. Perhaps he will make a few more attempts to free himself; but failure will only plunge him deeper into his stupor. Despised by parents, siblings, peers, and teachers, he is the submissive dunce, the opposite of the rebellious dunce (who is also despised by all, but who, far from giving up the competition, seeks superiority because of an expansive and primary vanity which incites him to supplant his peers by tyrannizing them). This submissive dunce gives up all competition, at least apparently. For, in truth, vanity-inspired competition is the only activity that will never be completely abandoned: unable to end in triumph, it continues to exist in a vexed, anxious form. The anxious comparison with his peers and his self-justifying tendencies will be the only forms of imaginative preoccupation that will not be completely drowned in fog. Resentments will spring from the feeling of being crushed and follow the prescribed paths of false justification. Self-pity will be accompanied by an accusation often wickedly concentrated on the teachers, one of the parents, a sibling, or one of his most prominent classmates owing to his success. Since competition can no longer be realized in its sensible form (emulation of qualities), nor in its perverse form of a quest for vanity-inspired superiority, the only path to its realization, ambivalently prescribed, will be that of collapse into the anguish of inferiority, reaching all the way to the feeling of nothingness. But this superlative of inferiority will cause a guilty torment that even the delights of laziness will no longer be able to compensate for. Abulic though these resentments may be, they will seek an outlet in vanity-inspired consolation which, at the limit, can be found only in oneiric megalomania. It could well be that the progressive etiolation of qualities is the deviated path that—followed all the way to its final outcome—in certain cases leads to hebephrenia, precocious dementia, and psychosis in children.

From the multitude of symptomatic and pathological manifestations in children, certain typical cases emerge. It is interesting to outline them, but it is even more necessary to isolate the traits common to all intermediary gradations of affectively deficient maturation.

All affectively backward children are characterized by the fact that they neither know how to play nor how to work.

The conflict between play and work is therefore superimposed in an increasingly acute manner, starting with school age, on the initial conflicts formed by the tangle of resentments against the frustrating parents or those inclined to spoil them.

These two forms of conflict mutually complement and amplify each other.

It would be wrong to explain the situation by two series of causes of which one, coming from the parents, would be the creation of the family atmosphere, and the other, imputable to the children, would be found in scholastic failure.

The truth is that the situation forms a legitimately structured whole.

The initial and essential cause of scholastic failure resides in the state of imaginative excitation in which the affectively backward child finds himself. This inner situation of the child—at once exalting and inhibiting—is composed of the imaginary escape to forbidden play and of perverse play with falsely justifying fantasies.

Ruminations, while reinforcing the affective backwardness originally due to the parents' educational deficiency, in the end determines intellectual backwardness.

Inattentive in school, the child draws no profit from the lessons: upset at home when he wants to do his homework, he is unable to do it. Settling down to work is a slow and interminable process, interrupted by the excuse of other tasks. Even when the child finally gets started, the work does not proceed unless he gets rid of it by doing it perfunctorily. There can be observed a reverse state of scrupulousness, which leads to a generalized panic due to the obsessive halting before the slightest obstacle, and which finally results in a perfunctory job in order to be completed at all costs. The constant state of absence of intellect or convulsive concentration causes a defective memory, and anxiety, which ends by attaching itself to the phenomenon, risks leading to a kind of paresis of the functions of registration and evocation. Daydreaming is the first stage of the somnolence of the superior faculties based on the mnemonic function. In order to function healthily the memory must above all be able to deliberately forget the elements it has learned. Forgetting constitutes the pre-conscious reservoir from which memory will automatically draw the registered elements by way of associative evocation. Exactly like every other unconscious function, it badly endures or resents anxious surveillance, which can only disrupt the automatic process. Having become anxious about his memory, the child does not dare to forget, for fear of being unable to find again the few elements he has painfully acquired. Anxiously supervised, the memory becomes convulsed and refuses to supply through association the registered materials, which in any case are themselves full of gaps. This generally deficient state of the memory will deteriorate seriously at the decisive moment of examinations and will produce, due to an excess of anxiety, an increased loss of capability. The anxious preparation for the examination cannot register the material, and once faced by the examiner, evocation risks being blocked more or less completely. Absence of intellect becomes total, and the child finds himself in a state of anguished self-hypnosis and guilty perturbation. Faced by the examiner, his habitual accusatory vanity toward his teachers collapses and turns against himself. It is transformed into an appeal for pity that induces the child, in the examination situation, to reinforce spectacularly the signs of his panic and thus provoke his failure even more decisively.

It is true that here as always, the outline needs to be rectified because it does not take into account all the gradations of such states and their ambivalent solution. It also happens that the anxiety of the person being examined, instead of being expressed by traits of submission, tries to disguise itself by insouciance and even insolence. This reversal will take place preferably in children, whether they are naturally gifted or deprived of intelligence. The lack of intelligence inspires a tendency to nonchalant withdrawal from scholastic competition, while a high degree of intelligence may drive the child to brazenly endanger his opportunity even when he is partly handicapped because of affective or intellectual backwardness.

Affective backwardness due to discord with the parents becomes the cause of intellectual backwardness as a result of transference of resentments to the duties. But the effect again becomes the cause of the progressive aggravation of the initial discord between parents and children.

Scholastic failure provokes the unceasing inculpation of the child, who in the end protects himself by becoming deaf to the reproaches, and thus exasperates the parents' impotent rage and its aggressive explosion.

Aversion to duties is but a special case of disobedient rebellion.

Re-education must take into account this entanglement between motivating cause and reactive effect.

In trying to elucidate and eliminate the motives of the affective discord, the re-educative effort also aims at the subconscious motives that determine the aversion to duties and its consequence, intellectual backwardness.

However, in order to be fully effective, the re-educational technique must be in a position to combat the specific causes of scholastic failure even more directly.

The analysis of affective retardation and of intellectual retardation nevertheless do join, because to the extent to which the child's hope for reconciliation with his parents through his own effort is born, the interest in his duties accepted as a means for reconciliation will be reanimated.

It is therefore important to explain to the child—in a manner suited to his ability to understand—the connection between his familial and scholastic difficulties. The explanation will give him grounds for hope. It will also free him from the feelings of inferiority that inhibit his intelligence and codetermine his surrender. By understanding that the scholastic failure is not due to an innate flaw but to motives that are reversible, the child finds himself in a better position to become reconciled to the ineluctable necessity to do his work.

But despite his desire to apply himself, he is still handicapped by his gaps and remains the prisoner of his retrograde habits. It is undoubtedly superfluous to emphasize the necessity to remedy the gaps, something which often is possible only by having the child undergo a regime of special tutoring and remedial courses. The inconvenience here is that they reduce the time available for organized play and they impose on the parents a financial sacrifice which often is beyond their means.

It is even more indispensable to try to disperse as rapidly as possible the daydreams, which impair the child's concentration and which, being an acquired habit, run the risk of persisting for a long time even after their deep-seated cause has been reduced: the affective and provocative intrigue that has determined the reveries of false justification and the deprivation of play, which in turn has motivated the reveries of escape.

In order to mobilize a technique capable of combatting obsessive inattention, that is, reverie, it is crucial to understand the conditions of attention. Imagination turns attention away from the surrounding reality presented to us by perception and in which reflection tries to orient us.

Reverie and lucidity coexist, in all degrees of the mixture. But as one of these conditions becomes accentuated, the other diminishes. Lucidity—whether it is perceptive or reflective—defines the presence of the intellect; reverie proves to be the deep-seated cause of inattention, the absence of intellect.

Sitting on a school bench, the daydreaming child is accustomed to being—although he is present bodily—in a state of spiritual or intellectual absence. His imagination escapes. He cannot help it, since it is precisely due to this state of absence that his mind is incapable of realizing this psychic scission, which is a veritable splitting of the personality. Turned away from his own environment, the child's perceptiveness is absorbed by images of his open-eyed daydream which figures forth a distant environment, the Far West, for example, which he has seen in a movie. In his reveries images of escape and justifying consolation intermingle. He is the admired hero. Sheriff or gangster, he triumphs over all opponents. His triumphant vanity consoles him for all his defeats and all his scholastic humiliations. The actual environment is no longer perceived. The teacher's voice is merely a distant noise, a murmur without distinct words. Now and then, the child awakens with a start from his imaginative flight. But his disappointment at seeing himself suddenly alight in the midst of his real failures carries him back to the distant places of his successes, where his charmed imagination overcomes with ease all obstacles and all difficulties. The return to reality is as painful as the flight was easy, and so the tendency to seek refuge in imaginative play is aggravated.

To the extent in which the child will understand the relationship that exists between his scholastic difficulties and his reveries, the relationship between the exaltation of the waking dream and the inhibition of his faculties, his attention will begin to fix itself on the phenomenon. Into these states of intellectual absence will filter— even despite himself—the warning that will awaken him from them. He will try to mobilize his perceptiveness to escape the ascendancy of imagination. He will cling to the teacher's words to prevent them from becoming merely a vague murmur. In the beginning the tendency to reverie will overwhelm him despite his effort at concentrating. But the conflict between imaginary pleasures and promises of real satisfaction, once introduced into the child's motivations, will result in his demand on himself for attention being produced at ever less distant intervals, and this will assure the possibility that the moments of mental presence will become increasingly frequent and prolonged. It is obviously advisable to support the child in this effort by clarifying more and more during the re-educational sessions the capital significance of the struggle against daydreaming with a view to overcoming his anxious obfuscation and achieving reconciliation with his parents.

The advantage thus gained will encourage the child to try to do his homework as well and as quickly as possible. Besides the intrinsic motives that determine his doing this so hesitantly and with such inhibiting scrupulousness, there are many incidental reasons that prevent the child from concentrating on his schoolwork at home. The apartments are often too small for the child to be able to isolate himself. Making him stay for the study hour after school protects him from familial annoyances, often complicated by the distractions offered by radio and television. But study in the scholastic environment will not stop him from daydreaming to his heart's content and from returning home with his homework badly done or sabotaged. It is not easy to find a remedy. It can only consist in the power of concentration. As long as he is not guided, the child is incapable of it, and his incapacity grows apace with his irritability. One must at least make sure that this situation, difficult in itself, does not become in the child's over-wrought imagination a principled excuse, used to sabotage radically the possibility of adaptation to what cannot be changed. Whatever the external difficulties, pacification or exasperation will take place on the secret plane of motivations. The capacity for concentration also varies according to the motives that ruin or support it. From an essential point of view, it is determined not only by the external and accidental situation but mainly by the psychic constellation.

The important psychological truth is that not only the mind's dissolution in daydreaming but also the concentration on work can transform disturbing noises into imperceptible murmurs. It is the false motives that in school are responsible for the perception of the teacher's voice as a vague noise, and at home are responsible for the concentration on work to be broken by the slightest perceptible incident. Attention is a function of interest. Proof of this is that the daydreaming child is incapable of concentration, even if he were beyond the reach of external disturbances. The essential cause of disturbances resides in his secret heart. The child is obsessed by temptations to escape and by his contempt for his duties.

At home the performance of work does not mainly require as in school auditory attention but rather reflective concentration. Now it is impossible to be at the same time imaginatively blinded and perceptively lucid, and it is even more impossible to be at the same time in a state of daydreaming and reflection. Reflection is activated with the help of precise concepts. Concepts are formed by way of abstraction. Reflection must make abstractions out of the emotional seduction exercised by vaguely pseudovisual images. Conceptual precision is the opposite of the soulful vagaries created by the escape into daydreaming which reels off its pseudovisual scenario at the behest of a purely associative fantasy freed from all the requirements of logic. Logical precision demands that concepts be formulated with the aid of inner language (hence the fact that the reflective state is accompanied by an imperceptible movement of the larynx). Attentive to the inner language, reflection is pseudoauditive rather than pseudovisual. It is true that imaginative exaltation in its no longer escapist and pseudovisual but ruminative and justificatory form also often unfolds with the help of an inner language. In that case it is not a reflective monologue but—as we have already said—a monologue turned dialogue by the illogicality of affect.

The difficulty of settling down and beginning to work is due to the fact that the daydreaming child, even when he wants to put himself in a state of reflection, cannot succeed in conceptualizing and precisely defining his thought. The inner language that should establish the logical link between concepts is constantly smothered by an associative surfacing of the debris connected with the underlying imagery. Re-education must grapple with the backwardness of the reflective faculty. Only the precise formulation of concepts—as soon as they are registered by the memory, or fixed in writing—can make thought unfold in prolonged reflection sentence by sentence.

However, a new complication may arise to the extent to which one succeeds in freeing reflection from the effects of escape into play. The child's hope becomes intensified, and instead of play it is duty that becomes obsessive. Instead of being content with doing it as well as possible (and as quickly as possible, in order to gain time for real play) the child demands of himself that he do it perfectly. The fantasy of escape is replaced by the fantasy of justification in quest of superiority. It will become manifest in the form of scrupulousness, no less conducive to a lack of concentration than escapist dispersion, and whose influence will underlie the work throughout the effort of execution. This convulsion of scrupulous concentration on detail proves to be just as harmful as the earlier slackness due to escape. The child, falling into ambivalent excess, cannot maintain a logical train of thought because of the survival of his inferiority feelings, which try to transform themselves into feelings of superiority. He finds himself unwittingly in a constant state of vanity-inspired competition. His obsessive desire to surpass his peers is transformed into anxiety at the thought of being surpassed despite his efforts. His exceedingly good intentions block the flow of thought from its source. His output is meager because it is impeded by scruples. The subconscious reference to the grades— good or bad—that he will receive and, thereby, to the criticisms or compliments of the teacher, parents, and re-educator, transform the desire to do well into inhibiting anxiety when faced by the opinion of others., The child loses all balanced self-criticism. The danger is great that, confused by qualms of conscience and fatigued by the convulsions of intention, in the end he will once more himself slip into resignation and laziness. Fantasies of escape will again begin to invade him.

Only knowledge of these implications allows the re-educator to intervene effectively. Mental backwardness—provided it is due only to affective deviations—will disappear to the extent in which the fantasies are stilled.

This statement is corroborated by re-educative experience. But because of its capital importance it is appropriate to sum up here, though briefly, its rooting in general psychic functioning.

The fact is that between abstract reflection and concrete imagination—even in its exalted form, which causes the benumbing of the faculties—there is no radical difference.

As creator of concepts, the function of abstraction consists in the elimination of the affective intensification attached to images. This fundamental relationship concerns not only the conditions of the healthy maturation of theoretical thought in the young student. The relationship of transformation that exists between imagination and reflection is of overriding importance for all of practical life. Its understanding is therefore of crucial importance for the technique of re-education: conceptualized, the images conform to real objects capable of expressing causal relations. Reflection, which is objectified imagination, takes into account the nature of the coveted objects and the obstacles that stand in the way of the realization of desires. With the help of reflection, the calculation of satisfaction obtains the sorting out of desires. It eliminates unrealizable desires and mobilizes the economized energy with a view to work destined to overcome the obstacles. At its utmost, reflection becomes theoretical. It no longer seeks the material possessions of objects. Its goal is a spiritual possession: truth. Its satisfaction is the joy of knowing.

Undoubtedly, the search for this satisfaction, even in its purely receptive form, is not advisable at the level of maturation of the school-age child. However, it already announces itself by the pleasure that the intellectually occupied child draws from his ability to handle concepts and organize his work. The feelings of inferiority of the affectively and intellectually backward child are ascribable not only to scoldings and meticulous or lax competition. They are more profoundly rooted in the obscure anguish of feeling backward in evolutionary terms in relation to one's more gifted or better disciplined peers, who are more advanced in the objectified deployment of their faculties and the maturation of their personalities. The result of this is the obsessive tenacity in the search for superiority that characterizes backward children. This search does not always end in inhibiting meticulousness. Very often, it will end with indulgence in a euphoric laxity caused by an imaginative escape into future extraordinary accomplishments. Children of this type value scholastic failure as the precursory sign of an unquestionable superiority. They feed on projects whose extravagance, in their eyes, exempts them from devoting themselves to their arid duties. Thus one frequently observes that characterological backwardness is accompanied by precocity in extrascholastic areas. It results in preoccupations that no longer belong to the domain of play (imaginative or active) but are condensed in plans and even in extravagant duties, which can only intensify the discord between parents and children. This deviating tendency is reinforced with age. It culminates at the time of adolescence. It is no longer manifested only on the sexual plane, but above all at the level of valuing spirituality, which is extremely liable to sustain and flatter hopes even if they are senseless. The fact is that most of the time this is only a phenomenon of purely imaginative overcompensation, which will produce obsessive adherence to an idealistic ideology (religious, artistic, political, etc.). It can also happen—in certain cases—to be a question of vocation; but vocations are rare and illusions are frequent. The deviant spirit, having become rebellious, will preferably attach itself to anticonventional movements or ideas (principled amoralism, which can run all the way to delinquency, or, conversely, overwrought moralism, which in our time often deviates toward a distorted Hinduism or any sort of mysticism. Also very frequent is the deviation toward revolutionary artistic movements and pseudosciences of all kinds). The most extravagant deviations are mistaken for spiritual manifestations and will not fail to become, in their turn, conventional due to the attraction they exercise over the growing masses of the disoriented. But even authentic vital impulses and real vocations are in danger of being influenced by them.

The deviation of vital impulse and its obsessive trait favor the formation of an exalted task. The flight from duty is converted into a game of the imagination involving a crushing duty that is beyond all possibility of realization. The exalted task—when it does not surrender in the face of the ineluctable exigencies of reality—will gradually become the crystallizing center of a neurotically nuanced characterological backwardness.

Nothing could be less superfluous than to emphasize these euphoric forms of affective and intellectual backwardness. Children and especially adolescents who suffer from this prove to be the most difficult to rehabilitate. They are in danger of becoming part of the multitude of neurotic adults who throughout their lives confuse authentic surpassing with imaginative overcompensation. Their good qualities are often real; but unfortunately they have often remained inhibited and undeveloped by dint of exaltation. The re-educator will also encounter such types of characterological backwardness among the parents, who often are the most recalcitrant. Crushed by their exalted task, which has turned into derision, and their vanity, which has become guilty and sentimental, they never cease deluging the child with accusations and exorbitant demands (unless their overwhelming exalted task induces them to neglect their educative task).

There are cases where the problem is whether it may not be preferable to propose a separation, at least a temporary one, between parents and children. The reason for this is the impossibility of obtaining an amelioration of the family intrigue due to a lack of sufficient understanding on the parents' part. In general one may say that if during the first weeks of treatment signs of amelioration are not incontestably apparent, the chance of obtaining a positive result is minimal.

The collective discipline that reigns in boarding schools is often good for the child, and the drawbacks can be overcome provided the re-educative sessions are not interrupted.

In all these cases, it is necessary to prepare the child for his new life and make sure that he sees in it help and not a punitive measure, since this could unleash sabotage on his part with the idea of getting expelled.

From the re-educational point of view, recourse to a boarding school is a last resort. It may be necessary for reasons which are often not at all ascribable to the parents. Children are frequently exposed to extremely harmful extrafamilial influences that prove to be the worst obstacles to recovery. This outside disruption of the collaboration among children, parents, and re-educator has its most baneful source in the social climate and its cultural aberrations: disintegrating ideologies, contradictory value judgements, perverting temptations.

Backward children, because of their tendency to extrascholastic precocity, form part of a group of young people that is most dangerously threatened by the disintegrative opinions of the times. Their affinity, based on secret motives, results in their trying to form clans in which the vanity of the too-mature backward children and their pose of rebellion pass all limits: each one has the ambition to surpass the others so as to be more admired. This is merely submission to the opinion of the clan. But the obsessive character of unleashed appetites and falsified judgments results in the re-educator having no leverage whatsoever on adolescents when they are led astray by the collective cynicism. The exception is those cases where the chief motives for deviation are not the triumph of mediocrity and a taste for the perverse but disappointed idealism and inverted vital impulse, which are susceptible to being changed into positive accomplishments. In certain cases the underlying guilt and accumulated disgust prepare the most propitious ground for re-educational work.

The treatment of young adolescents whose motivations are no longer exclusively influenced by the familial and scholastic milieu verges on adult therapy.

It has been necessary to enumerate the difficulties that re-education cannot fail to encounter. It is all the more justified to insist on the positive opportunities.

Insurmountable resistance from the children is the exception.

Provided one knows how to capture the imagination and guide it step by step toward reflective concentration, the child will not tire of listening. The analysis of motives will interest him as soon as his intelligence is awakened. As for the synthesis that results from this—the vision of the harmony of values—it will exert its suggestive influence without the need to develop it explicitly. Its comprehension goes beyond the children's ability to understand, with the exception of certain adolescents gifted with true impulse. For them, the guiding vision becomes the treatment's most effective tool.

The satisfying synthesis of ideas and characters has always been the ultimate goal of all profound reflection. But the harmonizing synthesis remains speculative without prior analysis of the extra-conscious, without profound investigation into the motives of disharmony and their subconscious roots.

The harmonizing synthesis, in which the analysis of motives is summed up, is based on the dynamic process of life. From imagination to reflection, from subconscious to superconscious, the psychic system forms a structured whole endowed with transforming dynamism. From childhood on harmony can be transformed into disharmony, but also disharmony into harmony; sublime into perverse, but also perverse into sublime; lucidity into blindness, but also blindness into lucidity. But lucidity demands that one never forget how the sublime and perverse can be defined only in relation to their immanent value of sensible or senseless satisfaction.

All possibility of re-education rests on the transforming dynamisms whose elements are the motives. All of life's concrete problems, all psychic conflicts are comprised in it. Founded on the study of transforming dynamism, the themes of analysis and synthesis are inexhaustible.

The re-educator thus finds himself armed with a tool that will never fail him, provided he knows how to handle it. Amelioration is achieved not only through a simple acknowledgement of the existence of false motives, nor even through knowledge of their categorized schema. The analytical technique consists in the incessant demonstration of the fallacious dynamic process that endlessly transforms the promise of satisfaction into anxious and inhibiting disappointment.

Since these pathological transformations are due to the fallacious dynamic process of the overwrought imagination, all diagnostic and therapeutic attention must be concentrated on the fantasies of escape (which follow the unfolding of three drives: sexuality, materiality, spirituality) and on the fantasies of false justification (which follow the unfolding of these three categories: vanity, sentimentality, repressed guilt). The fantasies of escape and false justification are the components of fallacious dynamism. They inevitably complete each other: the essential fault resides in the escape from the exigencies of reality, and thus this culpable fault seeks its pathogenic justification by means of vanity-inspired repression and sentimental and accusatory projection. Fallacious dynamism consists in the fact that escape seeks its justification, and the justification leads to further escapes.

It is not enough to acknowledge the presence of vexed or triumphant vanity, rancorous or aggressive accusation, aggrieved or moralizing sentimentality, repressed or projected guilt. Such a diagnostic observation is merely the means for the re-educational explanation which consists in exposing dynamically all the harm resulting from the deviation, the producer of pathogenic anxiety. Only an understanding of the harm one inflicts on oneself has the strength to mobilize the liberating impulse. Comprehension of the ills for which everyone—even the child—is essentially responsible carries with it a comprehension of the good that will come from the dissolution of imaginatively exalted temptations. It transforms destructive dynamism back into healing impulse.

The themes of dynamic analysis are inexhaustible, because the results of ambivalent decomposition and its false calculations of satisfaction are innumerable. The consequence of the repression of truth and producer of mendacious motives, the destructive dynamism begins with the splitting of one's feelings into ambivalent, anxious and inhibited resentments. It thus leads to the gradual impotence of the essential drives (sexual, material, and spiritual) and to the loss of all positive qualities (lucidity of intellect, intensity of emotions, voluntary decision). In the end the progressive loss of liberating lucidity produces psychopathic oneirism. The ravages that have thus taken place deep within render even the child unfit to incorporate himself healthily in the familial and social framework. Finally, at the adult level it determines the unhealthiness of social relationships.

If it is true that destructive dynamism, secretly operating at the level of motives, produces consequences of extraordinary gravity, ranging from mental illness and social malaise all the way to ethical collapse, how could one not help but concentrate all one's attention on this central phenomenon of life: the alteration of motives of action? How can one not try to perfect the re-educational technique that attempts to remedy evil at its very source, that is, the life of children?

Re-education, by the very fact that it proposes to intervene in the vital dynamic process, is an act of the highest responsibility. To the extent in which it succeeds in eliminating the disorder it is a creative act: it molds the psychic system, forms the character.

Like every creative act, re-education must avail itself not only of a perfectible technique but also a guiding vision. From the analytic technique derives the vision of values, and this vision in turn guides the analysis.

The re-educator-counselor can be content with dissolving falsely motivated resentments by means of an established and transmissible technique. Indeed, he must utilize the knowledge that has been transmitted to him, if not to enrich it, at least to realize in himself the indispensable condition of objectivity. The synthetic vision is not indispensable. The re-educator will be not only counselor but analyst in the full sense of the word to the extent to which authentic inquiry into what he has acquired will lead him toward a perfecting of the technique and the application of the synthesis.

Life itself demands this profound inquiry. For while life is evidently activity, it is first of all an intentional projecting, and the activity is its projection.

What children need for their life plan to ripen in a sensible manner, for them to become adolescents and fully matured adults, is a social and cultural superstructure rooted not in conventions and prejudices but in the judgement of just values, founded in the in-depth inquiry into the immanent meaning of life. The absence of such a superstructure is the true cause of the confusion, even more than the disorder of familial life that is its consequence.

In family life, what degrades the life of the children from the earliest age, perhaps even more than the discord and quarrels, is the parents' conversations the opinions they exchange, their judge-ments of events and people, all of which bear the mark of their conventional view of things and evaluation of common problems. The child witnesses all this not without deriving a picture of the life that awaits him. In these seemingly innocuous conversations are imprudently paraded reproaches and grievances, bad feelings and triumphs, perverse intentions, and plans for aggressive action. Before the disenchanted child pass and unfold all the problems of life as the parents, the adults, create and solve them, setting out from their false motivations.

APPENDIX: Case Histories

C.H.
Only child.
Attends school.
Scholastic difficulties. Abulic.
Suicide attempt.

The father is a foreman in a factory. A nervous type whose ambitions far surpass the potential inherent in his trade. His ambition would be highly praiseworthy if the absence of valid realization did not mar it with an underlying discontent with himself and life in general. His profound dissatisfaction is especially projected on his family life. He has fixed his disappointed hopes on his only child and imposes a strict regime on this daughter. His own unhappy childhood makes him meticulous in his decisions, uncertain in his actions, due to excessive scruples. His profound uncertainty is counterbalanced by a cramped assurance sought for in the rigidity of principles. These underlying traits produce a marked attitude of timidity. In order to overcome his weakness—dangerous in his job as foreman—he has read books on popular psychology, such as *How to Become Forceful*. He declares that from them he has drawn the means to face his difficulties on the job.

But this certainly has not helped him overcome his nervous hypersensitivity, which at the very most has changed in aspect. From such books he has drawn a reinforcement of his cramped ideal of wanting to appear strong-willed and forceful in all situations; and this has simply emphasized his tendency as a nervous, disappointed person, inclining him to play the despot at home. His exalted idealism has produced, among other deviations, a compensatory realization of a ceremonial nature which deserves to be mentioned owing to the influence it must have exercised over the child's nascent feelings. A nature lover, he introduced in his family the custom of bathing together in the nude. Having recently noticed in his daughter certain reactions of modesty, he ultimately renounced this practice.

The mother gives the impression of being very sweet, although a bit soft. In order to avoid confrontation, she has gotten into the habit of submitting to her husband's demands. She confesses that she has always had the tendency to spoil the child, more or less secretly, in order to make up for the father's severe demands.

It is useful to emphasize that the first contact with the parents was very difficult. They both answered questions in an evasive manner so as to protect their method of education against therapeutic intervention. Filled with good intentions, they wanted to give their child the best possible education, so it is difficult for them to admit that they may have made mistakes. According to what they say, the family life is exemplary. They have come to the laboratory with the firm conviction that the cause of the child's misconduct could only be organic in nature. However, only cases in which the predominance of the psychic factor is attested to by the medical examination and the evidence of tests are sent in for re-educational consultation.

The first contact with the girl reveals, in her case too, a tendency to protect the family life from all attempts to reveal an educational error. Invited to express herself freely, she avoids speaking about herself and gets bogged down in a long, somewhat confused account. She tries to give prominence to her mother's charitable concerns, which apparently impel the mother, it would appear, to a generosity toward the poor that often goes far beyond her budgetary means. The admiring tone leads one to think that the child is not only subjected to the father's idealistic demands but that on the mother's side, she is propelled toward a path of abnegation whose excessive demands may well be a root if not the principal root of her hidden conflict. The propensity for excessive compasssion is too marked and by that very fact invites us to look for complementary ambivalences. How could a sentimentality that compels one to give even beyond one's material means not provoke sentimental regret with a shade of guilt over more or less depriving one's family (and oneself) of the basic necessities? In order to appease one's conscience, guilt obsessively compels one to continue the sacrifice on behalf of those one protects and at the same time demands that the injustice done the family be paid for by a greater sacrifice on their behalf. Answers to the questions reveal that the desire for redemption has a tendency to manifest itself in the mother by excessive and meticulous housework, which almost makes family life intolerable because of the incessant reminders about cleanliness or—and this becomes even more intolerable—the sight of her sorrowful face expressive of silent reproach.

Such an atmosphere of sacrifice and reproach would be unlivable even for the person who created and maintains it if she could not find the vanity-inspired compensation of believing herself a better person than most. The others are soon considered ungrateful, never sufficiently appreciative of so much beneficence. Goodness, falsely motivated, is transformed into accusation. In cases where the sacrifices obsessively imposed by guilt finally become too burdensome, sentimental and vanity-inspired hypocrisy will unfailingly be subtended by an accusation tinged with hate.

What is true for the mother is also true for the daughter. The way in which she evades answering precise questions and in which, during the first interview, she gratuitously overflows with praise for her mother, forgetting completely to speak about her father, presents too illogical a nuance not to be revelatory of hidden motives.

Could the exceedingly ostentatious admiration for the mother's goodness conceal an underlying accusation, regarding herself as too neglected compared to her mother's charity cases? It will also be necessary to find out whether this whole story is not an exaggerated interpretation of rather minute negligible facts. The indisputable presence of marked illogicality justifies the hypothesis that this might be a point of crucial importance in the family constellation.

It is typical of all sciences to establish a hypothesis, even if it is modified in the course of further investigation. The hypothesis outlined here is not gratituous, because it is founded, beginning with the revelations which have been obtained, on the law of ambivalence that governs the secret calculation of satisfaction and whose knowledge permits one to uncover an underlying falsified motivation of a pseudosublime nature. In all cases, however, the initial hypothesis is only a means of approach that helps to orient the questions. The fact is that in the present case the parents' method of education can be suspected of being contaminated by a particularly serious error, because the child has tried to remove herself from its orbit by the most decisive kind of flight: suicide. At present not only the parents but also the re-educator are faced by the threat of a new suicide attempt. Behind a screen of exalted admiration (which it would have been imprudent to bring to light too brusquely), the girl conceals her educational errors. We must, however, identify them as rapidly as possible in order to ward off the dangerous blackmail of a new attempt at suicide. We had to try to obtain from the parents—in spite of their reticence—a clarification of the situation so as to modify or amplify the hypothetical pattern, according to the exigencies of reality and the particular circumstances.

In order to break down the parents' manifest resistance, it was deemed preferable to question them separately.

After long reticence, the mother confesses that the family atmosphere is far from being so benign as the first interview led one to believe. Frequent, even venomous quarrels take place between her and her husband, often in front of the child. These often break out on the occasion of the educational intervention of one or the other parent. The mother reproaches her husband for his harshness, and the father accuses his wife of weakness with the child. The possibility of an educational error is thus admitted. But this perspective, once opened up, merely serves to reinforce the reticence. The woman withdraws into a resistance that is as soft as it is tenacious. The fault is exclusively her husband's. Drenched in tears, she begins to complain of the cruelties she has had to suffer heroically since her marriage. The tearful hypersensitivity does not contradict the initial hypothesis, but it renders any verification of the details impossible. In such cases we must be guided by significant attitudes rather than by extracting a confession. An in-depth analysis of the parents is not our purpose. A reconsideration of their educational behavior is obtained by explanations composed of subtle and precise strokes, which demonstrate all the misdeeds of the falsely motivated behavior. The closer the initial hypothesis, founded on the laws of motivation, is to reality, the more it will permit applying the strokes with precision. In this resides the whole importance of psychological calculation. The essential is that the parents, feeling themselves fathomed and humanly understood, are by that very fact led to confess the fault to themselves and end by understanding its disastrous consequences. The guilty self-dissatisfaction thus awakened is modified by hope. To the extent that the parents feel profoundly understood, the idea is installed that the new educational method proposed by the re-educator will obtain more satisfying conduct from the child, and this obliges the parents, despite their apparent resistance, to accept the instructions.

The revelation of the secret family discord, a revelation obtained from the mother, enabled us to break down the father's resistance. Without speaking to him about his wife's complaints, we told him point-blank that it was impossible for the child to have become desperate to such a manifestly dangerous degree unless the family atmosphere—whatever one might say—were disturbed by quarrels and that, to help his child, he must assume his share of responsibility. This direct attack was necessary because of the urgency of the situation and was justified by our belief in the existence of a basic integrity and frankness in the nature of this simple man so full of idealism. He was shaken, and in order not to give him any time to get a grip on himself, it was best to confront him with his essential fault even at the risk of going too far. The risk was slight, because the premonition of his essential fault—the central cause of all of his educational errors—was based on the calculation that would allow us to uncover the presence of an exalted task and the falsified attitudes that spring from it. The admission—provoked purposely this time—is not long in coming. The man is ready to admit that he projected on the child both his idealistic task and his disappointments. Though at some cost, he admits that he has tried to impose on the child the somewhat exalted task of a rigid voluntarism that has dogged him throughout his life. He seems to grant the possibility that the success he sought was an overcompensation for his timidity and may have made him too demanding toward others and, above all, in regard to his child. It is possible that this admission contains a certain dose of vanity, because the revelation of an idealist task—painful though it may be—still flatters hidden pretensions. But this is only a matter of a detail, negligible at this point. All the same, his basic sincerity has been reached, because the man spontaneously begins to talk, saying that the birth of a daughter was for him a serious disappointment which he has not yet overcome. He would have preferred a boy. He insists that a boy seems to him more suitable to carry on his life's aspiration and achieve its success. Toward the end of this interview, the man seems in high spirits and animated by new hope. He understands the necessity of loosening his grip on the child so as to allow her to live her life in accordance with her abilities. He declares himself ready with his new attitude to do his best to help to break through the vicious circle in which the child is thrashing about. These good intentions, though expressed without too much exaggeration, undoubtedly need to be supported by a more profound investigation of secret motives. But vivified by the general explanation of the situation his good will even leads him to say on leaving, "I too could be helped by treatment."

The parents' idealism and good will are not a sufficient guarantee of a sensible education. In the present case, they led to two diametrically opposed exalted tasks (the mother's goodness, the father's severity) which, inculcated in the child, set up an insoluble and crushing conflict. One can surmise that the suicide attempt is related to this feeling of being crushed.

According to what the child says, the reasons for attempting suicide would appear to be her scholastic failure and the fear of being scolded at home. The girl, however, is far from unintelligent. In spite of her indolent mask, she follows the phases of the analytic process with growing interest. It would seem, then, that she is not only affectively deficient confronted by the exalted task imposed by her parents but also confronted by the modest scholastic task. The exaltation of intentions, by convulsing her abilities, inhibits her and thus brings about the situation of failure. The failure of her relations with her parents (the exaltation-inhibition of obedience) extends to the scholastic situation, where the deficiency manifests itself in the relations with the teachers (duties) and her schoolmates (play). The girl, who is being tutored in a special course, is attached to a teacher whom she intensely idealizes and finds herself radically separated from the other pupils with the excuse that she does not care for their games. So it is important to bring to light the individual constellation of a generalized deficiency, whose deforming motives extend gradually to all vital relations and end in the suicide attempt, the most decisive failure in life.

The accidental motives, as the girl presents them, are not false; but quite clearly by themselves they are insufficient to explain the decisive surrender, the flight into death. Suicide is never due to motives of an incidental order, even though such causes always have a precipitating role. Despair in regard to accidents, circumstances, and situations is merely a pretexual cause; the true cause is the despair about oneself. The gravity of the escape obliges us to search for the contribution of subconscious motives, which are due to a deeply mistaken calculation of justificatory and accusatory pseudosatisfactions. The presence of exalted and inhibiting ambivalent motives is underlined by the fact that the suicide itself turned out to be a failure. It failed, something that is almost never due to happenstance but to a chance left open and subconsciously prepared. With her suicide attempt the girl wanted to prove something to herself and her parents. The ostensible motives could not have been determining if they had not contained a summation of her secret despair and, in the background, a symbolic condemnation of the entire family situation and the child's entire subconscious constellation. So it is a matter of finding the source of the imaginatively overwrought anxiety when faced by scholastic failure and the parents' scoldings.

The suicide is suspected of being an act of rebellion that did not dare manifest itself openly. The child had assumed the twofold exalted task that was imposed on her since her very early childhood. Having become a young girl, she has taken the task to heart. She would have liked to realize it to please her parents, to escape their scoldings, and her entire life has become a failure due to these unrealizable demands. The suicide attempt, triggered by a casual fear when faced by scholastic failure and scoldings, assumes the significance of a punishment inflicted on the parents. It is an attempt to break with the overly demanding family milieu; but it is also an expression of the child's despair about herself and her manifest and growing inabilities. Since the inhibiting anguish vis-à-vis the exalted task finally extends to all real tasks, it is above all her deficiency in scholastic tasks that arouses a discouraging judgmental comparison with her classmates, which could lead to a complete abandonment of all competitiveness. The paralyzed impulse, which has become filled with anxiety, begins to vacillate between exaltation and inhibition: now meticulous, now lazy, it risks sinking into abulic exhaustion, which can end up in total surrender to despair. Subconsciously motivated, the suicide attempt is a desperate warning addressed to the parents to force them to moderate their demands; it is the most suitable way to frighten the parents and compel their indulgence even in regard to real deficiencies. The true motives of the suicide are the false motives acting subconsciously: guilty vanity (exalted task and real deficiencies) and accusatory sentimentality (abulic submissivness, ambivalently transformed into a threat and masked rebellion).

In fact, after the suicide attempt the parents did yield to some extent to the threat. They tried, as much as possible, not to irritate the child; but the pressure of this blackmail merely increased their irritability. Their annoyance, no longer able to be expressed by verbal explosions of reproaches, threatened to manifest itself in underhanded intonations, whose incessant inculpation were for the child perhaps even more disturbing than the old regime of more or less shortlived scoldings. The parents' increased irritability derived not only from their obligation to control themselves but also from the fact that the child was becoming a source of greater disappointment than before. Feeling less harassed, the girl settled into her old abulic habits.

The material needs of family life also have their share in worsening this tendency. The parents return home late in the evening and the child is often alone. She lives withdrawn into herself, sad and depressed. She loves her solitude and reads a lot, but indiscriminately: sentimental romances as readily as children's stories. The ambivalent split of her tastes is emphasized by a somewhat banal trait of backwardness: at the age of fifteen this young girl still plays with dolls. And here a comment imposes itself: the ambivalence of tastes and value judgements in the nervous adult lead to an alternation between the lofty and the base, sign of the presence of unrealizable aspirations, simultaneously overwrought and inhibited. In finding the germ of such an excessive split in the child, we would be wrong to neglect this indication and not see in it an invitation to search for its cause in the parents' aspirations and in their imposition, as excessive on their part as it is premature for the child. In the case of the young girl, the suspect contradiction does not manifest itself merely through her reading and the regressive love she devotes to her dolls, but also through the amusements she seeks outside her home. Avoiding sports and collective games, she loves—like all children—the movies, where she finds nourishment for her vagabond fantasies. But even more than the movies, she likes the theater, the *Comédie Française*. She is attracted, in more than an average degree, to the heroes and heroines of classical tragedy, to whom she devotes a cult of admiration that is quite extraordinary, even though somewhat muffled by her general state of abulia. Here the contrast with playing with dolls is too abrupt not to betray the amplitude of her affective disorientation.

This girl's most prominent trait is an excessive timidity that even goes as far as mutism. During the first interview she keeps her eyes lowered, her gaze, when she looks up, is shifty, and her voice is flat. The ensemble of these traits of prostration and submission suggest the idea that the exalted task as it is imposed by her father (activity, energy, success), is adopted only in the negative form of excessive guilt about her inactivity and lack of success. The fear of failure extends to her entire life and becomes anxiety over the future. She has a certain talent for languages and nourishes a vague hope of being able one day to become an interpreter, without even daring to believe this because of her bad scholastic record. Her laziness, which embraces her work in school, entails consequences typical of such a situation: gaps are created and through their accumulation transform the imagined difficulty into real difficulty. To this is added the disastrous influence of daydreaming, which creates a state of semisomnolence not very propitious to the act of concentration. The girl is definitely not unintelligent; during the reeducational sessions she gives proof of subtle understanding and sustained interest. But when confronted by schoolwork she finds herself in a situation of intellectual collapse, imputable to her anxiety in the face of difficulties that have become insurmountable. The typical outcome of such a situation is flight into imaginative and devaluing consolation: scholastic success is of small importance. There are more remarkable gifts, more ideal tasks.

The girl, in despair at having lost the hope of pleasing her father, turns to her mother. But by fleeing from and sabotaging the exalted task imposed by her father, she will receive her mother's protection only if she submits to the excessive aspirations for goodness that the mother imposes on herself, perhaps as a kind of protest or resignation faced by her husband's convulsive harshness. To satisfy her desire to please her mother, the child imagines a degree of the accomplishment of goodness that her mother doesn't even impose on her, and she falls into the trap of a new need for asceticism. True goodness is the sign of an exceptional spiritual strength, capable of dissolving all rancor; on the contrary, submission mistaken for goodness is but a falsely motivated pseudoideal. It is in any case easy to see that the mother's exalted ideal goes along with the child's passivity. Her abulia is thus reinforced under the pretext of goodness, and this falsely idealizing justification develops—as if it were an unadmitted revenge—in a direction contrary to all the father's demands. The child's abulic goodness—in contrast to the mother's—has no other path of expression than that of escapist fantasy. It expresses itself through a great compassion for all those who have suffered the injustices of fate. But this pity for others is only a transference of the pity she feels for herself, and not only because of her father's injustice. The girl's psychic system, hemmed in by these vicious conflicts, becomes "a point of least resistance" against which all aggressive tendencies—especially those of her peers—are unleashed even if only in the guise of contempt. Due to the excessive humiliation, the girl is exposed to the danger of feeling surrounded by bewildering threats. The danger is great that she will in the end imaginatively foresee aggressive intentions aimed at her, and that the increasing intimidation will lead her toward morbid interpretation, a tendency without which the suicide attempt is unthinkable.

At any rate, morbid interpretation is not a salient trait in this girl's case. It remains confined to the relationship with her parents. The interpretative anxiety is rooted on one hand in her fear of her overly severe father, who imposes his over-wrought ideal of sternness on the child, and, on the other hand, in the identification with her mother and her over-wrought task of goodness. The flagrant contradiction of these two impositions can only lead the child to a disorientation whose vast proportions must be grasped, because it certainly is not unconnected with the rebellion of suicide.

Abulic submissiveness is merely a disguised form of rebellion. In all cases of the exaltation of goodness, one finds an immense underlying need for hate-filled revenge and the imaginative unleashing of suppressed pleasurable sensations. Here—with the help of circumstances—excessive guilt leads to self-condemnation without appeal, the idea of suicide.

In a dream that the girl reports, she sees herself walking along a barrier. On the far side of the barrier is a meadow. She says that she goes down this road every day on her way to school. The barrier and the meadow exist in reality. For them to appear in the dream, the girl must certainly have endowed them with symbolic meaning on her way to school. The dream has perfect clarity and can be understood even without knowledge of an explanatory method. The dream images juxtapose duty and play. School life, experienced as painful and grim, is separated—by a barrier fence—from the joy of living (the meadow). This theme is singularly amplified by an association: the girl says that some time ago a gypsy camp was set up in the meadow. Every time she goes by there, she feels pity for these poor people and becomes indignant over their miserable living conditions. But behind her sentimental pity and her accusatory indignation hides the desire to lead the independent life that the gypsies symbolize. Much more than pity, it is because of this forbidden desire for escape that the place struck her to the point of reappearing without symbolic disguise in her dream; but, conversely, the need to repress the desire for escape is the reason why the gypsies do not appear in the dream picture even though they are its meaningful center. They symbolize the escape to adventure, imaginary horizons, travel, flight from the family environment, an intense desire for freedom, liberation at any cost, breaking loose.

The girl, until now reluctant to broach this counteraspect of her ideal of goodness and submission, spontaneously declares that the dream thus interpreted expresses the truth about her inner life. Unmasked by the dream, she finally dares to face the shamefully hidden truth that, so long as she remained repressed, had caused her despair about life and above all about herself.

These fantasies of escape constitute the exalted and obsessive countertask. They sustain the scholastic inability, they cause the terrifying fear inspired by one's scolding father, but they also heighten the overwhelming shame that becomes unbearable by comparison with her mother's goodness. They exacerbate the feeling of unworthiness in relation to one's parents and codetermine the excess of guilty self-condemnation.

It should be noted that an exalted task is too heavy a burden to carry at this girl's age. Before adolescence, the characteristic trait of the exalted burden—ambivalence between idealist exaltation and breaking loose—is only chaotically sketched in the case of unbalanced children. Overwrought idealism is prefigured by sporadic, exceedingly good intentions, and the breaking loose is announced by the collapse into disobedience. What then distinguishes the present case very markedly from the norm, and what explains the girl's excessive collapse, is chiefly the premature formation of an exalted task with a precise character. In this connection, one should perhaps not omit the determining role that could be played here by the parents' social position and cultural level. In an intellectual milieu, it often happens that at least one of the parents is affected by exalted aspirations that provoke a diffuse discontent with himself, or herself, and which he or she will tend to project on the children in a rather vague and imprecise manner. But in a culturally more primitive social stratum, aspirations—even though present—will usually have a simpler and less absolutist structure. It is quite rare to find in this stratum families in which both parents impose a crushing task on the (only) child so directly and imperatively as is the case with the young girl. Furthermore, in this milieu idealism will not be an intellectual game but a deep conviction of the entire being, and this will make its exaltation even more destructive.

We will not fully understand the extent of the girl's turmoil unless we also take in account her extrafamilial situation.

Her excessive feeling of guilt extends to play with her peers. She shies away from play, pretends she detests it, believes she detests it, she detests it. Locked into the solitary play of her imagination, she regresses toward puerile amusement in which the doll is her companion. The contrast between the exalted task of the adolescent, and even of the neurotic adult, and playing with dolls, here has the significance of a symbolic fixation. Living in isolation with her parents and subject to their impositions, she transfers her exalted task to the doll by punishing it excessively for the slightest imagined disobedience. The suppression of collective play and the transference of her exigencies to the doll become the only realization—so very abulic and backward—of her unhealthy idealisms. Since for her collective play has the significance of a breaking loose which she forbids herself and which the others allow themselves, she considers herself superior to her peers. Disdain for play extends to her peers. She is good; the others are bad. She considers herself uniquely good, and her misfortune is to see herself compelled to live among young people whose sensibility is not on a par with hers. Her isolation is without remedy. If she were to make contact and participate in the play, she would do so in a manner so inhibited, so shy, and so clumsy that this would make her even more ridiculous than her attitude of reserve. She has never exercised her capacity for making contact, nor her physical aptitudes. Her motor inhibition is striking. Her face is inexpressive, her gait is languid, her movements are monotonous and ungraceful. (It is not superfluous to mention here that the girl is far from beautiful; but her face—especially when a rare smile animates it—is not unpleasant.) Her physical ineptitude removes her from collective play even more definitely than her resentment. No matter how much she pretends that she herself does not want to be included, the truth is that she is excluded; she is banned by her peers, and suffers cruelly because of it. Withdrawn into herself, having removed herself from all realization and all contacts with the young people of her age, her life, having become exactly the contrary of what her task of goodness would aspire to, is by now only a dream of revenge, bitter rumination, boredom. All the centers of interest that tie a young being to life are cut off for her. Barely at the threshold of existence, she begins to play with the idea that the only sensible activity would be to put an end to her days.

At the beginning of the sessions, the girl is extremely wary about any revelation whatsoever of a possible fault on her part or that of her parents. The way in which she answers the questions reveals her feeling of utter prostration. She is completely disoriented about herself and what is happening to her. Her voice is toneless and barely audible. Even if one sits right in front of her, it is often difficult to catch her replies.

The communication of the pact made with her parents and the promise that starting from now she will no longer be scolded by her father for her scholastic failures, does not even kindle a gleam of hope in her eyes, but rather provokes an incredulous pout. The promise was at any rate only a first tentative approach, because it was only too obvious that the child suffered as much if not more from her mother's overly enveloping and inveigling attitude. At the question whether she in turn would agree to help her parents keep their promise by ceasing to irritate and even exasperate them with her excessive attitudes of frustration and surrender, a thin smile flits over her lips. Her head remains bowed, but out of the corner of her eyes she throws a surprised and probing glance. She listens—without giving a sign of agreement or denial—to the explanation of a possible change that her parents will do their best to facilitate, provided that she in turn will do her best to clear the way for a reconciliation. Her face remains inert; but when she leaves she regales me with a thin smile and it seems to me that I feel a slight tightening of her limp hand.

Later on the mother withdrew into sulky resistance. I saw her only one more time. She complained that the child was beginning to drift away from her. The attempt to make her understand that it would be necessary for her to relax her insidious grip had no success whatsoever. On the contrary, her husband did his best to adapt himself to the pact. He came regularly to report on the smallest details of the child's behavior. He took pleasure in talking with me, and he would even ask questions that were outside the subject that tied us together and concerned his own problems, or even offered opinions on matters of a general order about which he showed a naive and touching interest. After several conversations, this simple man ended by condensing the experience he had lived through in a very felicitous formulation. "In short," he said to me one day, "if I have understood properly what you ask of me, it is that I never ask the child to face her responsibilities without assuming my own. There is no doubt that I was too strict without being strict enough. Everything the child did seemed to me an attack on my authority, and I was in a constant state of rancor, which I exaggerated in order to prove to her that it could not go on like this. But it did go on, precisely, and even more so, with a vengeance, because all she did was imitate me. Since I met you, I've made an effort to be calm and firm without emphasizing my firmness with frowns. The child obeys without sulking. This doesn't always go smoothly, but, I can assure you, it is often bewildering to see how much good will she has despite her skittish moments, when one stops showing her at every opportunity that she is definitely unworthy, that it's over, that it's too much, and that one is fed up with her. If only her mother could understand. I believe she is jealous because the girl is beginning to attach herself to me. Oh, I don't say that she always prefers me, but sometimes it becomes very visible. When I think how much she must have detested me!"

Evidently it would have been preferable if the mother too had actively participated in the rehabilitation effort. Despite repeated invitations to come in, she stayed away with the excuse of being too occupied with her housework. However, it seems that her reticence did not go so far as sabotage and that willy nilly she adapted to the new situation, because signs that the child was living in the grip of emotional blackmail decreased.

In the course of the sessions, the girl opens up and participates in the tracking down of false attitudes and the disastrous profit she proposed to obtain from them. Her timidity disappears quite quickly, at least in the therapeutic situation. She supplies material— dreams and small daily incidents—that permits us to reveal in detail the false motivations and the imponderable false reactions that underhandedly impair the effort of rehabilitation. The review of the errors committed daily, by successively diminishing the affective deviation, dissolved the anxious disorientation. The discovery of the imponderables will produce a shock of surprise that will prove to be powerful enough to break down the abulic block. This shock was so deeply experienced that at first it provoked a temporary state of euphoric exuberance, which had to be checked in order to obtain gradually more thought-out calm attitudes.

Following inquiries, the school situation proved to be much less compromised than the abulic etiolation had led us to fear. The bad school report that had triggered the idea of suicide had merely been a pretext-accident. As family relations improved, it became first of all necessary to orient the therapeutic intervention toward the much more pronounced abulia with regard to peers and collective play. The girl agreed to get rid of her dolls, and shortly afterward her father confirmed that she had definitely put them aside. It was more difficult to obtain from her the decision to enroll in a youth movement. It was important not to press her as long as her apprehensions were intensified by the memory of an experience of inept adaptation that caused derision. Another failure risked provoking a relapse, which could compromise the improvement under way. As her progress became more noticeable and family relations were normalized, she began to consider more favorably the idea of throwing off her reserve and confronting the redoubtable judges represented by young people of her own age. This event could be decisive for the commencement of her recovery, but it again threatened to be harmful so long as her shaken imagination was dominated by the fear of ridicule, fastened vaguely and indefinitely on her old attitudes of vexed superiority and submissive inferiority. The essential thing was not to force a decision from her, but to prepare her little by little by raising to consciousness her imprecise fears and clearly defining them in order to transform the resentments directed at her peers into a precise awareness of her own corrigible fault. Quite a long work of analysis was necessary to introduce gradually into her imagination the vision of a new, more sensible behavior filled with promises of satisfaction unknown until now. To the extent in which her imagination, ceasing to obsessively conjure up the dissatisfactions that must be avoided, became oriented toward pleasant play with the newly introduced presatisfactions, the desire to realize them had every good chance to overcome the old anxious apprehensions. The day came when the girl began to ask questions—still somewhat embarrassed, it is true—about the conditions of enrollment in a youth movement. In the same period, she related with great joy the minute details of a relative success in some attempts at approaching certain of her classmates. She summed up these first experiences with a most felicitous formulation: "If they laugh at me, I'll laugh too instead of getting upset." Finally she asked, on her own initiative, to be enrolled in a youth movement. By chance the counselor was a fine psychologist. Aware of the present and past situation of her new protogée—who was just a few years younger than herself—she devoted friendly attention to her. Her understanding was undoubtedly an important factor in our final success. After the few weeks required to adapt to the group, the Easter vacation came. The troop prepared to go camping. Here are some details about this period of vacation that were collected and sent me by the girl's father. (The notes are transcribed without corrections. Coming from a man whose education did not go beyond elementary school, they bear witness to a fine ability to express himself.)

March 24: After she got up definitely late, we observed that her room was a complete mess. In order to avoid verbal remarks, I had the idea of placing this simple notice on her bed: "Tidiness is one of the most beautiful expressions of intelligence." She found this very nice, agreed with us, and without any need to be asked by us, she tidied up with the best of good will.

March 28: Letter from an English pen pal in correspondence with her for the past year, announcing that she is in Paris and expressing her desire to get together. Great joy, great plans.

March 29: Visit with this unknown young lady, after leaving the Gay-Lussac center. Return home, unusual exuberance, prolix on the details of the visit.

March 30: Went out to a show, excellent morale. Vacation period.

March 31-April 2: Vacation, not very loquacious. Period of physiological indisposition.

April 3: Awaits a telephone communication setting up an Easter outing. Answer inviting her to attend a meeting to decide upon departure. Meal cut short, precipitous departure. Triumphant return; she leaves for three days to Coulommiers with a troop composed of a dozen young boys and girls, a little older than she.

April 6: Return. Very happy and fully satisfied with her three days of escape to the country, rejoices in this atmosphere of active and joyful youth. Inexhaustible about the multitude of occupations and minute details.

April 7: Persistent euphoria; new departure to the home of her friends at Seine-et-Marne.

April 9-10: Days spent at home without obvious desire to go out, since the second camping trip is set for next Sunday. Comforting prospect.

April 11: Return to classes without apparent disgruntlement. In any case, little explanation on the resumed contact with school. Meeting set for Thursday evening with camping group to discuss another outing. Manifest hostility to our attending together with a cousin of her age, he too a fervent camper, so as to try to form an opinion on the tone of this club.

After three months of re-educative work, at a rate of two sessions a week, the father himself—having overcome his excessive demands—comes to declare that he no longer has anything for which to reproach the child. The treatment is temporarily interrupted in order to see how the girl, left to herself, will behave. Follow-up inquiries show that her behavior remains satisfactory and that adaptation in a positive direction persists. It will even be amplified, because the control of motivations, once acquired (and rudimentary though its teaching may necessarily be in re-educative work with children), creates inner determinants which militate against relapse into the old attitudes, provided their acquisition is not prematurely destroyed by external circumstances (relapse of the parents or bad companions).

P.A.
Only Child
Expelled from three schools. At present attends a trade school.
Instability.

The parents are small tradespeople in a district on the outskirts of town. The father is an authoritarian man with a stern look and brusque gestures. From everything he says transpires the style of his life: duty and discipline. The mother complains bitterly about her husband's severity. Her mimicry, even more than her words, expresses how much she has suffered from it. However, severity is also her predominant character trait. Looking at her and listening to her speak, one is tempted to depict her with two words: honesty and money. On the other hand, it is possible that her looks and manners are but a veneer of adaptation to her husband's character. But her cold eyes lead one to think that it is also a natural propensity.

The child resembles his parents in obstinacy and a not very refined sensibility. But as for the attitude in which his traits become manifest, the boy is the opposite of his parents. The duties imposed on him too rigidly have led him to hate all discipline. He only likes amusements, and their suppression, which has become increasingly necessary, has only intensified his need for them. Punishments, instead of breaking down his obstinacy, have made him rebellious. Frequently skips school with some of his delinquent schoolmates. He treats them to the movies and gets the money by filching quite considerable amounts from the cash register in the shop run by his parents. The band of kids spends whole afternoons going from movie to movie, enjoying adventure and gangster films. According to the parents, the child supposedly has vague ideas of becoming a mechanic, but they are aware that the realization of such a plan must seem to him too difficult. The boy does not like manual work, but he proves to be even more rebellious when it comes to scholastic effort. In order to escape school, he claims that he wants to work as a laborer in a workshop. Among his companions are "pals" who are older and already work in the factory, and the boy admires their presumed independence. By earning a living as they do, he would be less controlled by his father, and he imagines he could then do as he pleases. He responds to the threat of remaining an unskilled worker all his life by imaginatively harboring a vague plan of completing his education once he is free from paternal control, but even he himself undoubtedly knows that his will is too weakened by his appetite for amusement. Once an unskilled factory worker, he will remain one forever. Unless, in order to escape the conflict between work and amusement, the child realizes another plan of which the parents are indeed afraid: to amuse himself without working; to obtain or procure for himself, no matter how, the money necessary to live without working. His dipping into the parents' cash register has somewhat prepared them for this, and to cross the threshold that separates him from delinquency is but a step. It seems that his imagination is not yet set in this direction; but it is to be feared that it will try this path and that in the end it will become seductive and irresistible.

An urgent decision is imperative because the principal's office at the trade school has informed the parents that the child (already expelled from several schools) will be dismissed shortly if his behavior does not change radically and above all if he does not stop disturbing classroom discipline by his brutality toward his school-mates and his impertinence to the teachers. The urgency of the situation involves the risk that the time available for the re-educative work may be too limited.

At the first session, the boy appears with red splotches on his face, the sign of guilt. Confronted by the gravity of the situation and the decisive moment of the first re-educative contact, his good intentions have been aroused even before the psychological expla-nation could whet them. The parents have accompanied him in order to supply the necessary information, but also to be certain that he will not avoid coming to the appointment. At the moment when they go away to leave him alone for the interview, the boy hugs his father effusively, as if to seal a promise. He has the wide eyes of innocence, and his entire being expresses good will. But these clear signs of exaltation point to the danger of collapse at the first temptation, or the refusal of the excessive praise for which his vanity clamors.

It is to be foreseen that he will graft his vanity onto this new attitude of sentimental submission, just as he previously grafted it onto the accusatory insolence of his rebellion. The therapeutic work will have the goal of calming or placating the excess of vanity that is presently inverted in excessive guilt feelings, so that this guilty vanity will no longer produce either an excess of rebellion nor the present excess of ostentatious submission. The attempt to calm the emotional hypertrophy, grafted here on a nature that is in itself quite crude, is the only chance to obtain the abandonment of the exalted plans that verge on delinquency. Here as always the overwrought sentiments of a vanity-inspired and guilty order with their counterweight of accusation and sentimentality, too easily transformed into each other, end by closing the circle and —as long as they persist—do not leave any way out for sensible plans and more considered behavior. The entire problem consists in finding out whether it will be possible to obtain his straightening out within a limited amount of time that allows for only one kind of explanation, which is perhaps not very accessible to this boy whose intelligence is visibly quite weak and stultified.

The fundamental cause of his disorientation is the family entanglement, intensified to an alarming degree by the underlying hostility between the child and his parents. However, the touchiest point at present is the school situation, complicated by a character weakness that makes the influence of the "pals" irresistible. The threat of being expelled from school may become decisive for his entire life. When questioned, the boy does not conceal his fear of the crushing punishment that his father will not fail to inflict on him if he is expelled. He says that he has often been beaten to the point of being "left for dead." It is nevertheless to be feared that, because of more or less subconscious motives, he will do nothing to escape the threat hovering over him. The tangle of motives here is typical of certain cases of active rebellion in which the rebellion dares to explode despite the parents' exceeding severity. Oppressed at home, the child lashes out at his teachers before the audience of his schoolmates. The maintenence of school discipline requires recourse to exemplary, often individually unjust punishments that the child, because of his family situation, resents most. His aversion for the duties too severely imposed by the parents is transformed into hatred directed at the teachers; the hate-filled rebellion is concentrated more and more on studies and attendance at school. The child becomes less and less attentive in class. The rebellion of a child of higher than average intelligence—for this and other reasons—will only rarely go astray to the point of making delinquent plans. But intellectual deficiency, innate or affectively aggravated, can become a secret torment of unbearable intensity, when to it is attached the inhibiting anguish of being less gifted than the majority of one's schoolmates and not being able to compete with them on the scholastic plane. Lack of intelligence, stupidity, is the most inadmissable deficiency that exists, much less admissable even than moral deficiency. Wanting to conceal his intellectual deficiency even from himself and others, the child exaggerates his moral misconduct so that his scholastic misadventures can be charged to the latter. But the calculation of satisfaction, when it begins to deviate in this manner, runs the risk of straying more and more into false motivation. All feelings of inferiority tend to be repressed and transformed into feelings of superiority. The child in a state of active rebellion, when he suffers from intellectual inferiority, is almost automatically led to look for superiority in the courage of his rebellion. To the primary cause of rebellion, to the accusation accompanied by sentimentality, by self-pity fed by the injustice (imagined or real) of the provoked punishments, is added a new cause which is much more difficult to combat: the rebel's vanity.

The rebellion becomes a task to be fulfilled, an exalted task that cannot be abandoned, even though it is crushing. The child, crushed by the punishment, resists in order to prove to himself that nobody can do anything to him, that he is stronger than his father and his teachers. The accusation is aggravated and becomes the need for vengeance, and to the extent to which the threat of being demoted in rank because of his scholastic and moral misbehavior becomes more definite, the rebellion threatens to go beyond the family framework and extend to society and its injustices. The slightest flinching in the face of punishment is then felt by the exalted vanity as submissiveness, as an unforgivable cowardice that awakens an unendurable sense of guilt. The guilt is inverted. It no longer has only its original significance, which has a real foundation: it no longer attaches itself mainly to the remorse felt on exasperating the parents. By reference to the task of vanity-inspired vengeance, the sense of guilt becomes purely imaginative and obsessive, and revives in the self-accusatory form of not being sufficiently exasperating to the parents and the world. The inverted guilt suppresses all wish for a recovery which, moreover, is expected to surpass one's capacities. This is only vanity-inspired self-justification, which permits the desperate person to indulge in vengeance and laziness.

The interview with the boy sheds light on all these implications. His initial distrust quickly disappears, and he describes his transgressions with a certain complacency tinged with naive boastfulness. From this is shown that he proves to himself his superiority vis-à-vis his peers by playing the avenging hero in school. At the slightest vexation, at the slightest too quickly suspected injustice, he strikes. Showing his clenched fist, he says: "One of these can knock you for a loop." He is physically stronger than his schoolmates, and his courage would merely be a cowardly revenge against their superior discipline and scholastic success, if one didn't realize that he is quite capable of also attacking someone stronger than he. The result is that his schoolmates—with the exception of a few dunces to whom he is close—are united against him. Because of his rebellious courage, he ends by feeling so superior to these small, docile, and submissive imbeciles, as the majority of his schoolmates seem to him, that he becomes indignant at being compelled to go to school with them. He plays the adult; he would already like to be one. Questioned about this, he exclaims, nodding his head affirmatively and repeatedly: "Oh yes! I would like to be at least seventeen." Unfailingly when you speak to him about his fourteen years of age (and a few months), he corrects you: "Fifteen." He dons adult habits; he has the nicotine-yellowed fingers of a chain smoker. He would like to prove to the entire world what a "tough guy" he is and what he will dare to do when he becomes free of paternal and scholastic discipline. It is vanity above all that prepares in him the characteristic trait of the delinquent: the blindness that can no longer see the real consequences of a crime. He is incapable of thinking: "If I steal, I will probably be caught"; he believes he is smarter than everybody else, and his imagination obsessively suggests to him: "I steal, and I enjoy myself." In order to make up for the disdain by which he feels surrounded on all sides (and to which he will ultimately respond by disdain for society), he already prepares to play the "top banana" in a small circle of admirers. He steals in order to amuse himself with his "pals" by treating them to movies, cigarettes, and drinks. His vanity, even more than his need for amusement, determines the weakness of his will, his submission to his pals' opinion, his suggestibility, the ease with which he yields to bad influences. His vanity—despite the good intentions of which he is still capable—makes him succumb to the slightest invitation, the slightest temptation.

Because of this suggestibility and because of the gravity of the case, it would be better to put the boy beyond the reach of temptation by moving him to another school and preferably putting him in a boarding school. But such a change of environment in the middle of the school year has many drawbacks, and it is at any rate unlikely that he would have adapted to it without preliminary therapeutic preparation.

The boy listens attentively to the beginning of the explanation of his situation and this allows one to hope that it might be possible to reduce his good intentions, currently revealed but imaginatively overwrought, to what they contain of the real and realizable.

Following the first session he makes a certain real effort. Here is the report of his godmother, with whom he has spent the weekend. (It is important to point out that he hated going to visit her because he felt out of place in this well-off bourgeois milieu and inhibited by a feeling of inferiority compared to the son of the family, a twenty-year-old boy): "Attitude sensibly different from what it is habitually. More relaxed. More willing to talk. Tries to be helpful and even shows some consideration."

During the next session he supplies a dream in which he identifies with a bandit, the avenging hero in a movie he has recently seen. In the movie and in his dreams, the hero becomes reconciled with society (with the king of the country) and renounces his rebellion.

Without repeating here the dream and its interpretation in detail, it can be said that the king is a compression of his father and the therapist. The dream expresses his joy at becoming reconciled with his father by going along with the treatment. But, on the basis of the associations, his joy is due above all to the expectation of praise. The dream sums up the situation. It shows—superimposed on a real but too feeble vital impulse—a tendency to rejoice imaginatively over forgiveness and success instead of preparing it by a constant effort so as to reestablish confidence.

In view of this attitude, two paths of treatment became clear: to reinforce or to alleviate the anxiety-producing pressure surrounding the boy at the moment, which consisted in the threat of a crushing punishment if he is expelled from school. This pressure having triggered or at least reinforced his rebelliousness, it was not at all advisable to expect from its reinforcement a real support for a revision of motives. An improvement obtained in this manner risked being temporary and deceptive. To alleviate the stimulating oppression born from the anguish was just as great a risk. Nevertheless, one must take this risk, for lack of a better solution but also because, from the point of view of motivations, anxiety, if confronted by a real danger, when it is subconsciously deflected toward morbidity—as was the case here—absolutely cannot be utilized as a positive stimulant. It was more advisable to try to remobilize the courage—diverted into rebellion—for more positive goals, by setting real hope against the anxiety.

The boy was informed that, whatever he might do, his father agreed to no longer subject him to the humiliation of beatings, and that, as the result of a request made to the school principal, the latter had declared himself ready to hold off and wait for a possible rehabilitation. However, the therapeutic work offered only very limited chances for success. The procedure employed was too vulnerable not to evoke the fear of failure: that is, the impossibility of removing the boy from the temptation of going in search of his "pals." Life on the outskirts of town did not lend itself to effective surveillance and the parents, having been taught by experience, were only too right in pointing to their helplessness in this connection, and in expressing their skepticism. During the re-educative consultations—whatever the method employed—there is a necessity for prudence because the available time must be reserved for those cases where it is possible to organize the parents' effective collaboration. Certain cases must therefore be excluded straightaway, and among them especially delinquent children whose treatment requires precautions and organizational procedures unrealizable in consultation. As for predelinquents, they are on the borderline of admissibility. Here too their family, their scholastic, and above all their social situation must offer a minimum of guarantees, justifying the hope for success. In this case, should one attempt the impossible or interrupt the treatment despite the delay granted by the principal of the school? But was it permissible to tell the parents that in the given situation there was no hope? There exists no especially organized service for predelinquents, and in view of the impossibility of sending the boy elsewhere, it was better to make a final effort based on the good intentions that the boy showed, at least at the moment.

It was also necessary to decide whether the sessions devoted until now to analysis of the motives of rebellion against his parents and submission to his peers (the analysis quickly sketched in the preceding pages) had prepared the ground sufficiently to justify the experiment. Would he be willing to renounce the company of his friends? Such a promise given by him could not be considered a sufficient guarantee. But the way in which it was granted or in which the proposition was discussed could give a clue to the boy's good or bad will. Even beyond any psychological method, it was necessary to test the ground in this way, offering him a choice: either he would continue to go around with his friends and in a short while be expelled from school, which would allow him to realize his secret desire (or, rather, his feigned desire) of going to work in a factory; or he would try to become disciplined. In this case a choice had to be made between boarding school (which he tended to imagine as a sort of prision) and staying at home, a much more difficult situation because it would require an effort at self-discipline that might be beyond his ability but one which—at best—could seem realizable to him with the help of treatment. In order to give him the time to reach a decision, his answer was put off until the next session.

After the interval passed, the boy showed up with a magnificent report written by his father. He had spent his leisure time at home, poring over his books, or trying to amuse himself as best he could. He had shown perfect docility toward his parents, who in turn were doing their best to avoid all confrontations. It was too good to last, but it was enough to grant him a mark of confidence. The urgent measure to be taken consisted in trying to organize his leisure time, which, later, proved very difficult to implement.

An attempt to get him to join a soccer team proved fruitless. Neither by temperament nor by age was he suited to being a beginner, a rookie. The categorical refusal that he set against his father's insistence triggered the beginning of a relapse into insolence. Propose that he go into scouting? Better not even think of it. But what to do then? Sooner or later a relapse was almost inevitable.

However, the re-educative experience prudently guided could lead to a solution, precisely because of the foreseeable relapse and the massive discharge of guilt that it would certainly precipitate. The sporadic sessions could do nothing against the constant temptation and the seduction of the imagination, which sooner or later would prevail over explanations of the obvious danger and the blinding motivation. But the explanation presented would have to be able to undermine preventively the ground on which the boy enjoyed erecting his imaginative constructions. It could be foreseen that collapse would quickly follow the shock of the inevitable expulsion, which would immediately release all the underlying guilt. The work of elucidation, even while not hoping to prevent a relapse, could thus have as its goal only the intensification of the sense of guilt, in order to obtain—despite and even because of the current repression—its temporary increase. It also was necessary to preventively cut off, by the further discharge of guilt, the paths of escape to insolent false justification that might make his rebellion definitive. Only the analysis of motivation could prepare a positive change of direction: the acceptance of the boarding school, until now obstinately rejected but which, after the expulsion, would be the only way out. In short, the boy had struggled so valiantly with the conflict between staying in treatment and running away that a legitimate hope remained that once he was sufficiently prepared he would finally, under the shock of relapse, willingly and without risk of sabotage accept the idea of continuing his training for a trade in the "prison" of the boarding school, in order to avoid a real prison.

After some weeks, the signs of an impending relapse became clear. The boy showed up for treatment at times that suited him. He was increasingly tense, and the red splotches on his face—which had disappeared—were prominent, the mark of a recrudescence of guilt. This sign would have been the worst omen if the relapse had not been foreseen, because habitually even the most tormented faces (partly under the shock of the first therapeutic contact) at the very first sessions start to relax and regain their childish expression, a clear and objective sign of a positive reaction. During the interview, the boy seems absentminded. He no longer supplies dreams, nor does he report any details about his life and, finally, he no longer even brings his parents' reports, which leads one to think that he tears them up.

His mother appears without having been summoned. She has discovered that for some time now the child has been staying away from school and that he has recently commited another theft of an amount greater than ever before.

Is this a sign that the case is hopeless and that rigorous measures should have been taken rather than running the risk of being duped? After the discovery of his recent misdeeds, the boy, too ashamed to come for consultations, has stayed away, all the while letting his parents believe that he continued to attend the sessions. In order to stop him from avoiding the summons, his parents accompany him. He is completely hostile and close to withdrawing into mutism. He barely manages to report that one of his teachers supposedly refused to let him into class and had finally admitted him only by saying that as far as he was concerned he did not exist. And so the entire fault is attributed to the teacher. The boy states with determination that he is through with school. Asked whether he resents the treatment, he does not answer verbally, but vehemently shakes his head in sign of denial. It is impossible for the past interviews not to have made an impression on him; his stolid attitude is the result of his intensified guilt and the repression of the reproaches he brings against himself.

Nevertheless, the therapeutic contact is broken. Only a decisive shock could re-establish it in the brief time of an interview which threatens to be the last if this effort does not succeed in penetrating the facade of hostility behind which the young deviate is barricaded. The silent obstinacy cuts short any attempt at resuming the dialogue so as to uncover the events that have caused his relapse. But for the moment it is, everything considered, not indispensible to know them. The essential thing is to understand the secret motives in order to try to take apart the fabric of false justifications that formed the fantasy of escape, this time decisively delinquent and undoubtedly conceived by him as a last hope precisely because of the deep feeling of hopelessness about himself into which he is plunged by his relapse, the proof of the impossibility of his recovering.

This recklessness of despair—which renders obsessive the hopeless hope of escape—must be attacked with the assistance of an understanding of the false motives which form a protective screen. But the time available and the boy's present state of mind do not lend themselves to a new or further detailed explanation of motives. How can one be sufficiently incisive so as to give the argument the power to shock? It would first of all be necessary to avoid the mistake of using persuasive methods, which consist in the fact that the re-educator, because of vexed vanity, allows himself to be swept into false justifications of his point of view and false motivations of his desire to succeed. All sentimentality, but also any excessive accusation, would only result here in the worsening of vanity-inspired guilty resistance. The most serious fault one could commit would consist in being overbearing or preaching morality, imploring the obstinate child to come clean, or treating him disdainfully. The only possibility of penetrating the crust of his fantasies and interpretations, to touch to the quick the underlying guilt, resides here in an objectivity devoid of all affective attitudes and, perhaps, thereby able to release the obvious elements of an inexorable reality to which the boy is affectively blind. In the circumstance this reality was the fact that confronted by a decisive scholastic failure he did not—as he liked to think—have a choice between the pretext of going to work in a factory and the secret promises of amusement that he hoped to realize by delinquency. We must avoid depicting for him both the depised school and the supposedly desired factory in seductive colors contrary to reality, or even to show him delinquency in its extremely terrifying aspects. In order to circumvent his imaginative opposition, and to let the evidence which he knows in his innermost depths act, it is enough to show him that these are two forms of life, each of which can have its joys and sorrows, but which are diametrically opposed and between which he had to choose there and then. Whether he liked it or not, his answer or his silence would have the importance of a choice; and this choice, in all likelihood, would be forever decisive.

The explanation, simple as everything that is obvious, gained its objective. Coming out of his mutism, the boy makes a spontaneous confession. This shows that even the delinquent child—or at least a child about to become delinquent—is more or less accessible. His vanity collapses, his accusation is disarmed, if one does not accuse him exaggeratedly and if one does not try to work on his feelings (which, at most, produces good intentions that are more or less artificial and of short duration).

Any rigid position would have merely led him to take the opposite position. Only the situation's reduction to obvious facts could penetrate his present resistance. However, the proper re-marks could not have brought about the sudden change in attitude if the ground had not been prepared by the previous interviews.

The rebellion's change of direction into docility was certainly not definitive; but it was decisive at that crucial moment.

In the course of his spontaneous avowals, the boy says that the idea of living without working already took shape in him when he was ten years old under the influence, he says, of adventure stories, and in connection with a corporal punishment that was much more drastic than any previous ones. Having found out that the child, instead of going to school, had for a week roamed the streets and fields, his father, seized by rage, had beaten him savagely, not even stopping when entreated by the child. Instead of becoming disciplined as a result, the child went even further, egged on by a friend he had at that time, who was two years older. In their forays together they spoke about plans of escape, which they never actually carried out but elaborated in imagination down to the smallest details.

Nothing would be more mistaken than to think that these past events were the cause of the present condition. On the contrary, it is quite possible that these memories contained retrospective elements that long ago had been constructed imaginatively—or at least overestimated in importance—with a view to falsely justifying the present deficiency by projecting the fault on the father and the seducing friend. In everyone's psyche, buried in the extraconscious and capable of being associatively awakened, there are such memories, which have become representative of the entire fabric of past life. On the other hand, these overvalued memories are not necessarily negative and traumatizing. They may just as well have a positive and heartening nature. These memories, the effects of past overvaluation, become in turn—by virtue of their motivating survival—the cause of the healthy formation or unhealthy deformation of the psychic system. The essential thing, however, is not the past event but the affective valuation that has become attached to it, and which, extraconsciously rooted, escapes intellectual criticism. The overvaluation of a past event, susceptible of being used as a screen, forms a motivation that codetermines, unknown to the subject, his habitual reactions. These motivations acquired long ago thus reveal themselves in the present activity, and this leads to the fact that associatively produced memories do not add anything essential to an understanding based on the study of legitimate motivations. The therapeutic outcome is obtained much more quickly if, instead of dwelling on the interpretation of memories, one attacks the complex structure of the subconscious with the help of psychological calculation. Nothing is more likely to bring about

error—as we have already remarked—than the associatively reproduced past event, when it is interpreted without a sufficient knowledge of motivations. We therefore have here a fundamental difference in methods.

The fact that the subconscious rebellion had here been condensed
since the age of ten into a delinquent plan and that since that time
the child had given it his conscious support, does not prove that he
was a "bad case," if one attributes the meaning of "incurable" to
this term. The deviation of the escape fantasy toward delinquency
is at the present time one of the most frequent phenomena. In the
majority of cases it remains a purely imaginative temptation. Its
realization cannot take place without there being added to the
affective disorientation (acquired factor) a tendency to the crude
form of rebellion (innate factor). In the present case, it was certainly not a matter of simple imaginative play with a fantasy about
delinquency, even though the attempts at realization were left
dangling. The definitive fall was still to be feared. The precocious-
ness of the long-cherished plan proves this, as does its present
character of obfuscating obsession.

Whatever the case may be, the boy, after he had begun to confide
in me, became quite prolix. He told me, out of need to spill it out
rather than bravado, that he had been stealing since the age of ten
and that the greater part of his thefts went unnoticed. He dipped
into the shop's cash register or his mother's wallet, always with the
idea of preparing to run away, but always again immediately
spending the money or giving it away.

After beginning treatment, he wanted to break with his old
habits and subject himself to the demands of school. One must
understand that it was not easy for him to bring about a change in
his present scholastic environment, even if his good will had been
more persevering. According to what he says, one of his teachers
(whom he had undoubtedly exasperated before) continued to single
him out and provoke him with disobliging remarks. It is easy to
understand that his dependence on the opinion of his schoolmates
prompted in him the feeling that they expected his rebellion and
even, it seems, encouraged him to carry it out. To disappoint them
meant for him the loss of face, even dishonor. Nevertheless, he
made an effort to keep quiet in class, fixing himself in an attitude of
absentmindedness that was conducive to escapist reveries. In order
to escape the unpleasantness of conflict, he intermittently stayed
away from school. Although he was tormented by guilt at the
beginning, it did not take long for him to justify himself, and by
thus becoming increasingly opposed to the therapeutic influence,

he ended by getting in touch again with his old "pal," a young factory worker under whose influence he had been for a long time. Since their idle hours spent together were not very pleasurable because their pockets were empty, the inevitable took place. He committed a new theft.

The story is simple, but what gives it a particular value is his way of telling it: without excessive self-accusation and without attempts at justification. Also, his good will is total, at least for the moment. With determination he declares that he does not want to continue in that kind of life. He insists on being taken back into therapy. However, his refusal to go on attending school remains categorical, and in order to resume his effort in a new milieu he would like to get into a factory as soon as possible. With insistence and simplicity, he persists despite warnings about his illusions as to what awaits him. He assures me that he is not afraid of manual labor and that he will be able to adjust to it. Certainly this is merely another good intention. Yet something has changed. The boy's attitude— leaving aside the persistence of his senseless plan—does not present any kind of exaltation.

A change of milieu is indispensable. Nevertheless, despite his relative scholastic incapacity it is still obvious that he will find it even more difficult to adapt to the life of an unskilled worker. His preference for the factory remains suspect. After several sessions devoted to explanation of the real factors and to the elucidation of the blinding motives, his resistance begins to break down. The boy declares himself ready to continue his apprenticeship in another school. It would be necessary to put him in a boarding school and at the same time follow him therapeutically, but unfortunately that is impossible.

Thanks to the intervention of the institution, an apprenticeship center in the province declares that it is ready to accept the boy. A few days before his departure, his father—happy with the solution—comes to the office for a final discussion and clarification.

Having regained confidence, as much as was possible, he remarks that the boy "is goodhearted at bottom." But when questions as to whether he admits that despite his good will certain educational errors may have been committed, he answers in a voice whose intonations betray a sudden upsurge of anger: "That child has been spoiled! If he had my childhood, he would really have something to complain about!" And he tells how hard life was for him, the second of seven children in a worker's family, his older brother a good-for-nothing, the terror of the family, who one day disappeared to escape the family restrictions, and nobody was ever able to find out what had become of him. He, on the contrary, with the burden of looking after his younger brothers and sisters, had always been a good fellow. "Forget about having fun, Up very early at dawn, and at work often till late at night. And yet one mustn't neglect one's duties. And always doing his duty. But never shirking." His greatest joy was to please his parents. And besides, he's always been considered exemplary. "Nobody ever found fault with me." "I was above reproach." It is during the course of his childhood, and in part to triumph over his older brother, that he imposed on himself an iron discipline that made certain achievements possible for him on the social plane, but also later drove him to crush his child. He ends his story by observing bitterly: "Once a bad one always a bad one."

This belated flare-up of his repressed anger confirms the impressions of the first contact, which were founded exclusively on behavioral clues, since initially the man was far from willing to offer any confidences.

We cannot stress enough the fact that it is the most exemplary of children—whom one never sees in consultation—who at an adult age become the best intentioned parents, but who also, because of too many good intentions, can prove to be completely unfit for the educational task.

It was not in order to harass him that it was necessary to try to bring about a change in the father's rancor. By taking refuge in the idea that the child was "incorrigibly bad," he was prepared to destroy what little chance still existed for therapeutic intervention. His most recent attempt to justify himself by throwing all responsibility upon the child greatly risked poisoning the last days before the boy's departure for the boarding school. All one could still attempt during this last meeting was to help this man, who was suffering from an almost irremediable disappointment, to understand that he must not at the last moment spoil with reproaches and sermons the slim hope that still existed. The only chance that the child, deprived of therapy, could still keep going lay in giving him the feeling of being reconciled with his family. Only an understanding avowal from the father could lead to a reconciliation deep enough to avoid squabbles. How could one hope that the child would forget his resistances and make a long-term effort at the boarding school if he, the father—instead of making an effort at self-control, after all quite short-lived—let him leave with an example of unsurmounted grievances before his eyes?

The argument was too obvious to convince him. A mocking

smile, which he tried to repress, began to appear on his face. Clearly, he took this simple warning for a moralizing remonstrance.

What is sensible has always been known to be obvious. But by dint of speaking about it, by dint of imposing it on others, instead of realizing it oneself, the obvious is emptied of its meaning. In order to make sensible conduct admissible and realizable, we must impart to it the allure of novelty by means of the analysis of its extraconscious basis. Deeper investigation being impossible, it was important in this final session to make the obvious sensible by trying to condense it in a high-powered argument. "Quite possibly your son is a bad one; but in that case you have no hope left. Stop imagining that we are asking you to submit to the child's whims. Ask yourself to overcome the vexation, so that you may have the strength to help the child as much as possible. And even, since it is the truth, tell yourself that by helping him you are offering him a last chance to give you better satisfaction in the future. Admit your error, and you will immediately feel freed from all the bitterness of your disappointment. You will be surprised to see how easy it is to free yourself of rancor and how greatly relieved you will be. What right do you have to demand from the child the strength to confess and avoid his faults if you yourself are incapable of doing so?" After a moment's struggle between resistance and reflection, the ironic smile disappears. With a voice that he wanted to be firm but which still betrays bitterness he exclaims: "I've been too strict. A child needs some relaxation."

This is merely a verbal avowal. So be it. Perhaps he even gave in only momentarily to cut short the explanatory taking to task. No matter. The fact is that, despite himself, he has been touched by the highlighting of the fault that he was preparing to commit once again. It was quite possible that during the following days, until the child's departure, he would control his desire to let himself be swept away by his resentments and that he would abstain from "spilling his guts" (his subconscious), which would spoil everything.

A week later, on his goodbye visit, the young boy seems to be in very good state. He appears cheerful and relaxed. In speaking about his parents he does not show any reticence and seems to be in full accord with the decision to send him to boarding school. He assures me that he considers himself happy to escape in this way the companions that he would not have been able to shake off. The reference to his old plan to go to work in a factory elicits a smile.

His aversion to his life as a student no longer has the strength of an obsession. The boy even seems rather happy at the prospect of attending classes while still continuing his apprenticeship to become a qualified mechanic.

A few weeks after entering the boarding school, the boy visits his family during the Easter vacation. He does not fail to show up at the office and to show his pride in the attestation to his good behavior, which he brings with him. After the vacation, the father reports a considerable change in the child's attitude. He has not made any attempt to look up his old "pals." After having spent his time at home in an excellent mood, he has again left for the Center, not without pleasure at the thought of resuming his work there.

The future—as was to be feared—did not fail to bring some disappointments. For several months he seemed to adjust normally to boarding school life. From time to time the parents brought us news and the information showed that the child—except for a few not very serious pranks—continued on a satisfactory level, both in regard to conduct and work. The messages were sent by his father and conveyed on his part quite a remarkable thoughtfulness in comparison with his previous attitude, which was to play the discontented man at all costs. But, gradually, the news became more infrequent and less reassuring. Finally the contact was broken off.

A follow-up inquiry, undertaken much later, with the idea of completing his dossier, resulted only in vague answers that were in any case extremely disappointing. The parents had sold their business and had left town. It was impossible to obtain their new address. According to the information gathered from neighbors, the boy had apparently ended up by getting expelled from the boarding school. Egged on by his schoolmates, he had gotten into the habit of jumping over the garden wall to go and have fun in town. Later on, he supposedly signed up as a cabin boy on a merchant ship. The adventurous life of a sailor was certainly more suited to his aptitudes and temperament than the trade of mechanic. But the danger is that the vicissitudes of an existence full of adventures may further expose him to temptations. Has he been able to resist his inclination toward delinquency? Nothing could be more uncertain.

One thing is certain: this boy could have been rehabilitated, at least in principle. It would have been necessary to put him out of the reach of temptation, thus creating the best opportunity to try and lead him step by step toward completion of his apprenticeship. It would have been as easy to obtain, instead of this failure, a case with a positive outcome. But the story of this boy has been chosen by design. It permits us—before we conclude—to broaden the theme of re-education.

The story has many aspects typical of a whole category of young people. Predelinquency is much more frequent than one suspects. Most of the time this condition eludes all observation because it often is revealed only at the level of secret fantasies. The delinquent intention can subsist for a long time—above all in young people— without any outward manifestation. The boy in question committed thefts, but he did not come into conflict with the penal laws. He has remained at a predelinquent stage. But this stage has proven to be subtended by a whole fabric of escapist fantasies and motives of justification. Would it not be correct to devote special attention to this preparatory stage of *imaginative predelinquency*?

An isolated case is not proof. But it can encourage reflection.

It is true that in its purely imaginative form juvenile predelinquency often ends by turning into an adaptation to social norms. But very often the adaptation will be merely apparent. The forced submission will continue to secretly carry the germ of rebellion. *Every delinquent or criminal act committed in life after a more or less successful period of adaptation could well be suspected of being attributable to resurgence of an old state of imaginative predelinquency which has been temporarily repressed instead of being dissolved.* This to say that juvenile delinquency and the plan for its re-education comprise a problem of a purely psychological order which proves to be not only of individual but also social importance.

What is more, this fact is recognized, at least as regards juvenile delinquency once it has become manifest. But the problem of predelinquency has barely been noticed. Its rooting in the imagination is ignored, or at least not taken into consideration, as if it were a negligible phenomenon. Yet this hidden root is at the basis of the whole problem. The fantasies of escape and justification, often prepared since childhood, are the primary cause of delinquent rebellion, the soil from which are born the delinquent acts under the secondary influence of social conditions. Excessive deprivations due to poverty and destitution certainly play a role. The exalted and unhealthy hold they have on the imagination is indeed—if one goes to the bottom of the problem—the main reason, which calls for greater social justice. However, the boy in question was not exposed at all to deprivations of a material nature. To give its true value to the imaginative root, it may be well to remember that he was a member of a gang of young people in his neighborhood—the germ of a gang, it is true; such germs have existed always and everywhere, but they have developed under the influence of the present epoch's general disorientation to become veritable scourges of society. And must we also point to the great number of crimes committed by adolescents often belonging to the affluent classes, who, far from being frustrated children, were spoiled beyond measure? If it were not cumbersome to broaden the theme too far, it would be tempting to present the idea that delinquency is, at its base, a phenomenon of intrapsychic origin, one of the multiple forms of imaginative exaltation which, without exception, incline to either repression or symptomatic explosion. The reactive explosion becomes a banal and frequent phenomenon during periods of decline in which the mind, at the mercy of ambivalences, finds itself, even more than the body, deprived of its indispensable nourishment. Should we conclude that the true cause of the spread and increase of delinquency—above all in adolescence, the rebellious age—is the impoverishment of the mind and the misery of souls?

It will be appropriate to pay homage to the courts for their effort to take into account the causes operating from childhood on, among which the principal one is the deficient education received in family environments that themselves are suffering from the malaise of the times. But not everything is said by pointing to environmental causes. Outside the milieux concerned with investigating the problem, there remains a strong tendency to claim that when all is said and done, delinquent subjects are by heredity marked by the brutality of their temperament and an excessive suggestibility that infallibly predestines them to being led astray.

The boy in question had a very coarse temperament, and his face certainly showed it. Once caught in the cogwheels of social decline, progressive humiliation could have marked him to such a point that we could even be led to believe in an innate incorrigible brutality. Undoubtedly such extreme cases do exist. But there also exist all the lesser degrees of deficiency, and they are the majority. The boy proved his sensitivity to an extent that cannot help but be touching. As for his somewhat pronounced suggestibility, it certainly favored a pernicious loss of control. But his suggestible weakness did not prevent the boy from understanding the explanation of motives and proving accessible to therapeutic suggestions. The truth is that suggestibility predisposes not only to harmful influences but also to salutary ones.

So this is how the crucial question is posed: does imaginative predelinquency—the root of all delinquent states—necessarily imply the failure of re-education even when it is armed with a technique capable of fathoming the subject's secret intentions? The question cannot be answered by preconceptions but only by an experiment carried out on a vast scale.

It would certainly be utopian to think that such an experiment could be organized easily. Too many obstacles stand in its way. What matters here is to present the problem of education and re-education in its true dimensions.

On the answer depends the hope of being able to fight, thanks to re-education, juvenile predelinquency, the root of the social decadence of adolescents, in fact even of adult criminality.

The study of imagination and its sublimating and perverting power opens an entirely new path for comprehension of the problem. It shows that from the period of juvenile predelinquency until the manifest crime, suggestibility elaborates the crime on the imaginative plane under the influence of harmful suggestions. There is suggestibility without external suggestion; but the solicitations of the environment could not become motivating and determining without their being transformed into imaginative auto-suggestion.

This psychological analysis is too simple not to be evident. It moves the problem from the accidental and reactive plane, which does not permit empirical solutions, to the plane of inner motivation, subject to the laws that preside over the ensemble of human interactions, in which ensemble delinquency is simply a special case. Seen from this legally constitutive aspect, crime is the reactive explosion of impotent rage, accumulated as the result of the successive repression of resentments due to injustices undergone, injustices often provoked and rendered unbearable by ruminating self-suggestion. The fantasy of escape elaborates the criminal plan; the fantasy of justification makes it obsessive and so prepares its active projection. Morbid suggestibility is nothing but deficient deliberation, the pathologically falsified calculation of satisfaction. Delinquency is only one of its multiple consequences. It is true that in very rare, extreme cases crime is the result of an autosuggestion that has an exclusively impulsive origin, and it is then legitimate to speak of innate and irresistible impulses. But it is illegitimate to generalize about such cases. The only phenomenon of a general order is the false motivation, which in fact also has an impulsive origin because it is exercised in connection with desires arising from instinctual drives.

In most cases, delinquency—a psychopathic symptom among many others—should be accessible to re-education, at least in its purely imaginative juvenile stage.

The most decisive obstacle standing in the way of success does not concern the possibilities of a re-education founded on the analysis of motives. It lies in the lack of organization for the indispensable support. The motives that underlie predelinquency go beyond the family intrigue, the only area that offers a chance for success as long as re-education is not elevated to the rank of a social task. Predelinquency is thus condemned to survive in its latent state, and individuals are judged when the crime becomes manifest.

It is not a question of justifying the delinquent, nor of accusing society. It is a question of analyzing a situation, described by some as "the crime of society." Everyone knows that crime exists. To become indignant at this awareness would only attest to a repression that attempts to perpetuate the false collective justification. The penal law that regulates the life of society is itself marked by the injustice common to all human interactions. The crime of society does replace the penal laws: it is an infraction of the laws that preside over the healthy or unhealthy functioning of the psychic system. The sanction of crime by a common false motivation—in which the problem of juvenile delinquency is but one aspect—is not annulled by the growing number of delinquent individuals and criminal acts, a spectacular social scourge. The immanent sanction—deficient actions—extends to all manifestations of social life in disorder.

If re-educative prophylaxis is possible with the help of the analysis of the overwrought imagination, which is the vehicle of false motivations, it must be clear that, faced by the delinquency problem, it is incumbent on social justice to organize preventive assistance. This is not a sentimental wish but a social measure of self-protection.

It would, however, be senseless to expect any short-term realization. At present the determining importance of motivations is ignored, and even their existence is denied. Justice is sought on the external plane of human interaction, instead of its being understood that it is before all else an intrapsychic condition: the rooting out of false justifications. Justice is not a *de facto* state of affairs, but a guiding ideal in constant process of psychic elaboration. The problem of social justice can be posed in a just manner only by psychological in-depth investigation. This is to say that the problem of social justice, posed in all its amplitude, far surpasses that of delinquency. Re-education, even prophylactic, is uneconomical because it does not sufficiently protect the individual from the assault of the false valuations and erroneous ideologies that are current in today's society.

The problem of juvenile delinquency that imposes limits on re-education becomes, through a large scale and profound inquiry, the essential problem that no longer exclusively concerns the child but the human being in general. The only satisfactory solution of the human problem will be found in an education that teaches us to endure the truth about our inner motivations.

About the Translator

Raymond Rosenthal is a translator and critic who has been nominated for two National Book Awards. Among his translations are the two critical biographies *Goethe* and *Tolstoy* by Pietro Citati, *Cancerqueen and Other Stories* by Tommaso Landolfi, and *The Periodic Table* by Primo Levi. Mr. Rosenthal currently lives in New York City.

DA